MW00774450

Padre Island
Baptist Church

THE HOLY SPIRIT IN PURITAN FAITH AND EXPERIENCE

BY

GEOFFREY F. NUTTALL
D.D.

WITH A NEW INTRODUCTION BY
PETER LAKE

The University of Chicago Press
Chicago and London

The University of Chicago Press, Chicago, 60637
The University of Chicago Press, Ltd., London

Introduction © 1992 by The University of Chicago
Copyright 1946, 1947 Geoffrey F. Nuttall
All rights reserved. First published in 1946 by Basil Blackwell.
Second Edition, 1947
University of Chicago Press Edition 1992
Printed in the United States of America

99 98 97 96 95 94 93 92   6 5 4 3 2 1
ISBN 0-226-60941-3 (pbk.)

Library of Congress Cataloging-in-Publication Data

Nuttall, Geoffrey F. (Geoffrey Fillingham), 1911–
    The Holy Spirit in Puritan faith and experience / by
  Geoffrey F. Nuttall ; with a new introduction by Peter Lake.
        p.   cm.
    Originally published: 2nd ed. Oxford : B. Blackwell,
  1947.
    Includes bibliographical references and index.
    1. Holy Spirit—History of doctrines—17th century.
  2. Puritans—England—Doctrines—History—17th
  century. I. Title.
  BT119.N88   1992
  231′.3—dc20   91-38579
                                                  CIP

♾ The paper used in this publication meets the minimum
requirements of the American National Standard for
Information Sciences—Permanence of Paper for Printed
Library Materials, ANSI Z39.48-1984

MATRI TRANSLATAE
PRIMITIAS IAMDIV SPONSAS
DEDICAT FILIVS

CONTENTS

For synopses of argument, see beginning of each chapter

Introduction

THE purpose of this introduction is to attempt, in a brief compass, to set Professor Nuttall's book in the context of the slew of literature on Puritans and Puritanism published since the volume's first appearance in 1946. In many ways that is an impossible task; the volume of modern publication on this subject has been massive and effectively to review it would require a book in itself. Again, the argument of Professor Nuttall's book is itself compressed, subtle, and allusive. Satisfactorily to discuss and evaluate it would also be a major undertaking. What follows is a summary gesture at both those tasks: the first half an all too general discussion of Puritanism in the recent literature on early modern England, the second an attempt to come more closely to grips with Professor Nuttall's text as it fits into this discussion.

Nearly all the major historiographical trends and tendencies of the last forty years are reflected in and indeed run through the literature on Puritanism. Whig, Marxist, and revisionist historians have all produced rival renditions and explanations of the phenomenon. Political historians have always invoked and are now invoking with renewed enthusiasm 'Puritanism' in order to explain political change and conflict. Indeed, in recent years there has been a turn back toward religion as perhaps the most important single cause of the English civil war and the political upheavals (revolution?) which followed it.

This has been a logical result of the revisionist assault on the traditional political narrative, which saw the period as one of mounting political tension and crisis, as a variety of conflicts between the Crown and an opposition variously defined came together to produce first crisis, then civil war, and finally revolution. Of course, such a political narrative fitted quite neatly next to a traditional rendition of the polarity in the church between an establishment 'Anglicanism' and an oppositional Puritanism. On this view, just as there was a high road to civil war, running from the Commons' Apology through the opposition to the Union, the fuss over impositions and monopolies, various clashes over free speech and foreign policy, under James, to the petition of right and the early years of the Long Parliament under Charles, so there was a parallel religious story leading from the agitations of the Elizabethan Puritan movement, through the organized petitioning that preceded the Hampton Court Conference and various parliamentary and extra-parliamentary schemes to reform or modify the church to the assault on and eventual abolition of episcopacy in the Long Parliament. Similarly, while the process of political polarization and radicalization which followed the outbreak of war was seen to fit naturally enough between the nation's earlier gradual acceleration down 'the high road to civil war' and the regicide, so too, in religion, the inherently radical and fissiparous force of Puritanism was seen as in itself an explanation of the disappearance of Anglicanism and the dissolution of the godly cause into the chaotic and cacophonous world of the sects. On this view, 'the rise of Puritanism' was followed naturally, even inevitably, by the progress of the causes of 'liberty and reformation in the Puritan revolution', as the titles of William Haller's two great books on the subject described themselves.[1]

The greatest statements of this view of the period, particularly in religious affairs, were under construction precisely during and immediately after the period in which Nuttall's book was written and published. William Haller's two books came out in 1938 and 1955 respectively. While Haller's view of the religious history of the period was written against and assumed a background provided by S. R. Gardiner's political narrative, the assumptions of both were now read back into Elizabeth's reign in the work of Sir John Neale on Elizabethan Parliaments. In Neale's magisterial narratives the reign was seen almost as a dialogue between the Queen and her Parliaments. The elements of later conflicts between Crown and Parliament could now be discerned running throughout the reign but held in check by the mesmeric personal and political skills of the monarch. In Neale's account a crucial element underlying the frequent clashes between Crown and Commons, an element which served both to explain and organize the story he was telling, was provided by what emerged fully into the light of day in the work of Neale's pupil Patrick Collinson as 'the Elizabethan Puritan movement'. Here was Puritanism seen both as an ideology and a movement, complete, in the person of John Field, with a potentially revolutionary and certainly very radical leadership. Here in Elizabeth's reign, then, was the

---

[1] W. Haller, *The Rise of Puritanism* (New York, 1938), and *Liberty and Reformation in the Puritan Revolution* (New York, 1955).

precursor of that revolutionary Puritanism which helped both to cause and then to fuel the English civil war.[2]

Thus by the end of the 1950s all the elements were assembled for a coherent account of English politics and religion from the mid sixteenth century to the English revolution; an account dominated by the rise of Parliament and of Puritanism, a conflict-centered account which rendered the events of mid-century explicable in terms of long-term processes of political and religious change. As the last pieces in this politico-religious narrative fell into place in the 1950s, so various attempts were being made to describe the causes and chart the course of these same religious and political movements in sociological terms. Here the crucial work was done by Christopher Hill, developing and applying the earlier insights of R. H. Tawney. In Hill's work Puritanism played a crucial role mediating between the social and economic changes which Hill saw as central to the causes of the English revolution and the classic Whig political narrative. Initially, Puritanism was a mobilizing force; located in the social experience of the emergent middling sort, it both expressed and helped to forge a sense of identity and independence amongst a social group whose allegiance and zeal were taken to be central to the triumph of Parliament in the civil war. At this stage, most notably in his *Society and Puritanism in Pre-Revolutionary England* and in the pendant essays in *Puritanism and Revolution,* Hill was concerned with the sober, disciplined, and disciplining religion of the godly middling sort. Here Puritanism operated as a species of social control and class consciousness for groups anxious to differentiate themselves from and to exert increasing control over the rude multitude. The middling sort thus occupied an equivocal role in Hill's picture of the period. On the one hand they provided the popular element in the parliamentarian struggle against royalism; on the other, they represented anything but a 'popular' or radical force as they sought to exercise control and moral discipline over the mass of the poor, laboring classes.[3]

But Puritanism for Hill was always a multidimensional force. He was always insistent that Puritans were not the humorless, repressive figures of popular myth, and in *The World Turned Upside Down* he was able to

[2] J. E. Neale, *Elizabeth I and Her Parliaments 1559–1581* (London, 1953), and *Elizabeth I and Her Parliaments 1584–1601* (London, 1957); P. Collinson, *The Elizabethan Puritan Movement* (London, 1967), and 'John Field and Elizabethan Puritanism', now reprinted in P. Collinson, *Godly People* (London, 1983).

[3] C. Hill, *Society and Puritanism in Pre-Revolutionary England* (London, 1964), and *Puritanism and Revolution* (London, 1958).

vindicate those claims triumphantly with a kaleidoscopic tour of the radical sectaries and popular prophets of the later 1640s and 1650s. Here Puritanism, radicalism, and the people all met in the sects, which, he claimed, drew their support and membership from the bottom third of the population, the masterless men living in the forests and wastes, many of whom were gathered up into the New Model Army and helped to give that body its unique tinge or tone of political and religious radicalism. Again, Puritan thought had been sociologized. Instead of the ideology of the godly middling sort, Puritan radicalism was presented as the expression of a genuine popular movement. Hill presented the crucial notions of the radicals on antinomianism, free will, and the role of the spirit in overcoming sin as reactions against an earlier clerically defined predestinarian orthodoxy that in turn had reflected the class basis of respectable Puritanism's prewar support. Thus on Hill's account the relations between the different Puritanisms of *Society and Puritanism* and *The World Turned Upside Down* were in part at least adversarial. Indeed, at times he wrote as though the second was more a product of an underground radical popular tradition running 'from the Lollards to the Levellers' than any very obvious continuation of pre–civil war Puritan thought.[4]

The high water mark of the sort of views and approaches that I have been summarizing here was represented by the publication of *The World Turned Upside Down* and of Lawrence Stone's *Causes of the English Revolution* in the early 1970s. After that point a so-called revisionist reaction set in. First to go was the notion of long-term social causes of the civil war. These were skeptically discussed in a few pages by Conrad Russell in 1973 and dismissed by him in a few paragraphs in 1990.[5] Next came the attempted overthrow of the traditional Whig political narrative. So close had been the integration of traditional notions of the rise of Puritanism, of Puritanism as a freestanding view of the world, a religious opposition feeding into more secular strands of political activism throughout the period after 1559, that the shock waves from the revisionist assault on the political sphere could not but have their effect on Puritan studies as well.

The groundwork for a profound reassessment had already been laid by Patrick Collinson in a series of brilliant studies of what he termed the second age of the English reformation, the period, that is, after c. 1570

---

[4] C. Hill, *The World Turned Upside Down* (London, 1972), and 'From Lollards to Levellers', in M. Cornforth, ed., *Rebels and Their Causes* (London, 1978).

[5] L. Stone, *The Causes of the English Revolution* (London, 1972); C. S. R. Russell, ed., *The Origins of the English Civil War* (London, 1973), pp. 4–12, and *The Causes of the English Civil War* (Oxford, 1990), pp. 2–4.

when genuinely Protestant values were brought home to the English people for the first time. The roots of this re-evaluation were clearly visible in Collinson's great book *The Elizabethan Puritan Movement*. Centered on the underground classis movement and on the radical, indeed potentially revolutionary, efforts of John Field and his friends to take over the English church, the book was ostensibly written within a Nealean paradigm. However, a careful reading betrays a crucially important subtext, in which through a brilliant analysis of the social and political context of much Puritan activity Collinson revealed the myriad ways in which the Elizabethan establishment was shot through with Puritan attitudes and personnel.

In the short term, the most obvious casualty of this subtle assault was the traditional notion of a coherently Anglican establishment during Elizabeth's reign. But in the longer term Anglicanism's terminological accomplice Puritanism could not escape from this situation scot-free. For without an ideologically coherent Anglican establishment what price, in the traditional historiography, an equally coherent Puritan opposition? And indeed in a series of brilliant articles and studies published throughout the later 1970s and 1980s, culminating in his two lecture collections *The Religion of Protestants* and *The Birthpangs of Protestant England,* Professor Collinson proceeded to undercut that traditional view of a freestanding Puritan tradition. Instead, Puritanism was presented as the leading edge of the evangelical Protestant effort to proselytize the mass of the people after 1570, its theology a mere continuation of the English reformed tradition or synthesis propagated by the arbiters of orthodoxy in the church and universities; its spiritual or devotional style or timbre merely the pietistic consequence of both the successes and failures of that Protestant proselytizing effort.[6]

There are considerable tensions, ambiguities, and even contradictions in the resulting vision of Puritanism. On one view, we have merely the most intense form, a peculiarly zealous subset of that 'religion of Protestants' which dominated the early Stuart church before the rise of Laudianism. Here is Puritanism as one species of 'voluntary religion' rubbing along with other forms of religious expression without undue difficulty. This argument can be pushed so far that the very word or concept of Puritanism itself becomes a problem, even an obstacle to understanding. In this mode Collinson has dabbled with but not entirely succumbed to the notion that 'Puritanism' was merely the invention, the shadow or polem-

---

[6] P. Collinson, *Godly People* (especially chapters 15, 17, 18, 19, 20), *The Religion of Protestants* (Oxford, 1982), and *The Birthpangs of Protestant England* (London, 1988).

ically necessary alter ego of anti-Puritans. Yet on other occasions Collinson can write brilliantly about the genuinely disruptive effects of the values and practices of 'perfect Protestantism' in contexts which seem to cry out for the conventional deployment of the word.[7]

In large part, the ambiguity of Collinson's analysis and the tergiversations of his arguments serve to reflect and highlight the ambiguity and contradictions inherent in the subject of study. In other hands, however, the results of this same tendency have been rather less happy. Certainly, in the first flush of revisionist enthusiasm, when the results of Collinsonian research into the social provenance and political resonance of Puritan activities in the localities were being juxtaposed with Nicholas Tyacke's findings on the prevalence of Calvinist predestinarianism amongst the theologically sophisticated under both Elizabeth and James, the result was all but the death of Puritanism. The word might retain some force as a descriptive term for a particular style of personal or collective piety but in the arenas of political action and discourse it was of no consequence. Central figures like William Prynne or John Pym, previously called Puritans in the belief that the appellation told us something both about how they behaved and why, were now recast as conservative defenders of an essentially Calvinist establishment in church and state under assault from an insurgent Arminianism newly ensconced in power at the center. Thus the religious reaction to the Personal Rule could be described less in terms of a mounting Puritan radicalism or opposition than as a Protestant or Calvinist reaction against an innovating Arminian or Laudian establishment.[8] Interestingly, a similar change has been effected even in recent

---

[7] P. Collinson, *The Puritan Character: Polemics and Polarities in Early Seventeenth Century English Culture* (William Andrews Clark Memorial Library, 1989), and, for the divisive effects of 'perfect Protestantism', see especially chapters 4 and 5 of *The Birthpangs of Protestant England*.

[8] This was arguably the position adopted by Conrad Russell in his *Parliaments and English Politics, 1621–9* (Oxford, 1979); see pp. 26–32 and especially p. 28, n. 2. Russell was in many ways glossing and appropriating the early work of Nicholas Tyacke and especially his seminal article 'Puritanism, Arminianism and Counter-Revolution', in C. S. R. Russell, ed., *The Origins of the English Civil War*. More recently Dr. Tyacke has expanded and modified his position in *Anti-Calvinists: The Rise of English Arminianism c. 1590–1640* (Oxford, 1987) and of late he has returned to the subject in an important Dr. Williams Library lecture on *The Fortunes of English Puritanism, 1603–40* (London, 1990), a text of the greatest significance in reevaluating the role of Puritanism in early seventeenth century England. On John Pym see C. Russell, 'The Parliamentary Career of John Pym', in P. Clark, N. Tyacke, and A. Smith, eds., *The English Commonwealth* (Leicester, 1979); on Prynne see W. Lamont, *Marginal Prynne* (London, 1963). Lamont's book in many ways prefigured many of the central features of the school of thought later termed 'revisionism'.

writing on the Puritan emigration to New England. Where once there was an eschatologically informed errand into the wilderness intended self-consciously to build a New Jerusalem in the wastes of New England, there is now a Puritan diaspora to avoid the impact of Laudian reform and conformist crackdown and thus to achieve free access to the pure ordinances of God even at the expense of emigration. In this way the revisionist account of things religious paralleled perfectly the revisionist analysis of politics, for there too the mounting criticism of the Crown was portrayed as a reactive, even obscurantist defense of ancient precedent and local custom against a central government forced to innovate or at least to press against the limits of accepted practice by the exigencies of finance and war.[9]

Such a position at least had the advantage of consistency and coherence. But, under the inevitable pressure to address and explain the brute fact that, for all the localism and neutralism of the ruling class, the civil war did happen, certain scholars, most notably Professor Russell and Dr. Morrill, have returned to religion as the basic cause of conflict. This emphasis on religion represents in some senses the continuation of revisionism by other means, since religion is seen to have provided a cause for conflict which was seemingly irreducible into other categories or forces. Here, then, is an explanation for war which leaves a great deal of previous revisionist writing on the political system and culture of the period more or less untouched. Indeed, in the introduction to his Ford Lectures Professor Russell seemed to root the basic religious divide with which he was concerned (that between Arminians and Calvinists) in an unchanging human condition. Religious divisions conceived like this do not so much require explanation as documentation. Earlier attempts to link religion too closely to a given social or political context can be and have been (sometimes rightly) attacked as reductionist. The result is that religious conflict becomes something of a deus ex machina, an explanation for conflict not necessarily linked to other aspects of the mental world of early modern English people.

And to turn to religion has meant to turn ultimately to Puritanism. Professor Russell does so under the guise of another name, preferring to talk of those in favor of further reformation, or more loosely of the godly rather than of Puritans. But that shift of terminology hardly represents a

[9] T. D. Bozeman, *To Live Ancient Lives* (Chapel Hill, 1988); for a good summary of this version of the revisionist position, see R. Ashton, *The English Civil War: Conservatism and Revolution, 1603–1649* (London, 1978), especially part 1. For a more recent restatement see Russell, *Causes of the English Civil War.*

conceptual breakthrough or even a notably more precise use of language.
Dr. Morrill is readier to grasp the nettle of Puritanism as name and thing.
Both scholars proceed, uncontroversially, to present the impact of Puritan schemes for reform and various royalist and conformist reactions
against them as a crucial element in the outbreak of the war.[10] We are
back here with the civil war as a war of religion, back almost to the Puritan revolution and to Puritanism as a revolutionary ideology.

The wheel has not quite turned full circle, however; there remain considerable problems in establishing the extent of continuity and discon-
tinuity between Puritanism as scholars of the pre–civil war period have
described it and the Puritan radicalism, red in tooth and claw, of the
period after 1642. On the one hand we have a stable style of piety and a
tightly defined body of orthodoxy allied through the double bind of
magistrate and minister to the cause of social order, forced into unwilling
opposition to the Crown by the apparently popish policies pursued by
Charles and Laud. On the other we have the apparently boundlessly fissiparous radicalism of the period after 1642.

This is an important issue which revisionist scholarship has been unwilling to address. In large part this has been because one of the crucial
interpretational and rhetorical ploys of revisionism was to decouple
events after the outbreak of the war from events preceding it. Back in
1973 Professor Russell introduced his important distinction between the
civil war and the revolution, claiming that the longstanding assumption
that explaining the one was explaining the other was an illusion, an illusion which prompted too many scholars to beg central questions about
the nature of the event under discussion. After that crucial intervention, it
would never be possible again, as Lawrence Stone had done, to write a
book entitled *The Causes of the English Revolution* which effectively ended
in 1642. Indeed, the notion of a caesura separating events before and after
the outbreak of hostilities has now so much entered orthodox thinking as

---

[10] J. Morrill, 'The Religious Context of the English Civil War', *Transactions of the Royal Historical Society,* 5th series, vol. 34 (1984); 'The Attack on the Church of England in the Long Parliament', in D. Beales and G. Best, eds.; *History, Society and the Churches* (Cambridge, 1985); 'Sir William Brereton and "England's Wars of Religion"', *Journal of British Studies,* vol. 24 (1985); and 'The Impact of Puritanism', in J. S. Morrill, ed., *The Impact of the English Civil War* (London, 1991). And C. S. R. Russell, *The Causes of the English Civil War,* and *The Fall of the British Monarchies* (Oxford, 1991). For the rooting of the propensity toward Arminian or Calvinist views of the world in an unchanging human nature see Russell, *Causes of the English Civil War,* p. x. This is an aside, even a joke, but it perhaps betrays an underlying assumption of his argument.

to frame the terminal dates of the relevant volumes of the new Oxford history of England, which break in 1643.[11]

This was an effective and legitimate ploy in subverting or calling into question the whole problematic of the English revolution and of pre-revolutionary England as Hill and Stone had formulated it. But now that the wheel of revisionist fortune has turned something like full circle and religion and even Puritanism are back at the center of explanations of the civil war, is it not time to reopen the question of the links between the war and the revolution and indeed of the role of Puritanism in helping to forge those links?

We are back here with the gap between the world of Hill's *Society and Puritanism* and his *The World Turned Upside Down,* and at present there seems no real consensus on how to approach the problem. Some of the more revisionist historians who have dealt with the revolutionary period proper have avoided the issue by marginalizing it. Thus, Professor Kishlansky has sought largely to exclude religion from the process whereby the New Model Army became an independent force in politics, while Dr. Adamson has sought to concentrate on what he presents as the crucial, indeed the preponderant, role in the politics of the 1640s of a group of peers largely untouched by Puritan enthusiasm.[12] Other historians less skeptical of the importance of religion have adopted a number of approaches to the problem. Some have stressed the radicalizing role of Laudianism and then the experience of war itself in creating a radical Puritanism where there had been none before. Others, arguably more revisionist still and less convinced of the novelty or disruptive effects of Laudianism, have fallen back on an almost Walzerian view of Puritanism as always inherently subversive and destabilizing. Here, at least, Christopher Hill and Kevin Sharpe join hands positing a perennial strug-

---

[11] For the initial distinction see C. S. R. Russell, *The Origins of the English Civil War,* pp. 1–3. The first of the projected volumes on the seventeenth century, by Professor Russell, is slated to end in 1643; the second, by Dr. Morrill, to start in 1643.

[12] M. A. Kishlansky, *The Rise of the New Model Army* (Cambridge, 1979) and J. S. A. Adamson, 'The English Nobility and the Projected Settlement of 1647', *Historical Journal,* vol. 30 (1987). Dr. Adamson's attempt to categorize a subsequent clash of views with Kishlansky as a collision between Gardinerian Whiggery (personified by the unlikely figure of Professor Kishlansky) and a tough-minded revisionism (represented by Dr. Adamson) seems unconvincing. From the present perspective their views seem more like but different parts of a common revisionist assault on traditional views of 'the Puritan revolution' and of the role of religion in shaping the intentions and actions of the central agents in that revolution. The debate between Adamson and Kishlansky seems more properly described as a disagreement about whether and how Dr. Adamson's footnotes work.

gle between a largely static conformist case and an always radically oppositional Puritanism.[13] Other scholars more impressed than they with the incommensurability of the staid respectability of prewar Puritanism and postwar radicalism have even called the very usefulness of the concept of Puritanism into question. The whole subject has been recently subjected to the skeptical gaze of Professor J. C. Davis, a scholar who seems almost incapable of studying a subject without denying that it exists. For him there was nothing notably distinctive about the Puritan view of the world in the period before 1640. As one might expect, therefore, for him the word has little useful to tell us about the spiritual dynamic of what one might be tempted to term the religious radicalism of the late 1640s and 1650s—had not Professor Davis ruled that term out of court too. On this view, even so central a figure in the 'Puritan revolution' as Oliver Cromwell cannot sensibly be called a Puritan.[14]

At one level even as extreme a terminological iconophobia as this represents a salutary reaction against the overenthusiastic, indeed rather anachronistic, use of denominational tags and distinctions to describe religious opinion during this period. But at least in relation to Puritanism it might seem to be in danger of throwing the baby out with the bathwater. It certainly causes some interesting dissonances and difficulties; Professor Davis's remarks on the impropriety of calling Cromwell a Puritan were made in a book of essays in which Dr. Morrill, the editor of the volume, identified as the crucial event in Cromwell's early career what appears for all the world to be what would hitherto have been called a Puritan conversion experience.[15] Moreover, Davis's own terminological austerity has seemingly left us only with the general appellation Christian and the more particular category of antiformalism, which seems a little sparse for the analysis of a period in which the number of Muslims and atheists was very small and virtually no one would willingly have admitted to being a formalist (i.e., a devotee of empty outward forms).

Professor Davis's concern with these matters, while perhaps a little overdone, is prompted by a real problem, however. And that is where, at

[13] K. Sharpe, *Politics and Ideas in Early Stuart England* (London, 1989), pp. 29–31; C. Hill, 'Archbishop's Laud's Place in English History', in *A Nation of Change and Novelty* (London, 1990).

[14] J. C. Davis, 'Cromwell's Religion', in J. S. Morrill, ed., *Oliver Cromwell and the English Revolution* (London, 1990); on 'radical' and 'Puritan' as useful/less categories see J. C. Davis, 'Puritanism and Revolution: Themes, Categories, Methods and Conclusions', *Historical Journal*, vol. 34 (1991).

[15] J. S. Morrill, 'The Making of Oliver Cromwell', in Morrill, ed., *Oliver Cromwell and the English Revolution*.

last, we return to Professor Nuttall's book. Written in the 1940s against a backdrop of Collingwoodian idealism, the book represents an attempt to recreate, to imaginatively inhabit, and to analyze the thought world, the spiritual climate or atmosphere of radical Puritan piety and to relate that piety backward to trends and tendencies in prewar and contemporary moderate Puritanism and forward to the emergence of the Quakers. It is a model exercise in the study of change and continuity, organized around a central doctrine, that of the Holy Spirit, but using that single topos as an entry point into a much wider subject.

The book takes as its starting point of view of Puritanism as a tradition of faith and experience. Concerned with the role of a specific doctrine within that tradition, formal doctrine is still not quite the point. 'The interest is not primarily dogmatic, at least not in any theoretic sense, it is experimental. There is theology, but, in a way which has hardly been known since St. Augustine, it is a *theologia pectoris'* (p. 7). Identifying as a feature characteristic of the sects 'their claim to the liberty of the Spirit in faith and experience' (p. 8), Professor Nuttall yet seeks to locate that claim in a wider conception of the Puritan tradition. That tradition is itself seen as dynamic, a process of experience and experiment rather than a mere sediment of common belief and practice. It is defined variously throughout the book in a number of asides and aphorisms. 'Puritanism may be seen,' he observes at one point, 'as an increasing preoccupation with the conscience, till the strain proved too great, and Antinomianism set in' (p. 36). Elsewhere Nuttall observes that 'throughout this study the Puritan movement . . . has evinced itself to be a movement towards immediacy in relation to God' (p. 134).

This is a study of ideas, of experience, and of individual authors in motion, a study of the process whereby certain tensions and tendencies within Puritan divinity worked themselves out during the 1640s and 1650s. Nuttall's approach is holistic, an attempt to apprehend and define the object of study, Puritanism, in the course of an account of its development, by relating the parts to the whole, by collating and comparing the opinions and positions of individuals and groups as they changed and interacted through time. Thus, early on in the book the reader is told that 'here, Puritan faith and experience is itself the subject: what is endeavoured is . . . correctly to interrelate its own parts and to appreciate it as a whole worth contemplation in itself' (p. 19).

Accordingly, the Puritan tradition is defined as a series of affinities or tendencies, and the effort throughout is to establish a sense of a spectrum of opinions on a number of central issues. In this way, Nuttall is able implicitly to overcome the very compelling and important recent objections to the deployment of the terms "moderate" and "radical" as substantive labels in themselves.[16] They can only ever be licit as qualifiers, helping to locate an individual, a group, or an opinion on a spectrum of opinions. Nuttall's book, through its choice of subject, establishes such a spectrum, stretching from medieval Catholicism on the right to Quakerism on the left. Puritanism is located as a set of positions on that spectrum, and Nuttall then charts the movement along it of particular groups and individuals.

Thus in a brilliantly appropriated quotation from Troeltsch, which applies almost as well to the Laudian as to the medieval Catholic Church, Nuttall speaks of a church, 'with its highly articulated sacramental system' that 'had come to be regarded as in itself "the extension or eternalizing of the Incarnation"' (p. 21). Nuttall presents Puritanism as part of a Protestant reaction against such a system, a reaction which vouchsafed the individual direct access to God through some sort of balance between the word, the spirit, and the ordinances of the church. As we have seen, Nuttall conceives of Puritanism as a movement along that spectrum toward a greater and greater emphasis on the testimony of the spirit, almost to the exclusion of the other ordinances of the church, and with the Quakers almost to the exclusion of the word itself. The progression is from an appeal to the word and the spirit to an appeal to the spirit and the word and finally almost to the spirit alone. In this way he is able to present Quakerism as the culmination, almost the natural outcome, of certain tendencies central to the Puritan mainstream. At the other extreme from the eternalized incarnation of the sacramental systems of the Catholic or Laudian churches lies the incarnation of Christ in each believer, indeed in each human being, preached by the Quakers. It is an approach that renders what might seem to be *the* central question—were the Quakers really Puritans, then?—all but irrelevant. Whatever one calls them, they are inexplicable outside the context, the spiritual climate mapped out in this book.

In this way Nuttall is able to build up and justify his vision of the Puritan tradition as the argument of the book proceeds. At the outset he observes:

> Some of the Episcopalians within the Established Church, all the Presbyterians and Independents in it before 1662, most of the Separatist and sectarian leaders outside it, and the founders of Nonconformity after 1662, are

---

[16] C. Condren, 'Radicals, Conservatives and Moderates in Early Modern Political Thought: A Case of Sandwich Islands Syndrome', *History of Political Thought,* vol. 10 (1989).

thus all spiritually nearer to one another than is any of them to the Roman Catholic Church or to the Laudian party within the Church of England. They have their own internal differences, some of them sharp, and sometimes turning . . . on their doctrine of the Holy Spirit; but in a large sense they have much in common, and for this faith and experience which they share, and which in one regard is the subject of this study, there is no other name than Puritan. (Pp. 9–10)

By adopting such an approach to his object of study Nuttall is able to produce an account of a tradition of thought and feeling centered in many ways on mainstream, moderate figures like Sibbes and Baxter but encompassing in the earlier period Separatists and in the later period all sorts of mystics and visionaries, up to and including the Quakers. This is not some syllogistic attempt to define in fixed formulas the central beliefs or determining characteristics of Puritanism; here rather is a dynamic, open-ended approach to the process of definition which can only convince the skeptic and defend itself against nominalist criticism in and through the process of comparing, collating, and analyzing the various texts and persons with which the book deals. The proof of the pudding is very much in the eating.

A great deal, then, turns on the choice of texts and authors to be dealt with and the tact and skill with which they are compared and collated. The location of many of the themes discussed in the book in the mainstream moderate Puritanism of the period before 1640 is justified mainly through the deployment and analysis of a number of quotes from Richard Sibbes. The continuity of contact with that same respectable Puritan tradition is guaranteed by Professor Nuttall's frequent recourse to the works of Richard Baxter. Baxter is nicely balanced by a figure, as Nuttall puts it, from the left of the Puritan middle group, John Owen. Other more radical figures are deployed next to these focal points until finally the Quakers and George Fox are approached and encompassed. Baxter, in particular, provides a crucial point of reference, almost a moral center for the book. Time and again the links between radical and moderate Puritans are exemplified by an apposite quote from Baxter. But if Professor Nuttall's personal sympathies often seem to lie with Baxter's commonsensical moderation, it remains one of the book's great qualities that its perspective shifts constantly. If Baxter is prominent, so too, amongst the radicals, is Walter Cradock, and the claims of the Quakers to direct experience of the spirit's testimony and of Christ's presence within are vividly and sympathetically described. In short, the views of any one group or individual are never privileged over those of another. Rather they are constantly juxtaposed, compared, and contrasted so that the affinities and differences of tone and content amongst the various positions discussed are constantly being demonstrated to the reader.

To take just one example, in a discussion on the witness of the spirit (pp. 57–59) having started with a passage from Baxter on '"the objective and the sealing testimony"' of '"the Spirit of adoption"', Nuttall proceeds through passages from John Forbes and Richard Sibbes to locate such attitudes in the earlier moderate Puritan tradition before proceeding through quotes from Samuel Petto and Walter Cradock to show how these notions were taken up in the more exalted and enthusiastic language of the 1650s. In conclusion we are told 'Baxter would not express himself in such enthusiastic language' but we are also shown that 'the same spirit breathes' in his own works and writings. The same approach animates Nuttall's analysis of the differences and divisions between his various types of Puritan. Writing of John Owen's anti-Quaker polemic Nuttall splendidly describes how the likes of Owen could take the Quaker notion of the light within as a reference to the natural power of human conscience rather than one to the supernatural testimony of the Holy Spirit. These misunderstandings, he argues, arose because of Owen and his friends' 'failure to consider what Fox meant rather than what they would have meant had they used his language' (p. 42). The book abounds with such careful distinctions, grounded both in a sensitivity to the language used to describe certain feelings and doctrines and to the overall tone, the emotional climate, the underlying 'spirit' of Puritan piety and experience. In this sense the book represents both a vindication of the concept of a Puritan tradition and a practical demonstration of how such a concept should be used as a heuristic device in the conduct of historical research and writing.

Professor Nuttall's account of that tradition turns on a number of tensions, even potential contradictions, within the Puritan impulse—tensions between the word, the Spirit, and the sacraments, between the claims of personal experience and spontaneous response to the promptings of the Spirit and of providence and the limiting influences of reason and education. These internal tensions could be multiplied almost infinitely to include, for instance, those between lay autonomy and clerical authority, respect for conscience and the drive for order, respect for individual experience and the massive stress on the collective identity and mutual obligations of the godly; or, inside the spiritual economy of Puritan piety, between dread and self-loathing at sin and spiritual hope and assurance of salvation. Indeed, the capacity to sustain and indeed to inhabit and live out these sorts of dialectical contradictions and tensions might be taken to represent a defining characteristic of Puritan piety. In the period before the war, a series of practical, institutional, and emotional accommodations between the various parts of the Puritan impulse and between that impulse and external reality were established. With the rise of Laudianism and the coming of war these accommodations increasingly broke down. This was a source of dread and of wonder to the godly. The resulting dialectical interactions between the constituent parts of the Puritan impulse and between that impulse and events in the world produced the chaotic outburst of creative energy and spiritual experience that forms the subject of Professor Nuttall's book. In locating the spiritual dynamic of Puritan thought and feeling within these contradictory tendencies and tensions Nuttall has provided a crucial means of explaining the links and continuities between pre- and postwar Puritanism—between, if you like, the Puritanism of this book and that depicted in, say, *The Religion of Protestants*.

As Professor Nuttall explains, the movement from left to right traced by the argument of the book was also a movement through time as the Puritan tradition developed and transformed itself. Many of the individuals discussed in the text themselves moved leftward through a variety of the positions which make up the spectrum of opinions described in the book. But while there is an implicitly chronological structure to the book, its arrangement or structure is not formally chronological. Rather it is analytic or logical. Here is an account of the logic of Puritan ideas with the dynamic for change proceeding from within the ambiguities and tensions of the ideas themselves. This, then, is an internalist, even an idealist account of the Puritan tradition, with little attention paid to the political or social context in which these ideas were promulgated and developed.

This might be thought a weakness, and if the book were intended as a total account of or explanation for radical Puritan thought during the 1640s and 1650s that would be a more legitimate objection. As it is, the book stands as a considerable testimony to the unique insights into the religious culture of the early modern period that can be gained by taking the ideas of contemporaries seriously and on their own terms rather than assuming almost immediately that they can be interpreted as a code for talking about something else entirely. Only after that has been properly done can historians have any real confidence that they know precisely what it is they are looking for a context for. The fact that this account was written from within the Christian tradition, in the course of training for the ministry, may serve to reinforce the point, although I would like to think that even those located outside that tradition can and should aspire to an effort at empathy and imaginative recreation similar to that performed in this book.

It is, moreover, worth observing that in the forty or so years since the

book's publication we have had arguably quite enough context to be
going on with. While it would certainly not be true to say that we have
emerged none the wiser it remains remarkable, as the historiography
moves through its revisionist to its postrevisionist phase, how many of
the insights and themes of Nuttall's book seem fresh and relevant to current historical problems. Indeed, much of the recent historical writing on
the Puritan tradition either has been organized around those very ambiguities and tensions that provide the dynamic element in Nuttall's story
or has picked up and developed crucial elements in the book's approach
to its subject matter. Thus Dr. Brachlow's recent monograph on radical
Puritan and Separatist ecclesiology has confirmed the good sense of an
approach to Puritanism that foregrounds the huge areas of common
ground, particularly over questions of piety and doctrine, uniting Separatists and semi-Separatists to mainstream Puritan opinion. Other work
on moderate Puritans has similarly stressed the links of thought and feeling binding together moderate and radical Puritans and has eschewed
definitions founded on the outward signs of Puritan commitment in
church ceremonies and government in favor of a more experiential approach. John Morgan's perceptive study of the Puritans' contradictory,
conflictual attitudes to reason and education finds many parallels in
Nuttall's account of these issues. For the later period, Nigel Smith's very
fine recent account of radical religion during the 1640s and 1650s likewise
stresses the links between the radical thought that provides his subject and
earlier Puritanism. N. H. Keble's examination of *The Literary Culture of
Non-Conformity* spends a great deal of time examining the literary forms
and voices appropriate to the heart religion founded upon the testimony of
the spirit located by Nuttall at the center of Puritan experience.[17]

But perhaps most notably Professor Davis's recent concern with antiformalism as an organizing concept for the study of the religious thought
of the 1650s and his related deconstruction of Whiggish construals of the
relationship between Puritanism, liberty, and toleration are anticipated
and encapsulated in Nuttall's almost throwaway remark that 'if freedom
be a keynote in Puritanism, so is theocracy; freedom is demanded, but in
order to facilitate obedience to God; those in whom the Spirit of God is
must bear their responsibility in judging the world and in ruling others;
the obverse of "the liberty of the Spirit" is "the government of the Spirit"'
(p. 119). In fact, what Professor Davis seems to be trying to do through

---

[17] N. Keble, *The Literary Culture of Non-Conformity in Later Seventeenth Century England*
(Leicester, 1987). See also S. Brachlow, *The Communion of Saints* (Oxford, 1988); P. Lake,
Moderate Puritans and the Elizabethan Church (Cambridge, 1982); J. Morgan, *Godly Learning*
(Cambridge, 1986); N. Smith, *Perfection Proclaimed* (Oxford, 1989).

his notion of antiformalism parallels very closely what Professor Nuttall was getting at through his explication of the doctrine of the Holy Spirit in radical Puritan thought and feeling. Moreover, Nuttall like Professor Davis is more prepared than some recent commentators to admit that such priorities did have effects in the running of church and state. His claims that 'this new-found spiritual liberty expressed itself both in a broad tolerance of difference within the fellowship of the Church, and in a demand for toleration as an established policy' (p. 113) and that 'toleration in the State, like tolerance in the Church, was a natural outcome of faith in "the liberty of the Spirit"' (p. 113) find considerable echoes in Professor Davis's recent brilliant account of 'Cromwell's religion' and the relations between that religion and the tolerance and toleration of the protectorate church.[18]

More generally still, to the extent that religion is back on the agenda for historians of the civil war and revolution, and to the extent that the links between that war and that revolution are once more a subject of concern, the general significance of this book both in terms of the thesis that it argues and of the methods it adopts to argue that thesis is considerable. In penetrating to the heart of the Puritan impulse, in explaining the links between mainstream and radical Puritanism, between the Puritanism of before and after 1640, we are arguably approaching a central strand in the events that produced the regicide and the republic, the protectorate and, indeed, the restoration.

To argue this is not to argue either that the authors cited above were all working under Professor Nuttall's direct influence (although many of them undoubtedly were) or that the value of this book only or mainly resides in the extent to which its findings and tone accord with more recent historical writing. Nor is it to contend that the value of studying religious thought and feeling lies mainly in the light it throws on other political, cultural, or social matters. It is rather to note the abiding value of a genuinely historical and sympathetic account of religious thought and feeling of the sort that is exemplified in this book: a book that remains perhaps the best single account of English Puritan thought in the later 1640s and the 1650s.

Peter Lake

---

[18] J. C. Davis, 'Cromwell's Religion', in Morrill, ed., *Oliver Cromwell and the English Revolution*. For a rather different view of the relationship between Cromwell's religion and toleration see B. Worden, 'Toleration and the Cromwellian Protectorate', in W. J. Sheils, ed., *Persecution and Toleration: Studies in Church History,* vol. 21 (Oxford, 1984).

FOREWORD TO THE SECOND EDITION

THE unexpectedly wide welcome to this book is reflected in generous reviews representing many types of Christian thought. From these emerge two points, brief reference to which may be useful to later readers.

Regret has been expressed that I have not related Puritan piety to similar kinds of faith and experience: in the Middle Ages, among the Anabaptists, in contemporary Continental Catholicism. Adequate treatment of this larger subject is most desirable, but was not possible in a detailed exposition of one particular period. Nor did I think it possible at all without the prior provision of that exposition. Cf. pp. 15 f., 19.

The other point relates to my treatment of Presbyterians, Congregationalists, Baptists and Quakers as representing, for our purpose, 'a largely logical development' (p. 14), and of Quakerism as indicating 'the *direction* of the Puritan movement as a whole' (p. viii). How few will study Church History without some *parti pris* ! Some are uneasy at the thought of fathering, or grandfathering, Quakerism; others accept my treatment as if it showed Quakerism to be the inevitable end, whether for evil or for good. But a logical development is not an inevitable one; and *direction* does not imply right *or* wrong direction. For the historian, who sees history as process, direction in itself, as of a river, is a regulative conception. That in this case 'the passage of individuals through the whole gamut' (p. 14; cf. pp. 13, 162) was, over and over again, in the one direction and almost never in the other, is, therefore, something of first importance. (To its perception, indeed, the book owes, in part, its very shape and method.) For its significance more widely I can but urge afresh the reading of Dr. Sippell's works (cf. p. 13, n. 8). These gain in impartiality from his Lutheranism. The geographer of the Rhine is not concerned to argue the superiority of residence at Basel, in the Rhine valley or on the flats of Holland. He loves the river as a whole, in whatever reaches he feels most at home. I have indicated on p. 177 where I feel most at home.

This edition includes a dozen small improvements or corrections, for some of which I must thank attentive readers.

G. F. N.

NEW COLLEGE, LONDON
Spring, 1947

FOREWORD

IN the earlier years of the present century, the centrality in the Christian religion of the doctrine of the Holy Spirit, with its manifold implications for Christian faith and experience, and the need for a fresh presentation of the doctrine, received frequent recognition. In 1901, for instance, Professor Moberly declared the indwelling of the Spirit of Christ to be the very essence of the Christian religion.[1] In 1913 Professor Royce called the article of the creed regarding the Holy Spirit the really distinctive and therefore the capital article.[2] In the same year Dr. Workman asserted a theology of the Holy Spirit to be the great need of the age.[3]

It cannot be said that the doctrine has received yet the attention which it deserves. In the last two decades more especially, the general moral upset and mental chaos have not been without their effect upon theology. The incursions of psychologists into religious spheres have caused alarm over what many had come to regard as faith's inner and impregnable fortress. The desire to lean upon a powerful external authority, which politically found expression in Fascism and National-Socialism, has favoured the claims both of the Roman Catholic Church and of a 'Word of God' in Scripture which judges but may not be judged. Rudolf Otto and Karl Barth have proclaimed a God Who is *ganz Anderes* and a revelation which is purely divine and given, *sui generis*, containing no element of human, and therefore fallible, creation or even discovery. Neo-Thomists and Neo-Calvinists agree in laying emphasis upon dogmas and confessions, and tend to treat faith as assent to a static deposit, to a closed system, of doctrine, rather than as an ἐνέργεια springing directly from living, personal experience. In the reaction against an optimistic humanism which seemed hardly to need any doctrine of the Holy Spirit, human incapacity through Original Sin has been so exaggerated latterly as virtually to deny the doctrine.

Over against a degree of moral despair, on the one hand, and, on the other, over against the unbalanced psychology of the 'Group Movement', which seems to have hardly less distrust of the normal activities of reason and conscience, a fresh presentation of the doctrine of the Holy Spirit and of the doctrine's implications would be of great value. It is to such a presentation, from a particular historical angle, that this study is intended as a contribution. As a thesis, it was approved by the University of Oxford for the award of the degree of Doctor of Divinity.

[1] Cf. R. C. Moberly, *Atonement and Personality*, p. 90.
[2] Cf. J. Royce, *The Problem of Christianity*, III. 15.
[3] Cf. H. B. Workman, *The Dawn of the Reformation*, II. xi.

As is shown more at length in the historical introduction, the doctrine, with its manifold implications, received a more thorough and detailed consideration from the Puritans of seventeenth-century England than it has received at any other time in Christian history. Puritan discussion and interpretation of the doctrine may be treated, indeed, as a vantage-ground from which to survey, and better to understand, the various contributions and emphases of the Puritan movement as a whole. It is hoped that the present study may provide not only stimulus to fresh contemporary thinking but a new appreciation of Puritanism, an appreciation of a synoptic nature.

In particular, an attempt is made to present early Quakerism in its immediate historical context. Quaker writers tend to concentrate upon mediaeval and sixteenth-century mystics, the similarity of whose teaching with that of the early Quakers is primarily of academic interest, and to neglect the spiritual climate in which, as a matter of fact, Quakerism arose. Non-Quaker writers, on the other hand, tend to ignore Quakerism as an unimportant and extreme vagary in seventeenth-century piety. In the present study early Quakerism is treated as of the first importance, because it indicates the *direction* of the Puritan movement as a whole. Attention is drawn to the numerous similarities, as well as to the fundamental difference, between Quakerism and the radical Puritanism of which in many ways it was the logical outcome; and because of its mediating position, radical Puritanism receives particularly careful consideration. This accounts for the small place given to certain aspects of theology and ecclesiology, to which orthodox Calvinists devoted much thought; the radical Puritans, with their more qualified admiration for Calvin, had a different centre of reference.

In a work of this kind there is bound to be much quotation, but an attempt has been made to quote no more than is needed for the purpose of the immediate argument. The presence of dots indicates where excisions from passages quoted have been made. The references in the footnotes make it possible to discover what has been omitted from any passage, or to read passages more at large in their several contexts. The extreme frequency of reference to the *Dictionary of National Biography* is unusual, but calls for no apology. The *Dictionary* has the unevenness of all symposia; but at the least it is a useful biographical and bibliographical directory, and, where writers are as eminent in their own field as are, for instance, Gardiner, Firth, and Alexander Gordon, to neglect their contributions would seem an excess of preciosity.

My thanks are due, and are expressed very gladly, to Dr. Theodor Sippell of Marburg, who in the course of almost daily conversations during the winter of 1936-7 inspired me with his own interest in radical Puritanism, and most generously made me free of his exceptionally fine collection of the relevant literature. In the autumn of 1938, when the present study first took shape in my own mind, Dr. Sippell again warmly supported me. His published work, in particular his *Werdendes Quäkertum*, more than the work of any other scholar, represents the path which led me to my own researches. It has been with regret that since the outbreak of war in 1939 I have been unable to turn to him for continued advice and criticism.

In a work of this nature it seems desirable that passages written in languages other than English should usually be quoted as they stand. To this rule I have made one exception: passages quoted from Welsh are translated in the text, and the originals are printed in an appendix. For assistance in the translation of these Welsh passages I am indebted to the Rev. Dafydd Ap-Thomas, M.A., B.D., of the University College of North Wales, Bangor. For the loan of many books I must also thank the Librarians of Dr. Williams' Library, London; of Friends House, London; and of Mansfield College, Oxford. Dr. Roderic Dunkerley, B.A., B.D., and Mr. P. A. Spalding, M.A., have given generous help with proof-reading.

Of the many friends who have helped me with unfailing interest in my work, I will mention only three: my Father; the late Dr. W. B. Selbie, of Oxford; and L. Hugh Doncaster, of Woodbrooke, who read this book in manuscript. To these, and to many whom I do not name, I am deeply grateful.

Finally, I would acknowledge my great debt to the Council and Readership Committee of Woodbrooke, in the Selly Oak Colleges, Birmingham, who, by inviting me to take up a Research Fellowship for the year 1943-4, enabled me to devote the major part of my energies to the writing of this book. In the Bevan-Naish collection of Quaker and other literature, including some thousands of rare seventeenth-century pamphlets, which is now housed within its walls, Woodbrooke provided much material to my purpose. Woodbrooke also provided something of yet more importance in 'the life and fellowship of the Spirit', which I shared throughout the year, and out of which this book was written.

GEOFFREY F. NUTTALL

New College, London
Spring, 1946

THE HOLY SPIRIT IN PURITAN
FAITH AND EXPERIENCE

The following abbreviations are used for works to which frequent reference is made:—

B.Q.   = W. C. Braithwaite, *The Beginnings of Quakerism* (1923 edn.).
C.R.   = *Calamy Revised*, ed. A. G. Matthews.
D.N.B. = *Dictionary of National Biography*, ed. Sir L. Stephen and Sir S. Lee.
P.G.F. = A. N. Brayshaw, *The Personality of George Fox* (1933 edn.)
Q.S.M. = A. N. Brayshaw, *The Quakers: their Story and Message* (1938 edn.).
R.B.   = *Reliquiae Baxterianae*, ed. M. Sylvester (quoted by part and section).
S.P.Q. = W. C. Braithwaite, *The Second Period of Quakerism* (1921 edn.).

HISTORICAL INTRODUCTION

SYNOPSIS OF ARGUMENT

i. Great questions engaging men's minds sometimes like underground
streams;
questions about Holy Spirit of this type.
Long-continued neglect of doctrine of Holy Spirit before Reformation:
reasons for this:
vagueness attaching to conception of Spirit
linguistically
imaginatively
theologically;
line of development taken by Christianity in the West:
Hellenism
hierarchic system
clericalism;
no reference to Holy Spirit in St. Thomas' treatment of revelation;
official condemnation of Montanism and Joachism.
ii. Recovery of interest in doctrine of Holy Spirit at Reformation:
reasons for this:
dissolution of hierarchic system
translation of Bible into vernacular
renaissance of learning, with encouragement of private
judgement.
At first, little direct or detailed attention paid to doctrine of Holy Spirit:
perception of issue by Erasmus
E. Campion
but not by Protestant controversialists of sixteenth century.
iii. Pioneer thinking on subject in seventeenth century, with interest in
religious experience: this characteristic of seventeenth century
in England generally: illustrations from other spheres: effect in
religious sphere.
The period 'an age of excitement': 1640-1660 the subject's *Blütezeit*.

iv. Use of the term *Puritan*:
> in narrower sense, exclusive of Separatists
> in wider sense, inclusive of Separatists and of Nonconformists of
>> 1662.

The parties within Puritanism:
> middle party led by R. Baxter (right wing)
>> J. Owen (left wing).
> conservative party Presbyterians: distinction between Scottish and
>> English Presbyterianism: L. Seaman, T. Hall,
>> R. Hollinworth.
> radical party Congregationalists *or* individualists:
>> S. Petto, M. Llwyd, W. Cradock, P. Sterry,
>> J. Saltmarsh, W. Dell, R. Williams, W.
>> Erbury.

The Quakers the conservatives' fiercest foes
> but extend and fuse much in radical Puritanism.

The Baptist position, in relation to doctrine of Holy Spirit, not essentially different from the radical Congregational.

v. A broadly chronological treatment, by denominations, possible
> but inevitably an over-simplification
>> in some cases a falsification
>>> lacking in clarity.

A logical analysis preferable.

vi. Influences on the Puritans largely subterranean: the radical Puritans' repudiation of tradition.

Influence of Boehme and
> Cambridge Platonists on Quakers over-estimated.

Independent lay searching: illustrated from Lucy Hutchinson
>> Mary Springett.

Puritan faith and experience itself the chosen universe of discourse.

THE great questions which engage men's minds across the centuries are like streams which flow partly underground. Above ground the stream's appearances are discrete. Below, it is itself continuous. It is continuous, not identical; for lower down not only is it fuller from the rains it received in its upper reaches, its colour also is altered by the new soil through which it now flows. So, of the questions which men ask in any age, it is inevitable that some, at least, should be related, and even similar, to questions asked by other men in earlier generations. Yet they will never be quite the same questions, partly just because they have been asked before, and partly because of the change in the conditions and mental framework in which they are asked.

Questions about the Holy Spirit are of this type. Quite early in the Christian centuries they may be found, and from time to time they reappear. Over the greater part of the first fifteen hundred years, however, they remain largely an underground stream. One reason for this may be found in a certain vagueness which attaches to the conception of Spirit, linguistically, imaginatively, and theologically. It is a fascinating study, to trace the linguistic development from the wind-breath[1] connotation of *rûaḥ* through $\pi\nu\epsilon\hat{\upsilon}\mu\alpha$ and *spiritus*, to such different associations as in English, French, and German, to go no further, have gathered about *spirit, Geist, esprit*. Through its welcome to Saxon and Romance words alike, English provides us with both *ghost* and *spirit*; and in both cases[2] the word has come to be used in a way quite foreign to the meaning attaching to the Holy Spirit. Again, although the Spirit is itself the *situs* of life and personality, and is defined in the creed as a person, men have not found it easy imaginatively to picture the Spirit as personal, in the way which it has been natural to picture the Father and the Son. In the popular mediaeval representation of the Trinity, while the Ancient of Days and the Crucified Christ are both portrayed anthropomorphically, the Spirit is shown as a dove.[3] Once more, theologically, there is within the New Testament itself a development, more marked even than the development in Christology, from the natural neuter $\tau o\hat{\upsilon}\tau o$ of *Acts* ii. 16 to the masculine $\dot{\epsilon}\kappa\epsilon\hat{\iota}\nu o s$ of *John* xvi. 13: a progressive *Christificierung des Geistes* may be traced.[4] Moreover, it might well be asked why the $\pi\nu\epsilon\hat{\upsilon}\mu\alpha$ $\Theta\epsilon o\hat{\upsilon}$ should be 'personified' more than the $\theta\dot{\epsilon}\lambda\eta\mu\alpha$ $\Theta\epsilon o\hat{\upsilon}$, or the $\pi\nu\epsilon\hat{\upsilon}\mu\alpha$ $X\rho\acute{\iota}\sigma\tau o\upsilon$ more than the $\nu o\hat{\upsilon}s$ $X\rho\acute{\iota}\sigma\tau o\upsilon$. Both for language, then, and for the imagination and thought which language expresses, there have been complications and difficulties which partly explain the comparative neglect from which the doctrine of the Holy Spirit has suffered.

There are also more local reasons for the neglect, reasons bound up with the main line of development followed by Christianity in the West. The dominance of Hellenic modes of thought was unfavourable to concentration on a doctrine antecedently and essentially

---

[1] As, in English, one *breathes* through the *wind*pipe.

[2] The use of *ghost* for 'a departed spirit' may be traced back, through such a phrase as 'he gave up the ghost' for $\dot{\epsilon}\xi\acute{\epsilon}\pi\nu\epsilon\upsilon\sigma\epsilon$, to the primitive identification of the breath with life (cf. *Gen.* ii. 7), and hence with the soul, represented in mediaeval painting in the form of a child issuing from the mouth of a dying man. The use of *spirit* for alcoholic liquor is interesting in view of the connexion between 'being filled with the Spirit' and drunkenness in *Acts* ii. 13–17 and *Eph.* v. 18.

[3] Occasionally the Spirit also is portrayed anthropomorphically: cf. F. Bond, *Dedications and Patron Saints of English Churches*, p. 260; J. E. Morris, *York*, p. 92, with n. 1.

[4] Cf. C. A. Anderson Scott, *Christianity According to St. Paul*, p. 144, with n. 1.

Hebraic. The establishment of Christianity in settled ways did not encourage enthusiasm. Its hierarchic and clerical system was bound to oppose any emphasis perceived to be dangerously individualist and lay. 'The long neglect into which the genuine Catholic doctrine of inspiration . . . had been suffered to fall'[1] receives incidental but striking illustration in the extraordinarily small number of ecclesiastical dedications to the Holy Spirit.[2] 'Aquinas treats the whole subject of revelation without referring to the Spirit.'[3] Where the stream did appear above ground, as in Montanism or Joachism, its waters were quickly condemned by authority as heretically defiled and poisonous.[4] *Prêcher un évangile du Saint-Esprit, c'était bouleverser complètement l'économie des âges du monde.*[5]

It was thus not fortuitous that a return of interest in the doctrine of the Holy Spirit, and a fresh conviction of its centrality for Christian faith and experience, are characteristics of the Reformation. Only through such a revolution as was effected in the break-up of the Middle Ages was such a recovery possible. The ecclesiastical system, with its centralization in an ultimate, single source of authority, was dissolved. The Bible was translated into the vernacular, for men to read for themselves, unchecked. The Renaissance of learning encouraged men to think for themselves, and the spirit of individualism became as potent in theological as in other mental disciplines. These and other influences combined to direct men's attention, for the first time in their lives and with some suddenness, to the nature of religion in the Bible, and more especially in the New Testament, as something individually experienced, a living, personal relationship, open to Everyman, between God and his soul. The doctrine bearing most nearly upon this experience and relationship on its Godward side was the doctrine of the Holy Spirit.

For some time yet, however, little direct or detailed attention was paid to the doctrine. Many of those who first recovered for their own lives the experience of New Testament Christianity were quite content with the joy of living it, and had no wish to work out its theoretical implications or to consider the problems which it raised. The revolution, moreover, was a violent one, and in untrained,

---

[1] E. I. Watkin, in *Great Catholics* (*s.v.* D. Baker), p. 235. Mr. Watkin interprets the Quaker emphasis on immediate inspiration as a revenge for this 'long neglect'.

[2] Apparently only three such ancient dedications are known in England: at Basingstoke, Hants, and Marton and Wappenbury, Warws. Cf. F. Bond, *op. cit., s.v.*

[3] T. Rees, *The Holy Spirit in Thought and Experience*, p. 176.

[4] The Lollards also contrasted the priesthood of Rome with that of the Holy Ghost: cf. their conclusions presented to Parliament in 1395, in *English Historical Review*, xxii. 29.

[5] E. Gilson, *L'Esprit de la Philosophie Médiévale*, ii. 273, n. 13.

ill-balanced minds the wheel turned so completely as to alarm the
more reflective and conservative. Many of the questions with which
we shall be concerned are touched upon already by Erasmus. The
freedom of the Spirit, he says, had been the burden of his message;
but by 1527 he had come to regret it. *Rarum est donum discretio
spirituum*, he had remarked earlier. Was not the spirit which inspired
the Reformers the spirit of folly, even the spirit of Satan? There were,
he thought, both moral and intellectual grounds for fearing so. One
wonders how far in the end he accepted the judgement expressed
by Sigismund I's physician, Benedicti, that it was absurd for the
Lutherans to preach their possession of the Holy Spirit

> *tanquam ob humanam fragillitatem numquam spiritus ab hominibus recederet,
> ignorantes . . . in nullo Spiritum Sanctum remansisse excepto Christo. . . . In
> Lutheranis ergo non est . . . Spiritus Sanctus, qui est spiritus mansuetudinis . . .
> qui non est autor conffusionis, sed pacis.*[1]

To *discretio spirituum, fragillitas humana* and to *mansuetudo* and *pax* or
ordo we shall find the discussion insistently returning as we proceed.

Fifty years later, another brilliant controversialist, Edmund Cam-
pion, had sufficient penetration to perceive that in the doctrine of the
Holy Spirit lay the fundamental difference between Protestantism and
Roman Catholicism, a difference deeper than that over Scripture, for
which in fact it was the basis. To Campion's accusation that the
Protestants are *opifices bibliorum, qui sua lima politula et elegantula vetus
novumque Testamentum raserunt*, they reply, he says, *non se veras
Scripturas exscindere, sed excernere supposititias*; and to his question, *quo
iudice?* their reply is *Spiritu sancto*. Campion then presents an impres-
sive list of critical reformed judgements on biblical books (many of
which are now accepted), and concludes with fine scorn, *credant suo
quisque spiritui*.[2] Here, again, we have in little the whole problem,
which is to concern us, of the relation between the Spirit and the
Word.

That Erasmus and Campion thus recognized where the essential
division lay is an indication of their genius. Their perception was far
sharper than that of Protestant controversialists, who for the most
part were unwilling to face the problems both of ethics and of
psychology which in time the recognition was bound to present.

---

[1] Cf. *Opus Epistolarum Erasmi Roterodami*, ed. P. S. and H. M. Allen, *Epp.* 1887, 1384, 948,
1483, 2601; G. F. Nuttall, 'Towards an appreciation of Erasmus', in *Congregational Quarterly*,
July 1936, p. 342.
[2] E. Campion, *Rationes Decem, prima ratio* (ed. J. H. Pollard, 1914, pp. 41 ff.); cf. *tertia ratio*
(p. 48), where the heretics give as their authority *Nos, qui divinitus edocti sumus*, and to Campion's
query, *Fabulae qui credam?*, reply, *Si arderes fide, tam scires hoc, quam te vivere.*

Die Furcht vor dem Geist ist unter den Vertretern kirchlicher Frömmigkeit gross:[1] it is a principle of the widest application. In the earliest teaching of Luther, it is true, there are 'spiritual' emphases, to which later *Spiritualisten* sometimes refer for support;[2] but in his later teaching, especially after the Peasants' Revolt, still more in the teaching of his followers, such emphases are quickly overlaid. Calvinism, again, included a distinctive doctrine of the witness of the Spirit; but after Calvin this 'tended to recede into the background'.[3] Calvin himself, for all his stress on the Spirit's witness, yielding an intuitive certitude of Scripture as αὐτόπιστος,[4] has been pronounced justly *kein Geistesmensch.*[5] From time to time individuals under persecution were driven by the force of events (perhaps rather than of logic) to fall back in assertion on their possession of, and dependence on, the Holy Spirit;[6] and such sectarian movements as Anabaptism on the Continent,[7] or the Separatism of Browne and Barrow in this country, were bound up with a reassertion of the doctrine.[8] As a rule, however, neither martyrs nor leaders had the mental powers or the leisure of spirit to perceive the importance of this, and to examine its implications for faith and experience. Such a state of affairs obtained largely up to the end of the sixteenth century.

It may thus be seen how, with the growth and increasing power of Puritanism in the seventeenth century, the way was clear for some pioneer thinking about the doctrine of the Holy Spirit. Richard

---

[1] E. Schaeder, *Das Geistproblem der Theologie*, p. 59, n. 1.

[2] Cf. E. Troeltsch, *The Social Teaching of the Christian Churches*, II. 934, 947 f., 962 f.

[3] A. Dakin, *Calvinism*, p. 202. In Reformed Protestantism the fear of the self-deceits of enthusiasm is so strong, *dass das testimonium spiritus sancti regelmässig erst nach den andern Zeichen und Ueberzeugungsgründen aufgeführt, ja nicht selten in die übrigen signa aufgelöst wird*: M. Schneckenburger, *Vergleichende Darstellung des lutherischen u. reformirten Lehrbegriffs*, p. 72.

[4] *Institutio*, I. vii. 5.

[5] P. Wernle, *Calvin*, p. 49. For Calvin the Holy Spirit is a necessity of thought rather than something known in experience. *Damit hängt es zusammen, dass er so korrekt biblisch vom Geist redet; aus dem Persönlichen hat er nichts darüber zu sagen.*

[6] Cf., e.g., Anne Askew, when examined by Christopher Dare in 1545: 'he asked me if I had the Spirit of God in me? I answered, if I had not, I was but a reprobate or cast-away': J. Bale, *Works* (Parker Soc.), p. 151; Henry Barrow, when examined by Lancelot Andrewes in 1590: 'I have the spirit of the Apostles': F. J. Powicke, *Henry Barrow*, p. 93.

[7] The kind of extravagance which prevented conservative minds from giving serious attention to the matter may be illustrated from the remark of a Strasburg Anabaptist: *meinst du, dass mein Geist sich nach dem Maas des Paulus einschränken müsse?*: cf. J. Adam, *Evangelische Kirchengeschichte der Stadt Strassburg*, p. 117.

[8] Cf. E. Troeltsch, *op. cit.*, II. 661 f.: 'Browne believed that the spirit was all that mattered' and based 'the life of the Church solely upon the inward power of the Spirit'. Barrow's anticipation of Quaker practice in rejecting the democratic principle of discovering majorities by voting, for the charismatic principle of seeking the unity of the Spirit in 'the sense of the meeting' is noteworthy in this connexion: cf. H. Barrow, *A Plaine Refutation of M. Giffards Booke*, p. 78.

Baxter, with the forthright penetration characteristic of him, declares the doctrine to be 'a most practical article of our belief';[1] and the Puritan approach throughout the century is with practice clearly in view. When John Owen, in the preface to his Πνευματολογία, declares, 'I know not of any who ever went before me in this Design of representing the whole Oeconomy of the Holy Spirit',[2] he is neither ignorant of, nor antagonistic to, the work of the early Fathers. Indeed, he explicitly combines 'the Suffrage of the Ancient Church' with 'the plain Testimonies of the Scripture' and 'the Experience of them who do sincerely believe' as the foundation on which 'the substance of what is delivered' securely rests. Neither Owen nor any of his fellow authors is concerned to deny or to controvert the classic expositions of the doctrine.[3] Their concern is rather to draw out its implications for faith and practice. What is new, and what justifies Owen in his claim to be among the pioneers, is the place given in Puritan exposition to experience, and its acceptance as a primary authority, in the way indicated in the passage just quoted. The interest is primarily not dogmatic, at least not in any theoretic sense, it is experimental. There is theology, but, in a way which has hardly been known since St. Augustine, it is a *theologia pectoris*.

This stress on experience is, indeed, a characteristic of the seventeenth century in England, the century which has Hamlet as its prototype and exemplar, and one could be only surprised if there were no corresponding emphasis in theology. At what other stage in philosophical development would it be argued *cogito, ergo sum*?[4] It is the age of diaries, often intensely introspective and finding in the slightest events God's personal dealings with the writers' souls;[5] and of the earliest memoirs and autobiographies. In painting Rembrandt speaks for the age in his recurrent fascination with himself: perhaps

---

[1] R. Baxter, *Works*, ed. W. Orme, II. 189.

[2] J. Owen, Πνευματολογία, 'To the Readers'.

[3] There was a small amount of Socinianism among the seventeenth-century Independents but it appears that John Bidle stood alone in denying the Godhead of the Holy Spirit, in this connexion expressly dissociating himself from Socinus. Owen's *Vindiciae Evangelicae* was a reply to Bidle's *Catechism*, which was considered so blasphemous that all copies which could be found were ordered to be burnt; cf. A. Gordon, *Heads of English Unitarian History*, p. 18; A. B. Grosart, in *D.N.B.*, *s.v.*, as Biddle.

[4] A. Dakin, *op. cit.*, p. 204, compares Descartes' *cogito, ergo sum* with Calvin's *testimonium internum spiritus sancti*; cf. E. Caird, *The Philosophy of Kant*, p. 30, for a comparison of Luther with Bacon: 'this return to experience is the point of union between the revivers of learning and the Reformers'.

[5] For an analysis of Puritan diaries, cf. M. M. Knappen, *Two Elizabethan Puritan Diaries*. It is significant that the early diaries of Presbyterian Scotland vastly outnumber those of Roman Catholic Ireland.

no painter has left so many, or such penetrating, *Selbstbildnisse*.[1] Rembrandt's picture, again, of Dr. Tulp at his anatomy class in Amsterdam (1632) is representative of much else besides: indeed *anatomy*[2] is one of the period's catchwords, Burton's *Anatomy of Melancholy* (1621) being only the most famous of a plethora of publications in whose title it occurs.[3]

In religion, consequently, it is the age of 'prophesying', of 'telling experiences',[4] of preaching 'what I felt, what I smartingly did feel',[5] activities which will fall within our purview. In 1645 were held the first meetings of what afterwards became the Royal Society, for inquiring particularly into 'what hath been called the new philosophy or experimental philosophy'.[6] Less than two years later, George Fox 'heard a voice which said, "There is one, even Christ Jesus, that can speak to thy condition," . . . and this I knew experimentally'.[7] The identity of the epithet is not coincidental or subditious, as will become abundantly evident from what follows.

Macaulay rightly calls the period 'an age of excitement',[8] an excitement which 'broke bounds with the civil war'.[9] The civil war also 'gave centrifugal religious forces a long-sought opportunity', so that 'by the year 1644 the constant appearance of new and fantastic sects became a scandalous but insurmountable fact'.[10] A feature natural to most of these sects is their claim to the liberty of the Spirit in faith and experience, and their claim forced consideration of the matter even upon those who found it abhorrent. Much discussion of the subject had been published earlier, and works such as those by Owen, Howe, and John and Thomas Goodwin did not appear, at least in print, some of them posthumously, till well on in the Restoration period; but the sectarian activity of the middle years makes the two decades 1640 to 1660 the subject's *Blütezeit*.

It is desirable to say something of the use and meaning of the term *Puritan*. Apart from its popular contemporary use, in common with other religious sobriquets, as a term of mockery or abuse,[11] the name

---

[1] F. Ried, *Das Selbstbildnis*, pp. 61 ff., calls attention to Rembrandt's *Selbsterforschungsfanatismus*.

[2] *Analysis* was not used in a logical sense till 1680: cf. *Oxford English Dictionary*, *s.v.*

[3] Cf. also the title of R. Brereley's poem, *Self Civil War.*

[4] Cf., e.g., the minister who 'burst out Into a passion & saide hee coulde speake his experiences as well as I': G. Fox, *Journal*, ed. N. Penney, I. 54.

[5] J. Bunyan, *Grace Abounding*, § 276; cf. J. Brown, *Puritan Preaching in England*, pp. 56 f.

[6] *D.N.B.*, *s.v.* J. Wilkins.   [7] G. Fox, *Journal* (1901 edn.), I. 11.

[8] T. B. Macaulay, *Essays* (1863 edn.), I. 136.

[9] A. Gordon, in *D.N.B.*, *s.v.* M. Hopkins, in connexion with 'witchfinding'.

[10] P. Miller, *Orthodoxy in Massachusetts, 1630–1650*, p. 269.

[11] Cf., e.g., R. Baxter's remark of his father that, 'only for reading Scripture when the rest were Dancing on the Lord's Day, and for praying (by a Form out of the end of the Common-

in its narrower sense may be contrasted with the name Separatist. Both parties desired greater purity in the worship and government of the Church, and in the lives of the Church's members; but, while the Puritans had hopes of further reform within the Church as at present established, and therefore stayed, often in some discomfort, within its fold, the Separatists, in despair of any early or sufficient reform within the confines of the Established Church, felt driven to form entirely new congregations on an independent, extra-parochial basis. Robert Browne's *Treatise of Reformation without Tarying for Anie* (1571)[1] was the clarion-call of the Separatist movement, and Browne, though he later conformed, was then clear that complete Separatism was imperative. Many later Separatists, however, dissociated themselves from Browne, and the movement included all shades of opinion how far, if at all, it was justifiable to have communion with the Established Church.

In this contradistinguishing sense, the Separatists were not Puritans; but their taking the final step of Separatism left undestroyed the greater part of those ideas and ideals which still, as hitherto, they had in common with the more conservative Puritans from among whom they came. In this wider sense Puritanism must be held to include Separatism. Similarly, the ministers who held livings within the Established Church during the Interregnum were by that very fact not Separatists; when in 1662 some of these were ejected from their livings, they became Nonconformists,[2] but remained Puritans no less than before. Some of the Episcopalians within the Established Church, all the Presbyterians and Independents in it before 1662, most of the Separatist and sectarian leaders outside it, and the founders of Nonconformity after 1662, are thus all spiritually nearer to one another than is any of them to the Roman Catholic Church or to the Laudian party[3] within the Church of England. They have their own internal differences, some of them sharp, and sometimes turning, as we shall see, on their doctrine of the Holy Spirit; but in a large sense they have much in common, and for this faith and experience which they share,

Prayer Book) in his House, and for reproving Drunkards and Swearers, and for talking sometimes a few words of Scripture and the Li e to come, he was reviled commonly by the Name of *Puritan, Precisian,* and *Hypocrite*; and so were the Godly Conformable Ministers ...': *R. B.*, i. 1.

[1] There is a modern edition by F. J. Powicke (1903).

[2] The terminology is apt to be confused by the use of the term Nonconformist for those outside the Established Church after 1662, whereas earlier it had been used as a synonym for the radical Puritans within the Church: John Owen describes his father as 'a Nonconformist all his days' (*Works*, ed. W. H. Goold, XIII. 224); cf. *R.B.*, i. 19: 'I daily disputed against the Nonconformists; for I found their Censoriousness and Inclinations towards Seperation (in the weaker sort of them) to be a Threatning Evil'.

[3] What Baxter calls 'the New Prelatical way (Dr. Hammond's)': *R.B.*, i. 140.

and which in one regard is the subject of this study, there is no other name than Puritan.

The situation will become clearer if we consider the position of representative leaders. Baxter and Owen have been quoted already, and will be used largely in the sequel. Baxter is usually considered a Presbyterian, but in point of fact he never was one.[1] 'Till Mr. Ball wrote for the Liturgy and against Can and Allen, etc., and Mr. Burton published his *Protestation Protested*,' he says revealingly, 'I never thought what Presbytery or Independency were, nor ever spake with a man that seemed to know it. And that was in 1641.'[2] In 1638 he had been ordained deacon by John Thornborough, Bishop of Worcester. 'The known facts preclude the possibility of his having proceeded to the priesthood',[3] but both his curacy at Bridgnorth and the first year of his vicarage at Kidderminster were held within the Established Church before episcopacy had been abolished, and later he used his influence to prevent the inhabitants of Kidderminster and of Worcestershire generally from taking the Covenant.[4] Furthermore, the Worcestershire Agreement of 1652, Baxter's scheme of voluntary association comprehending Episcopalians, Presbyterians, and Independents, was based, in contrast with Parliamentary Presbyterianism, on the rectoral rights of the parish clergyman, and for the government of the parish Baxter preferred the old system of churchwardens.[5] In 1662 his conscience forced him to vacate his living and to become technically a Nonconformist, but throughout the years of persecution he continued to oppose, as savouring of Separatism, the formation of Nonconformist congregations, and for himself declined any pastorate even after 1689.[6] Baxter's title for himself was a 'meer Catholick';[7] the only description which fits him throughout his ministry, and which he would not have repudiated,[8] is Puritan.

Baxter thus led what may be called the right wing of the middle party in Puritanism, and his convictions about the subject of our study will be found to be always judicious and never extremist.[9] The leader of the middle party's left wing was John Owen. Owen, though episcopally ordained, and only a year or less Baxter's junior, was already a Presbyterian, and ready to defend the Presbyterian

---

[1] A. Gordon, *op. cit.*, p. 63.   [2] R. Baxter, *True History of Councils*, p. 90.

[3] F. J. Powicke, in *Times Literary Supplement*, Jan. 22, 1925, p. 56. Dr. Powicke remarks that 'no question of "status" was raised . . . when he was offered the see of Hereford' in 1660: *ib.*, Feb. 5, 1925, p. 88.

[4] *R.B.*, i. 100.   [5] A. Gordon, *op. cit.*, p. 64.   [6] *Ibid.* p. 83.   [7] *R.B.*, i. 140.

[8] Cf. his acceptance of the description of himself as one *qui totum Puritanismum tantus spirat*, towards the end of the unpaginated foreword to his *Church-History*.

[9] Cf. G. F. Nuttall, 'The Personality of Richard Baxter', in *Friends' Quarterly Examiner*, April 1945.

system,[1] when in 1643 he accepted his first living at Fordham. By the time he became Vicar of Coggeshall he had been converted to Independency,[2] and to the end of his life, whether as Dean of Christchurch and Vice-Chancellor during much of the Commonwealth, or as a Nonconformist minister after 1662, he may justly be called 'the leading figure among Congregational divines'.[3] On this account he has received perhaps somewhat excessive attention. Owen was more decidedly Nonconformist than Baxter, and became the pastor of an Independent congregation in London[4] (though he escaped imprisonment, which Baxter did not); but his having been one of those Independents who had sought to combine Congregationalism with a State Church system had its effect in keeping him in the middle way,[5] opposed to extremer Separatism, and Stoughton is not wrong in summing him up as 'in theology, and in some ecclesiastical respects likewise, a very decided Conservative,' 'an Aristotle among Puritans'.[6] Baxter himself couples Owen with Francis Cheynell as 'the two over-Orthodox Doctors';[7] and of the two strands which went to the making of Congregationalism,[8] the Calvinist and the Anabaptist, Owen's sympathies were with the former.

In the fully conservative Puritan party, in Presbyterianism, there were, again, two wings. There was the Scottish tradition, the 'presbyterian government dependent', with its fully articulated hierarchy of kirk sessions, presbyteries, synods, and general assembly, defended in England in 1645 by John Bastwick[9] and represented in the Westminster Assembly pre-eminently by the Scottish commissioners. There was also the English tradition since the days of Cartwright and Bradshaw, the 'presbyterian government independent', that is, the system of autonomous congregations, the internal government of which was Presbyterian. This distinction explains why the Presbyterianism even of such a supporter as Stephen Marshall, who held the internal polity to be *iure divino*, 'was never sufficiently severe for the

---

[1] In his *Duties of Pastors and People Distinguished* (*Works*, XIII).

[2] Cf. his *Vindication of the Treatise on Schism* (*Works*, XIII. 222 f.).   [3] *C.R.*, *s.v.*

[4] He had already put Congregational principles into practice at Coggeshall; cf. his *Eshcol; or Rules of Direction for the Walking of the Saints in Fellowship* (*Works*, XIII).

[5] What in the preface to his Presbyterian treatise mentioned above (*Works*, XIII. 5) he calls the 'habitable earth between the valley (I had almost said the pit) of democratical confusion and the precipitous rock of hierarchical tyranny'. The words added in parenthesis reveal which peril he feared the more, and he did not change his temperament with his denomination. In his *Brief Instruction in the Word of God* (1667; *Works*, xv), 'he giveth up', as Baxter remarks, 'two of the worst of the Principles of Popularity' (*R.B.*, iii. 141).

[6] J. Stoughton, *Religion in England*, II. 249, 406.

[7] *R.B.*, ii. 55; for Cheynell, cf. *D.N.B.*, *s.v.*

[8] The combination is studied in detail by P. T. Forsyth, *Faith, Freedom and the Future*.

[9] In his *Independency not Gods Ordinance ... Wherein is evidently proved that the Presbyterian Government Dependent is Gods Ordinance, and not the Presbyterian Government Independent*.

Scottish delegates';[1] their stricter system was in England 'an exotic novelty'.[2] So far as our subject is concerned, it is, as a rule, only the moderate Presbyterians who so much as take notice of it, and then always with a strictly conservative bias. Lazarus Seaman, who in the Westminster Assembly maintained the *ius divinum* of Presbyterianism, and who had a controversy with the Independent Sidrach Simpson over lay preaching, is an exception. Generally speaking, the few Presbyterians with whom we shall have to do are the more accommodating, such as Thomas Hall, a man 'of a quick Spirit',[3] who was unable to join Baxter's Worcestershire Agreement but signed Baxter's petition for the retention of tithes and a settled ministry, or Richard Hollinworth, whose *Holy Ghost on the Bench* well represents the moderate conservative point of view among the Puritans.[4]

In the party at the opposite pole within Puritanism, the fully radical party, we find no longer two wings, as in the conservative and middle parties. We find, rather, a series of positions which shade off, through increasingly complete Separatism, into pure and acknowledged individualism. There are, for instance, Samuel Petto and Morgan Llwyd, who hold livings in the Established Church before 1662 but are convinced Congregationalists[5] of a much more enthusiastic type than John Owen. There are Walter Cradock and Peter Sterry, the one voluntarily abandoning his vicarage, the other never beneficed, Congregationalists of the type which Cromwell liked to have about him as his chaplains. There are John Saltmarsh and William Dell, both army chaplains[6] and both more extreme Congregationalists and already inclined to be 'free lances' in their judgements. There are Roger Williams and William Erbury, who finally dissociated themselves explicitly from any existing denomination, preferring a frankly individualistic position. All these men have much to say of the doctrine of the Holy Spirit.[7] Finally, from 1650 onwards, there are

---

[1] A. Gordon, in *D.N.B.*, *s.v.*   [2] *Id.*, *ib.*, *s.v.* P. Nye.   [3] *R.B.*, iii. 203 (8).

[4] All these men are the subjects of articles in *D.N.B.*; cf. also F. J. Powicke, 'Thomas Hall', in *Bulletin* of John Rylands Library, VIII. 1; 'Thomas Hall' in *Proceedings* of Birmingham and Midland Institute, XIV; C. W. Sutton, 'Richard Heyrick and Richard Hollinworth' in *Transactions* of Lancashire and Cheshire Antiquarian Society, VII.

[5] The appellation *Congregational* has the advantage over the appellation *Independent*, that it lacks the latter's political connotation; it was already in use in the 1640s, cf. the titles, *A Defence of Sundry Positions, and Scriptures alledged to justifie the Congregationall-way* by S. Eaton and T. Taylor (1645); 'Ιχνογραφία; *Or A Modell of the Primitive Congregational Way*, by W. Bartlet (1647). The appellation *Presbyterian* also acquired a political connotation (cf. *C.R.*, p. x), but for this there is no alternative.

[6] 'the two great Preachers at the Head Quarters': *R.B.*, i. 81.

[7] All these men are the subjects of articles in *D.N.B.*; reference may also be made to E. Lewis Evans, *Morgan Llwyd*; G. F. Nuttall, 'Walter Cradock', in *Transactions* of Congregational Historical Society, XIII. 1; V. de S. Pinto, *Peter Sterry*; T. Sippell, *William Dells Programm einer 'lutherischen' Gemeinschaftsbewegung* (*Zeitschrift f. Theologie u. Kirche*, drittes Ergänzungsheft, 1911).

George Fox and the Quakers, who in the exclusive sense are not Puritans but the Puritans' fiercest foes,[1] but who yet repeat, extend, and fuse so much of what is held by the radical, Separatist party within Puritanism,[2] that they cannot be denied the name or excluded from consideration.

No reference has been made above to Baptist writers, partly because they were fewer, and partly because for our subject their writings present no important differentia from Congregationalist writings. The Owen of the Baptists was John Tombes, 'reputed the most Learned and able Anabaptist in England',[3] who entitled his Treatise against the Quakers *True Old Light exalted above pretended New Light*, and who ended his life as a lay conformist. At the other extreme is Thomas Collier, whose approach has not a little in common with Quakerism.[4] The Baptist position falls between the Congregational and the Quaker, and many of those who 'posted up and down',[5] 'posting most furiously in a burning zeal towards an unattainable end',[6] passed through a Baptist period before finally coming to rest among the Quakers.[7] Probably most of these men felt alone in their spiritual pilgrimage. Actually, they illustrate the result of the two parallel movements in Puritanism, *die Ueberspitzung des kirchlichen Legitimätprinzips* and *die Erschütterung der Heilsgewissheit*, which have been traced in illuminating detail by Dr. Sippell.[8] In 1671 Quakerism was referred to as 'the fag-end of Reformation'.[9] Some, it may be, will approve the taunt and see in Quakerism primarily a warning against

[1] For implicit Quaker repudiation of the name, cf. R. Barrow, in T. Taylor, *Works*, p. vi: 'about Two Years after George Fox came into Westmoreland . . . many of those called Puritans was Convinced and Broken by the Power of God'.

[2] 'Walter Cradock, William Arberey [Erbury], Joshua Sprig [cf. p. 64, *inf.*], . . . John Webster [cf. p. 178, *inf.*], . . . Peter Sterer [Sterry], William Dell, John Saltma⟨r⟩sh, Morgan Floyd [Llwyd]' are included in a list of 'some of these Men's names that we used to hear in those days' by A. R., *A Tender Exhortation to Friends at Bristol* (1700), p. 13, who says of them, 'they preached of the two Seeds [cf. pp. 158 f., *inf.*], though we did not know what they meant in that Day. And I pray what difference is there between that they Preached and that Friends came forth in:'. The identification of the author with Ambrose Rigge (cf. *D.N.B.*, *s.v.*, as Rigg) in the copy at Friends House, though accepted by E. L. Evans, *M. Llwyd*, p. 3, seems unlikely on account of Rigge's North-country *provenance* and the date of his birth (*c.* 1635). 'T. [i.e. J.] Saltmarsh, W. Dell, W. Erberry [Erbury] . . . & Webster his Works' are included, again, in a list of 'Books forrunning Friends appearance', in a letter written by William Penn in 1693 and printed in *A Quaker Post-Bag*, ed. S. F. Locker-Lampson, p. 4. cf. p. 184, *addendum*.

[3] *R.B.*, i. 137 (10).   [4] Both these men are the subjects of articles in *D.N.B.*

[5] F. Howgill, *Works* (*The Dawnings of the Gospel-Day*), ed. E. Hookes, p. 40.

[6] J. Salmon, *Heights in Depths*, Foreword; Dr. Sippell has reprinted this in *Werdendes Quäkertum*, pp. 199 ff. For Salmon, cf. p. 105, n. 5, *inf.*

[7] Cf. *B.Q.*, index, *s.v.* Baptists; cf. also p. 162 *inf.*

[8] Cf. T. Sippell, 'Ueber den Ursprung des Quäkertums', in *Christliche Welt*, May 12, 19, 26, 1910; 'Zur Frage nach dem Ursprung des Pietismus', in *Zeitschrift f. Theologie u. Kirche*, XXVII. 263; *Zur Vorgeschichte des Quäkertums* (*Studien z. Gesch. des neueren Protestantismus*, 12. Heft); *Werdendes Quäkertum*.

[9] R. H., *The Character of a Quaker*, p. 1.

the end to which what they consider to be an undue emphasis on the doctrine of the Holy Spirit is bound to lead. Others may hold that Quakerism is true Puritanism, purged of extraneous elements and carried to a conclusion not only logical but desirable, and that in Quakerism, with its fresh perception of the implications of the doctrine of the Holy Spirit, is the beginning of a new cycle, full of promise for the future.

From the last few paragraphs it will be clear that to some extent the subject is susceptible of a chronological treatment. It could be shown that Presbyterianism represents not only the most conservative but the oldest party in Puritanism, Quakerism the youngest as well as the most radical. Moreover, the rise in turn of the Presbyterians, the Congregationalists, the Baptists, and the Quakers, and, after the appearance of Quakerism, the passage of individuals through the whole gamut, repeating the sequence in their own lives, might be presented, so far as concerns the doctrine of the Holy Spirit, as a largely logical development. Such a treatment would have its advantages and would not be wholly untrue. In three ways, however, it would fall short.

It would be, in the first place, an over-simplification. The order of denominations given above does represent a genuine movement of men's spirits; but in some things an Episcopalian like Baxter, a Congregationalist like Owen, and a Baptist like Tombes had more in common with one another than had any of them with a Congregationalist like Cradock. Secondly, a chronology used in the interests of a theory is likely in some cases to falsify the actual sequence. It appears, for instance, that a large influence in directing the Puritans' attention to the doctrine of the Holy Spirit was the preaching of Richard Sibbes,[1] whose *Bruised Reed* played a part in converting Baxter, and whose writings were published, both before and after his death in 1635, every year from 1633 to 1641 inclusive. Now Sibbes' interest was primarily devotional, not controversial. Consequently his influence was felt without regard to party differences, one of his works being edited by the Presbyterian Seaman, others by the Congregational Thomas Goodwin and Philip Nye. Thirdly, a chronological treatment would lack the clarity of a treatment confessedly logical. If Puritan faith and experience are to be studied as a whole, then fundamental questions, which to the Puritans presented

---

[1] Robert Bolton, Thomas Hooker and John Rogers had already described the working of the Holy Spirit on man's heart but in a way, in comparison with what followed, still 'low and legal' (W. Erbury, *Testimony*, p. 67) and so precise as likely to exercise the young believer with many doubts (cf. *R.B.*, i. 6).

themselves sometimes quite late, must be dealt with first; equally, issues which temporarily were magnified by extrinsic circumstances, but which now are seen to be peripheral, must receive no more than secondary consideration. In this study, therefore, while neither the general denominational movement nor the actual sequence of events is forgotten, the analysis is a logical one.

One other matter invites attention, namely the chief influences at work upon the Puritans. Here something depends upon the universe of discourse. Every whole not only has its parts but is itself part of a larger whole. The thought of an individual may be related to that of his time, the thought of a period to mental development through the centuries. To relate both at once is hardly possible; which of the two courses is attempted will vary according to the point of major interest. In the present case, as has been remarked, there had been latterly so little explicit orthodox teaching about the doctrine of the Holy Spirit that what influences there were must have come largely by heretical channels, subterranean tributaries of the hidden stream here so suddenly breaking forth into the light of day. *Spiritualisten* abroad, such as Schwenkfeld, Denk, Frank, and Coornhert, preceded Puritanism and in some cases anticipated radical Puritan convictions,[1] but any direct influence is far to seek.[2] *Post hoc, non ergo propter.* Moreover, the more radical the position taken, the more inclined Puritans are to repudiate the traditions intervening between the New Testament and themselves, Fox going so far as to speak of 'ye Apostacy yᵗ has beene since ye Apostles days'.[3] True it is that 'Fox and his friends are steeped in images and convictions that have grown up amongst, that have been handed down by, concrete, historical men, and concrete, historical institutions and cultual acts.'[4] The fact

---

[1] All these men are the subjects of chapters in R. M. Jones, *Spiritual Reformers in the 16th and 17th Centuries.* To call Denk and his followers 'in reality sixteenth-century Quakers' (p. 31) suggests anachronistic *parti pris.* Fox possessed a copy of Frank's *Forbidden Fruit* in English; cf. J. L. Nickalls, 'G. Fox's Library', in *Journal* of Friends' Historical Society, XXVIII. 18.

[2] It is noticeable that Benjamin Furly, who translated the Collegiant tract, *Lucerna super Candelabrum* (accepting the identification in R. M. Jones, *op. cit.,* p. 128, n. 2), for a time supported John Perrot in his 'imaginative' but 'negative mysticism', in disaffection from the main body of the Society of Friends (cf. *S.P.Q.,* pp. 237, 232, 242), and that at the end of his life 'the probability is that he silently acquiesced in being considered . . . as a nonmember' of the Society (W. I. Hull, *B. Furly* (Swarthmore College Monographs, v), p. 159). William Ames definitely opposed the Collegiants as 'out of the way of the Lord' (W. Sewel, *History of the Society of Friends,* 1722 edn., p. 379).

[3] G. Fox, *Journal,* ed. N. Penney, I. 44; John Howe, in a letter of 1685 'to such in and about London, among whom I have laboured in the work of the Gospel', refers with more reserve to 'the discernible restraint and departure of that blessed Spirit from the church of Christ in so great a measure, for many foregoing generations, in comparison of the plentiful effusion of it in the first age': H. Rogers, *Life of J. Howe* (1863 edn.), p. 229.

[4] F. v. Hügel, *Essays and Addresses,* I. 231.

remains that consciously they are not traditionalists but spiritual pioneers, who with Barrow would condemn 'traditional divinity'[1] as wholly derived from other men's books and writings, and not springing from the fountain of God's spirit in themselves.

For the radical party, more particularly for the Quakers, the influence of Jakob Boehme is more specious. All Boehme's *Works* were translated into English between 1644 and 1662,[2] and without doubt aroused considerable interest. We know Boehme was read by Baxter[3] and Thomas Hall,[4] by Llwyd[5] and Erbury,[6] by Lodowicke Muggleton,[7] and, among the Quakers, by Thomas Taylor,[8] William Smith,[9] and Benjamin Furly.[10] If the identification of Justice Hotham of Cranswick with Boehme's biographer[11] be correct, it is certainly interesting that in 1651 he told Fox, after some discourse with him, 'hee had knowne y^t principle this 10 yeere'.[12] Nor is it difficult to trace striking resemblances between Fox's own language and Boehme's.[13]

---

[1] H. Barrow, *Discoverie of the False Church*, p. 56.

[2] *Encyclopaedia Britannica* (11th edn.), *s.v.* J. Boehme; 1692 in *B.Q.*, p. 40, would appear to be a slip for 1662.

[3] Cf. *R.B.*, i. 10 and 124, as Behem and Behmen.

[4] Cf. catalogue of Hall's library now in Birmingham City Library (Reference Department).

[5] The works by Boehme translated by John Sparrow as *True Resignation* (1654) and *Supersensual Life* (1655) were translated into Welsh by Llwyd as *Yr Ymroddiad* (1657) and *Y Discybl ai Athraw O newydd* (1657) respectively. For Boehme's influence on Llwyd, cf. E. Lewis Evans, *op. cit.*, ch. vi, 'Morgan Llwyd a Boehme'. The interpretation of *Yr Ymroddiad* by H. W. Lloyd, in *Y Cymmrodor*, viii. 1, followed by D. Ll. Thomas, in *D.N.B.*, *s.v.* M. Llwyd, is misleading.

[6] Cf. W. Erbury, *Testimony*, p. 333.

[7] Cf. L. Muggleton, *Spiritual Epistles*, pp. 45 f. *et passim*, as Bemon.

[8] Cf. T. Taylor, *Works*, p. 86, as Bewman.

[9] Cf. L. Muggleton, *A Looking-Glass for the Quakers*, p. 5, as Behmont.

[10] Cf. C. R. Simpson, 'B. Furly and his Library', in *Journal* of Friends' Historical Society, xi. 73. For Furly's later relations with Quakerism, cf. p. 15, n. 2, *sup.* T. H. Green (*Works*, ed. R. L. Nettleship, iii. 295) remarks 'the family likeness' between Boehme's writings and those of Sir Henry Vane the younger, who in 1655 was 'very loving to Friends, but drunk with imaginations' (J. Nayler, in *Letters of Early Friends*, ed. A. R. Barclay, p. 39; cf. H. Vane, *The Retired Man's Meditations*, p. 184), but in 1657, after an interview with Fox, 'woulde have put mee out of his house as a mad man' (G. Fox, *Journal*, ed. N. Penney, I. 314). Samuel Herring, who was perhaps a member of Thomas Goodwin's church, petitioned Parliament to encourage the study of Boehme; cf. *Original Letters*, ed. J. Nickolls, p. 99. Boehme was also read by John Webster and by such fanatics as T. Tany and T. Tryon (cf. *D.N.B.*, *s.vv.*). Cf. also p. 17, n. 8, *inf.* All those mentioned in the text are the subjects of articles in *D.N.B.*

[11] The identification is suggested by N. Penney, in his edition of G. Fox, *Short Journal*, p. 277 (correcting the note in his edition of G. Fox, *Journal*, I. 400), and is accepted by R. M. Jones, *op. cit.*, p. 210.

[12] G. Fox, *Journal*, ed. N. Penney, I. 18.

[13] Cf. R. M. Jones, *op. cit.*, pp. 221–7. Professor Jones follows R. Barclay, *Inner Life of Religious Societies of the Commonwealth*, p. 214, in detecting Boehme's influence in Fox's use of the phrase 'the flaming sword' (*Journal*, 1901 edn., I. 28); but the phrase is used also by J. Nayler, *Discovery of the First Wisdom* (1656 reprint of 1653 edn.), p. 4, by W. Dewsbury, *Discovery of the great enmity of the Serpent* (1655), p. 13, and by I. Penington, *Some things Relating to Religion* (1668), p. 22, and proves rather that Fox had read *Gen.* iii. 24, to which Dewsbury has a marginal reference, than that he had read Boehme. Mr. E. Lewis Evans' comment (*Morgan Llwyd*, p. 153) is also pertinent: 'he could scarcely have drawn these heartfelt words from a book

Alexander Gordon has pointed out the psychological similarities between the two men,[1] and it would be strange if these had not expressed
themselves in linguistic similarities also. Muggleton refers in 1663
to a Society at Nottingham which 'was the Beamonists mix'd with
the Quakers';[2] but, if we may assume its identity with that in which
his correspondent, Rice Jones, of Nottingham, was 'a private speaker
amongst the Bemonists and Quakers',[3] this was the society known as
'Proud Quakers' in separation from the main body.[4] Muggleton's
decided derivation of Quakerism from Boehme[5] must as decidedly
be rejected. To any one who reads Boehme's and Fox's writings
consecutively and comparatively, the utter difference between their
respective spiritual climates[6] is soon apparent, and not least precisely
in this, that in Fox's sense Boehme has no *Christian* doctrine of the
Holy Spirit.[7] Further, in 1660 we find a Quaker, John Anderdon,
writing directly against the 'Behmenists'.[8] Professor Rufus Jones'
argument that Anderdon would not have done this, 'if he had not
been impressed with the general marks of likeness in other respects'
than their use of the sacraments 'between the "Behmenists" and his

published in English in this year,' [1648] 'and not in 1641 as Barclay supposes'. (Actually
Barclay prints both 1641 and 1648 on the same page.) It is true that Fox's *Journal* was written,
or dictated, long after 1648; the point is that Fox could hardly have been influenced by
Boehme *at the time of the experience* which he describes in terms of 'the flaming sword'. 'What is
the flaming sword?' is no. 18 of the Quakers' Queries answered by R. Baxter, *The Quakers
Catechism* (1655), p. 15.

[1] A. Gordon, 'The Origin of the Muggletonians', in *Proceedings* of the Literary and Philosophical Society of Liverpool, April 5, 1869, pp. 256 f.

[2] L. Muggleton, *The Acts of the Witnesses of the Spirit*, p. 83.

[3] *Id.*, *Spiritual Epistles*, p. 141. Another correspondent whom Muggleton describes (*ib.*,
p. 106) as 'wrapped up and entangled with Jacob Bemon's principles and disciples, with a little
smatch of the Quakers', Richard Sudbury, was also of Nottingham, and may be presumed to
have belonged to this same society.

[4] For the 'Proud Quakers', of *B.Q.*, pp. 45 f.; P. J. Cropper, *Sufferings of the Quakers in
Nottinghamshire*, 1649–1689, pp. xi f. Fox condemned Rice Jones for his 'imaginations &
whimsys' (*Journal*, ed. N. Penney, I. 11).

[5] Cf. L. Muggleton, *A Looking Glass for the Quakers*, p. 5: 'Jacob Behmont's Books were the
chief Books that the Quakers bought, for there is the Principle or Foundation of their Religion;
for they cannot go beyond that, but there they build'; *eund.*, *Spiritual Epistles*, pp. 90, 141
(quoted in n. 7 below). So, similarly, Henry More, according to a passage quoted in *B.Q.*,
p. 40, but the reference is incorrect, and I have not succeeded in tracing the passage. In his
writings against the Quakers (cf. *Works*, xx. 299; *R.B.*, i. 124) Baxter associates them with the
'Behmenists' but has too much judgement to attempt to derive them from Boehme.

[6] What W. Struck, *Der Einfluss J. Boehmes auf die engl. Literatur des 17. Jahrhunderts* (*Neue
Deutsche Forschungen*, ed. H. R. G. Günther & E. Rothacker, LXIX), p. 118, calls a *Verschieden-
geartetheit der Religiosität*.

[7] In the same paragraph in which Muggleton says, 'there is very little difference betwixt the
Bemonists and the Quakers', he also makes the vital distinction, 'neither revelation, which you
call the spirit within you, nor, as the Quakers say, the light of Christ within them': *Spiritual
Epistles*, p. 141. Cf. W. Penn, *Works*, II. 812, quoted on p. 44, *inf.*

[8] In his *One Blow at Babel*; cf. W. Bayly, *Works*, unpaginated 'Testimony of the Light in me
from my Childhood', *ad fin.*: 'Then I heard Jacob Behmen's Books . . . but this and all the
other gave not Peace and Rest to the Immortal Soul'.

B

own people'[1] has small weight, when one recalls the prodigious extent of controversy at this time. The opinion of another Quaker, Roger Longworth, is probably representative of those Quakers who were at all familiar with Boehme:

> Though a candle was lighted in him at the beginning, yet he hunted before the Lord; and those who have Behme's books are puffed up in their knowledge.[2]

Much the same may be said of the Cambridge Platonists, whom Braithwaite describes as 'a circle with close affinities to Quakerism'.[3] In actual fact there is, again, an utter difference of spiritual climate between the rationalist Cambridge men's Logos theology and the theology of the Holy Spirit which the untutored Quakers worked out in their own experience. Henry More's phrase, 'the Light within me, that is, my reason and conscience,'[4] sufficiently marks him off from Fox, in conversing with whom, on the apparently only occasion on which they met, 'he felt himself, as it were, turn'd into Brass'.[5] Later, it is true, More so far retracted his opposition to Quakerism as an 'Enthusiastick Freak'[6] that he acknowledged part of Robert Barclay's *Apology* to be 'golden words indeed';[7] but Barclay was of the doctrinaire second generation, a theologically trained Scot who 'belonged to a fundamentally different school of thought from that in which the leaders of Quakerism moved'.[8] Even so, Barclay was personally attacked by another of the Cambridge School, John Norris.[9]

More instructive for the independent way in which the Puritans came to their convictions than any careful elaboration of lines of influence would be are two parallel stories related of the Hutchinson and Springett families. The first may be told in Lucy Hutchinson's words:

> When formerly the presbyterian ministers had forc'd him for quiet-nesse sake to goe and breake up a private meeting in the cannoneer's

---

[1] R. M. Jones, *op. cit.*, p. 232.

[2] R. Longworth (1676), in C. Fell Smith, *Steven Crisp and his Correspondents*, p. 38. There is a biblical reference to *Gen.* x. 9.

[3] *S.P.Q.*, p. 392. Cf. M. H. Nicolson, *Conway Letters*, p. 379: 'Henry More and the Quakers were integral parts of the same movement . . . the message was the same'.

[4] H. More, *The Grand Mystery of Godliness*, x. xiii. 7.

[5] R. Ward, *Life of Henry More*, p. 197.

[6] H. More, *op. cit.*, preface, p. viii.

[7] *Id.*, *Divine Dialogues* (1713 edn.), p. 373; cf. More to Lady Conway (1676), in M. H. Nicolson, *op. cit.*, p. 418: 'there are some things which I hugely like in the Quakers'.

[8] R. M. Jones, introd. to *S.P.Q.*, p. xxxii; cf. pp. 334, 386.

[9] In his *The Grossness of the Quakers' Principle of the Light Within* and *Two Treatises concerning the Divine Light*.

chamber, there were found some notes concerning paedobaptisme, which being brought into the governor's lodgings, his wife having then more leisure to read then he, having perus'd them and compar'd them with the scriptures, found not what to say against the truths they asserted . . . she, hap'ning to be with child, communicated her doubts to her husband, and desir'd him to endeavour her satisfaction; which while he did, he himselfe became as unsatisfied, or rather satisfied against it. First, therefore, he dilligently search'd the scriptures alone, and could find in them no ground at all for that practice; then he bought and read all the eminent treatices on both sides, which at that time came thick from the presses. . . . After this, his wife being brought to bed, that he might, if possible, give the religious party no offence, he invited all the ministers to dinner, and propounded his doubt, and the ground thereof to them.[1]

They were unable to resolve it, and the infant was accordingly not baptized. This was in 1647.

In the Springett household in 1644 Gulielma, later the wife of William Penn, was not baptized for similar reasons. In her mother's words:

We tore out of our Bibles the common prayer, the form of prayer, and also the singing psalms, as being the inventions of vain poets, not being written for that use. We found that songs of praise must spring from the same source as prayers did; so we could not use any one's songs or prayers. We were also brought off from the use of bread and wine, and water baptism. . . . In this state my dear husband died. . . . When he was taken from me, I was with child of my dear daughter Gulielma. . . . When I was delivered of her, I refused to have her sprinkled, . . . Such as were esteemed able ministers (and I formerly delighted to hear), were sent to persuade me; but I could not consent and be clear.[2]

It is important to remember how much there was in the first half of the seventeenth century of such independent, sincere, lay 'searching'.

In the present study, in any case, no attempt is made either to trace the nature and extent of the influences at work upon Puritan faith and experience, or to compare and contrast Puritan teaching with that of Boehme or the Cambridge School. Here, Puritan faith and experience is itself the subject: what is endeavoured is, rather, correctly to interrelate its own parts and to appreciate it as a whole worth contemplation in itself.

[1] L. Hutchinson, *Memoirs of Col. Hutchinson* (1810 edn.), ii. 103 f.
[2] M. Penington, *Experiences*, ed. N. Penney, pp. 26 ff.; it is not surprising that the writer and her second husband, Isaac Penington, both later became Quakers.

CHAPTER I

THE SPIRIT AND THE WORD

SYNOPSIS OF ARGUMENT

i. The Reformation characterized by a return to the Bible
as God's Word;
a primary authority:
its writers inspired
its readers illuminated by the Holy Spirit:
Puritan acceptance of the former
discussion of the latter office.
ii. Puritan emphasis on conjunction of Spirit and Word: R.. Sibbes.
Question whether Spirit ever speaks apart from Word: answered
affirmatively in principle by radicals:
O. Cromwell, W. Cradock,
R. Brereley, S. Petto.
iii. Conjunction between Spirit and Word first systematically disturbed by
Quakers:
Quaker devotion to the Bible accompanied by a claim to the same
Spirit in themselves as in the Word;
Quaker insistence on the Spirit as the criterion.
iv. Question whether the Spirit *can* thus be in contemporaries *as* in the
Word;
the Spirit's indwelling in the Apostles was
ordinary
or extraordinary.
Such contemporary indwelling denied by middle party:
Baxter, Owen;
accepted in principle by radicals:
Saltmarsh, Erbury.
v. Quaker tendency to dissociate Spirit in Word from Spirit in themselves;
give primacy to latter as criterion
illustrated from Fen Stanton disputes.
vi. Fresh insistence on conjunction of Spirit and Word:
T. Higgenson, R. Hollinworth, Baxter, Howe.
Conclusion: The Spirit speaks in, by, or through the Word
and if (in extraordinary cases) without
yet according to it.

20

'My spirit that is upon thee, and my words which I have put in thy mouth' (*Isa.* lix. 21).

'The sword of the Spirit, which is the word of God' (*Eph.* vi. 17).[1]

THE rediscovery which men made at the Reformation was two-fold: '*Wort und Geist' ist die Parole der Reformation.*[2] Hitherto, it is true, the Bible had been the basis of Christian doctrine, and had been studied with assiduity.[3] Very largely, however, for reading, and for interpretation entirely, it had remained a purely clerical reserve.[4] The Church, with its highly articulated sacramental system, had come to be regarded as in itself 'the extension or eternalizing of the Incarnation'.[5] To ecclesiastical tradition, consequently, the highest authority was attributed. When men came to read the Bible in the vernacular, they found something so different from current Christianity that this they summarily rejected and sought to drink, not only intellectually but spiritually, *in ipsis fontibus.*[6] No longer ecclesiastical tradition, but 'the Bible, I say the Bible only',[7] was to be regulative.

Later, in and through their reading of the Bible, they further rediscovered a religious experience. This is not to belittle what had gone before. Of religious experience, as of biblical study, there had been much; but mediaeval religious experience had necessarily been coloured by the ecclesiastical medium.[8] The experience now apprehended as specifically Christian, and on that account as desirable, was an experience of directly biblical type, the experience which Scripture terms 'being filled with the Spirit'.

This, however, is to anticipate. At first, men were content, as the Lollards had been, to find Scripture itself 'so deliteful as her lijf';[9] and, if one reads Tyndale's version together with Erasmus' *Paraphrases*, one can still in imagination recapture something of the first fine careless rapture. The rapture was itself a new experience, which in its own right, apart from any controversial Protestant motive, led men to consider the nature and authority of Scripture. The name which they believed Scripture to claim for itself, and which they used, was the

---

[1] The texts printed at the beginning of the chapters are those which, from the frequency of their occurrence in Puritan writings, may be regarded as definitive for Puritan thought.

[2] P. Wernle, *Calvin*, p. 182.

[3] Cf. B. Smalley, *The Study of the Bible in the Middle Ages.*

[4] Richard Rolle's glossed English psalter was the only biblical book which the laity might use without licence. Some gospel harmonies were licensed, as safer reading for the laity than vernacular gospels. Cf. M. Deanesly, in *Modern Language Review*, xv. 349–58.

[5] E. Troeltsch, *op. cit.*, I. 92, of the episcopate.

[6] *Opus Epistolarum Erasmi* (cf. *sup.*), *Ep.* 541. 145.

[7] W. Chillingworth, *The Religion of Protestants* (1836 edn.), p. 465.

[8] A comparison of *La Divina Commedia* with *The Pilgrim's Progress* is suggestive here.

[9] R. Pecock, *Repressor*, ed. C. Babington (Rolls Ser.), I. 274.

Word of God, or simply the Word. And what made Scripture to
be God's Word? The Holy Spirit. πᾶσα γραφὴ θεόπνευστος. ὑπὸ
Πνεύματος Ἁγίου φερόμενοι ἐλάλησαν ἀπὸ Θεοῦ ἄνθρωποι.

Again, how was Scripture apprehended to be God's Word? The
naïve might be satisfied to accept Scripture's claim unexamined; the
more thoughtful were conscious that God's Spirit was the agent here
no less. Luther points the way in his insistence that the Word of God
is the preached word: *non de evangelio scripto sed de vocali loquor:* . . .
Christus herrscht allein durch das mündliche Wort oder Predigtamt.[1] Dell
does no more than draw out what is implicit here when he says,
'They who preach the Outward Letter of the Word, though never
so truly, without the Spirit, do . . . wholly mistake the Mind of
Christ in the Word for want of the Spirit'.[2] This work of the Spirit
in preaching will fall for consideration later. Here, it is to be noticed
that the Puritans went beyond Luther in acclaiming the written word
as 'able to save' not only in public preaching but in private reading as
well.[3] They found that they read the Bible in a different way from
the way in which they read other books. When they read the Bible
something took place in their hearts, not only in their heads. The
Holy Spirit was at work, illuminating what was written and enlightening their minds to understand it.

The work of the Holy Spirit in connexion with Scripture is thus
twofold: the Spirit both inspired its writers and enlightens its hearers
or readers. Belief in the former of these offices—the inspiration of its
writers—is axiomatic among Puritans. Calvin describes the writers
of Scripture as *certi & authentici Spiritus sancti amanuenses,* . . . *verba
quodammodo dictante Christi spiritu.*[4] Such a conception, with the
infallibility of the writers as a corollary, does not come under dispute.
Only 'the acutest and most liberal of Puritan controversialists',[5] John
Goodwin, 'one of the broadest minded men of his time',[6] so much as
raises the issue.[7]

---

[1] Cf. R. Sohm, *Weltliches u. Geistliches Recht,* p. 46, n. 2.

[2] W. Dell, *The Tryal of Spirits,* p. 24; cf. R. Sibbes, *Works,* ed. A. B. Grosart, IV. 219: 'For
if it were not the Spirit that persuaded the soul, when the minister speaks, alas! all ministerial
persuasions are to no purpose.'

[3] Baxter says his father was converted 'by the bare reading of the Scriptures in private,
without either Preaching, or Godly Company, or any other Books but the Bible' (*R.B.,* i. 1);
cf. J. Robinson, *Works,* ed. R. Ashton, II. 232; 'whether by preaching the Gospel by a true
Minister, by a false Minister, by no Minister, or by reading, conference, or any other means of
publishing of it . . .'; R. Sibbes, *Works,* IV. 211: 'when we go to hear a sermon, when we take
up the Bible to read a chapter alone by ourselves, or in our families, . . . we should say to
Christ, Lord, join thy Spirit . . .'

[4] *Institutio,* IV. viii. 9 and 8.   [5] *C.R., s.v.*

[6] A. Gordon, *Addresses Biographical and Historical,* p. 97.

[7] Cf. J. Goodwin, πλήρωμα τὸ πνευματικόν (1857 edn.), p. 361: 'How far, and in what respect the apostles themselves were infallible is worthy of consideration. Certain it is that their in-

It is over the second of these offices, the work of the Holy Spirit in the believer, that discussion arises. 'The Spirit and the Word' denotes this, one of the major controversies of the time. That the assistance of the Spirit is necessary for the saving knowledge of Scripture is doubted by none: the bare word, the letter of Scripture cannot save by itself. But can the Spirit save, or even speak to, man apart from the Word in Scripture? or is the Spirit tied to Scripture? Is the Word to be interpreted by the Spirit? or should the Spirit's leadings, rather, be tested by the Word? How can men know that it is God's Spirit which speaks to them, and not their own fancy? To what in them does the Spirit speak? Some of these questions, in which the predominating psychological interest of the period may be observed, must be deferred to the following chapter on 'the discerning of spirits'. For the present we will confine ourselves more narrowly to an analysis of the first and fundamental question: does the Holy Spirit work only in conjunction with God's Word in Scripture?

The normal, central emphasis throughout Puritanism is upon the closest conjunction of Spirit and Word, a conjunction such as is indicated by the texts quoted at the beginning of this chapter. Writing before controversial matters within Puritanism had come to a head, Richard Sibbes is a fair representative of the general Puritan approach in this, as in several other subjects:

> God, joining with the soul and spirit of a man whom he intends to convert, besides that inbred light that is in the soul, causeth him to see a divine majesty shining forth in the Scriptures, so that there must be an infused establishing by the Spirit to settle the heart in this first principle, . . . that the Scriptures are the word of God.
>
> There must be a double light. So there must be a Spirit in me, as there is a Spirit in the Scripture before I can see any thing.
>
> The breath of the Spirit in us is suitable to the Spirit's breathing in the Scriptures; the same Spirit doth not breathe contrary motions.
>
> As the spirits in the arteries quicken the blood in the veins, so the Spirit of God goes along with the word, and makes it work.[1]

---

fallibility . . . did depend upon their care and circumspection; so that . . . they might deviate and swerve from the truth. . . . the apostles themselves, as infallible as they were, yet without a serious, close, and conscientious minding of what they had received from the Holy Ghost, might mistake.' Baxter goes so far as to argue, 'if we could only prove that the Holy Ghost was given to the penmen of holy Scripture, as an infallible guide to them in the matter, and not to enable them to any excellency above others in the method and words, but therein to leave them to their natural and acquired abilities; this would be no diminution of the credit of their testimony, or of the christian faith' (*Works*, xx. 119).

[1] Sibbes uses this image again of the relation between the Spirit and the ordinances; cf. p. 91, *inf*.

The word is nothing without the Spirit; it is animated and quickened by the Spirit.

Oh! the Spirit is the life and soul of the word.[1]

The question whether the Holy Spirit ever speaks apart from Scripture here hardly raises its head; but it is clear that, if it had, Sibbes would have answered it decidedly in the negative.[2]

Bolder inquirers, however, did ask the question and gave it, in varying degrees of assurance, an affirmative answer. In his farewell address John Robinson is reported to have said, 'The Lord has more truth and light yet to break forth out of his holy word';[3] and those who looked eagerly for more light were in some cases prepared to look for it not only out of but without 'his holy word'. Oliver Cromwell, for instance, a keen believer in 'more light',[4] says, God 'speaks without a written word sometimes, yet according to it'.[5] Robert Baillie goes so far as to include 'contemplations of God without Scripture'[6] among his grounds for condemning the Independents in general.

On the whole, it remains true that in earlier Puritanism even those to whom the doctrine of the Holy Spirit was most central were careful not to separate the Spirit from the Word. Cromwell's qualification 'yet according to it' is typical. Thus Cradock, who is very sure that 'God comes now with more light than wee had before', and who says, 'the spirit is all in all in religion,' also says, 'I speak not this as if the Spirit were contrary to the Word, as some men to advance the Spirit, set the Word and Spirit by the ears; but the Spirit leads by the Word.'[7]

One of those who was thought to be 'setting the Word and Spirit by the ears' was Roger Brereley, of Grindleton in Craven, whose position as a link, geographical as well as spiritual, between Elizabethan Separatism and early Quakerism, has not yet been adequately ex-

---

[1] R. Sibbes, *Works*, III. 427, 434; v. 427; VII. 193, 199; II. 62. Cf. F. Rous, *Works*, p. 721: 'the light of the Word, and the light in our souls are twins, and resemble each other, and agree like brethren'. For Rous, who was Provost of Eton, Speaker of the Nominated Parliament, and a Congregationalist, cf. *D.N.B.*, *s.v.*

[2] As does John Forbes, *How a Christian man may discerne the testimonie of Gods spirit, from the testimonie of his owne spirit*, p. 14: 'nothing els doeth the spirit witnes, but that which is contayned in the word'.

[3] J. Robinson, *Works*, I. xliv; A. Gordon, in *D.N.B.*, *s.v.*, remarks that this address, 'recollected after twenty-six years or more, owes something to the reporter's controversial needs', but this does not destroy its representative value, which is borne out by many Congregational church covenants, binding members to walk together in all the ways of God known or to be made known. I cannot accept Dr. Sippell's judgement (expressed in conversation) that the address is *völlig apokryph*.

[4] Cf. O. Cromwell, *Letters and Speeches*, ed. T. Carlyle, Letter II: 'I dare not say, he hideth his face from me. He giveth me to see light in his light'.

[5] *Ib.*, Speech IV.

[6] R. Baillie, *Dissuasive from the Errours of the Time*, p. 130; for Baillie, cf. *D.N.B.*, *s.v.*

[7] W. Cradock, *Gospel-Libertie*, p. 41; *Divine Drops Distilled*, pp. 215, 168 f.

plored;[1] but he, too, is guarded. Like others, he is conscious of
'Halcion dayes, which God hath sent,' and his teaching is strongly
Antinomian; nevertheless, he thinks it wise to add a qualifying phrase
such as the following:

> Nor that the Spirit doth without the Word
> Unto our Souls sufficient light afford.
> But this I saw, that there's a rest of faith,
> Which sets Believers free from sin & death.

Or again,

> Not that I dream of such a rule erected,
> As that Gods word should so become neglected;
> But that th' spirit, which from the word ne're swarves,
> Guides all Gods Children as occasion serves:
> And leading them to what's there spoke or meant
> In expresse words, or by good consequent;
> Whereof the very scope, the mould, and frame
> Is in the heart deep written by the same,
> And is to every one his heap of Treasure,
> According to his several pitch and measure.[2]

The tone of this is unusual and is advanced, if Dr. Sippell's suggested
date, 1625,[3] may be accepted, but in form it is strictly regular.

Another writer says:

> In all these discoveries I had nothing but came with this, *As it is
> written*, and so I did wonderfully esteeme and value the Scriptures; and
> my heart was wonderfully set against those that pretend to Revelations
> without, or not agreeable to or against the Scriptures.[4]

Once more, Samuel Petto, who describes the Holy Spirit's operations 'within' before dealing with those 'without', and who is concerned because 'the more Immediate testimonie of the Spirit is very
little insisted on, by any that I could ever yet see,' is yet careful to
explain what he means by 'immediate':

> The Spirit witnesseth more Immediately by itselfe: I say *by it selfe* not
> in opposition to the written word; but to distinguish this way of witness-
> ing, from those by water and bloud, 1 *John* 5. 8. . . . Ordinarily, the
> Spirit maketh use of the written word in this way of witnessing: he
> maketh the word without a voyce within; by the effectuall application of

---

[1] 'Tis probable they are the Offspring of the Grindletonians'; Roger Williams, *George Fox
digg'd out of his Burrows*, ed. J. L. Diman (Narragansett Club Pubs., v), p. 42, of the Quakers.
Cf. Appendix I on the Grindletonian Movement, p. 178 *inf*.
[2] R. Brereley, *Of True Christian Liberty*, pp. 16, 6, 44.
[3] Cf. T. Sippell, *Zur Vorgeschichte des Quäkertums*, p. 25, n. 1.
[4] A. M., in S. Petto, *Roses from Sharon*, p. 18.

it unto a particular soule. Or if it be not by an expresse word; yet it is by some Scriptural consideration, or in or presently after waiting upon the Lord in wayes of his owne appointment by the Word: as prayer, it may be for the very mercy of Assurance, &c., and so it is not properly an Immediate Revelation, because in the use of meanes. It may seem very improper to call it Immediate, and yet assert it to be by the Word. But, the expression may be borne withall.[1]

Those who first, in any systematic way, disturbed this conjunction, upset this equilibrium, between God's Word in Scripture and the Holy Spirit were the Quakers; and it is important to observe that the disturbance was brought about partly because of their very devotion to Scripture. 'Though the Bible were lost', it was said, 'it might be found in the Mouth of George Fox';[2] and the boast was justified, if ever, in Fox's case. Again, the early Quakers' practice of going through the streets 'as a sign' naked or in sackcloth, with face blacked, or with ashes or a pan full of fire and brimstone on their heads,[3] is itself convincing evidence of the seriousness with which they read the Old Testament prophets. It was this seriousness, making them regard prophetic behaviour as a model for their own,[4] which also made them so insistent that the same Spirit which was in the prophets, and in the writers of Scripture, was in themselves. This was their fundamental conviction. Theoretically and with qualification, it was regularly accepted by the Puritans. The Quakers brushed away all qualification, and turned theory into burning assurance and consequent action.

> What had any to do with the Scriptures, but as they came to the Spirit that gave them forth? You will say, Christ saith this, and the apostles say this; but what canst thou say?

So said Fox, according to Margaret Fell, and with effect, for

> it cut me to the heart; and then I saw clearly we were all wrong. . . . And I cried in my spirit, to the Lord . . . 'We have taken the Scriptures in words, and know nothing of them in ourselves.[5]'

What canst *thou* say? In *ourselves*. In itself, this message of Fox, the appeal to individual, personal experience, is, we can see now, the

---

[1] S. Petto, *The Voyce of the Spirit*, 'To the Reader', and pp. 25 f.

[2] G. Croese, *The General History of the Quakers*, p. 14; cf. G. Fox, *Journal* (1901 edn.), I. 36: 'I had no slight esteem of the holy Scriptures, but they were very precious to me'; it is his reason which is significant: 'for I was in that Spirit by which they were given forth'.

[3] For examples, and a discussion of what was involved, cf. W. C. Braithwaite in *First Publishers of Truth*, ed. N. Penney, pp. 364–9.

[4] Cf., e.g., T. Ellwood, *History*, ed. C. G. Crump, pp. 27 f., on 'the example of Isaiah, who went naked'.

[5] M. Fell's testimony, in G. Fox, *Journal* (1901 edn.), II. 512; cf. G. Fox, *Journal*, ed. N. Penney, I. 66, 257: 'I have that spirit dwellinge in mee of ye father which speakes to you'; 'hee . . . askt me . . . whether I had ye same spiritt as ye Apostles had & I tolde him yes'.

authentic voice of the seventeenth century, is precisely the Puritan emphasis and contribution; but the man who first applies a newly discovered principle to the heart of the citadel itself, as the Bible then was, must expect misunderstanding and opposition from those with a less penetrating perception than his own, and, no less, exaggeration and perversion of his principle by those who will apply it to the exclusion of all other principles. Sometimes Fox met men with no grasp of the real issue, who led up to the wit which was one of his strong suits, as when

> one priest Jacques[1] saide yt ye letter & ye spiritt was Inseperable. And I saide if soe then every one yt has ye letter has ye spiritt & they may then buy ye Spiritt with ye letter of ye scriptures. Upon this Judge ffell and Coll West reproved ye preists seeinge there darkñesse: & tolde ym yt then they might carry ye spiritt in there pocketts as they did ye scriptures.[2]

At other times, Fox was guilty of the abruptness of expression common in pioneers, and perhaps especially noticeable in the early Quakers.[3] Thus once, when a minister preaching from 2 *Peter* i. 19 on 'a more sure word of prophecy'

> told the people that this was the Scriptures . . . the Lord's power was so mighty upon me, and so strong in me, that I could not hold, but was made to cry out and say, 'O no, it is not the Scriptures'; and I told them what it was, namely, the Holy Spirit, by which the holy men of God gave forth the Scriptures.[4]

Here, apart from the interruption of the preacher,[5] one can hardly be surprised that Fox was thought to be attacking the Scriptures, so that 'the officers came and took me away and put me into a nasty, stinking prison'.

In his *Short Journal* Fox describes this minister as calling the Scriptures 'the touchstone and Judg' and himself as saying, 'ye holy ghost yt gave them forth was the Judg and Toutchstone'.[6] This mention of

---

[1] i.e. John Jacques (cf. *C.R.*, *s.v.*, as Jaques). [2] G. Fox, *Journal*, ed. N. Penney, I. 71.

[3] Cf. A. Gordon, in *D.N.B.*, *s.v.* G. Fox: 'admitting no weapon but the tongue, they used it unsparingly'; T. Seccombe, *ib.*, *s.v.* R. Williams, also observes the Quakers' 'talent for obloquy'.

[4] G. Fox, *Journal* (1901 edn.), I. 43. The phrase 'I could not hold' suggests identification with Jeremiah (cf. *Jer.* xx. 9, a verse which may also lie behind Fox's expression, *Journal*, ed. N. Penney, I. 15, 'ye word of ye Lorde was like a fire in mee').

[5] On only one other occasion is Fox known to have interrupted the preacher (cf. *P.G.F.*, p. 23, n. 3). Such interruptions must be distinguished from the legal right until 1656 to speak 'after the priest had done' (cf. R. Barclay, *op. cit.*, ch. xii; *First Publishers of Truth*, ed. N. Penney, pp. 348 ff.).

[6] G. Fox, *Short Journal*, ed. N. Penney, pp. 1 f.; cf. G. Fox, *Journal* (1901 edn.), II. 217: 'one of the priests undertook to prove, "that the Scriptures are the only rule of life" . . . after I had plunged him about his proof, I had a fit opportunity to open unto them "the right and proper use, service, and excellency of the Scriptures; and also to show, that the Spirit of God . . . is the most fit, proper, and universal rule, which God hath given . . ." '

the touchstone is of the first importance. Hitherto, God's Word in Scripture has been treated as the criterion by which to test faith and experience. Now, the Holy Spirit is introduced as the touchstone by which all else is to be tried, including the Bible itself. A contrast, though not necessarily an opposition, is thus created between them. Throughout the years from 1650 onwards there is a perpetual controversy, whether the Word is to be tried by the Spirit, or the Spirit by the Word.

Logically, this controversy is preceded by the question whether the Spirit which was in those who wrote the Scriptures *can* be in contemporaries; and, if so, whether, or how far, in the same mode. This question therefore falls for prior consideration.

The keywords of the arguments used are 'ordinary' and 'extraordinary'. That the Holy Spirit dwelt in the biblical writers is agreed by all; the more conservatively minded regard the indwelling as extraordinary, the more radically minded as ordinary. The middle party claim a greater reverence for the apostles and foresee dangerous implications of infallibility, if an identical mode of indwelling be admitted to contemporaries. The radicals, believing that 'the plentiful pouring out of the Spirit, is the great priviledge which is promised unto the latter dayes',[1] and that, in point of fact, 'no generation since the Apostles daies had such powerful preachers and plenty of preaching as this generation',[2] see themselves as spiritually close to the apostles, and are less concerned to guard against assumptions of infallibility.

For the middle party, Baxter says succinctly:

> The Holy Spirit, by immediate inspiration, revealed unto the apostles the doctrine of Christ, and caused them infallibly to indite the Scriptures. But this is not that way of ordinary illumination now.[3]

Owen says, similarly, of the Holy Spirit that

> In the continuation of his Work he ceaseth from putting forth those extraordinary effects of his Power which were needful for the laying the Foundation of the Church in the World.
>
> Upon the ceasing of Extraordinary gifts really given from God, the Gift also of discerning spirits ceased, and we are left unto the Word alone for the tryal of any that shall pretend unto them.[4]

---

[1] S. Petto, *op. cit.*, 'To the Reader'.

[2] V. Powell, *A Word in Season*, p. 9, as quoted by T. Richards, *The Puritan Movement in Wales*, p. 171.   [3] R. Baxter, *Works*, II. 104.

[4] J. Owen, Πνευματολογία, II. ii. 4; I. i. 22. In the former passage, however, Owen continues: 'But the whole work of his Grace according to the Promise of the Covenant, is no less truly and really carried on at this day in and towards all the Elect of God, than it was on the day of Pentecost and onwards'.

For the radicals, we may instance Saltmarsh, who believes in the Holy Spirit's continued indwelling, though he fails to find such indwelling as he seeks:

> I know not any of us that either preach or write on Scriptures in such a light of Spirit as the Apostles writ the Scriptures.[1]

Erbury so strongly believes not only in the possibility but in the necessity of such continued indwelling that he regards its absence as completely condemning existing Christianity:

> Will ye say of this . . ., as ye do of the gifts of the Spirit, that 'twas extraordinary onely for those Apostolique Churches? this indeed is the Popish distinction, which Protestants have learnt from them. . . . If those gifts were extraordinary, are Gospel-graces so? for their Faith you cannot shew, nor their Love we cannot see, not a shew of it. . . . This shews, the falling away is come upon you and the Apostacy foretold by the Apostles is come upon you in perfection, having no gift of the Spirit, nor yet the grace of Faith.[2]

Not every one was equally pessimistic. Another writer says:

> it was brought in, that it was the same Spirit I now felt, that Spirit that did write the Scriptures. . . . I did see, and could not doubt of it, that the very administration was given to me, which was given to the Apostles and Saints of old.[3]

The further question whether the mode of the Spirit's indwelling is to be regarded as in the fullest sense personal, we shall inquire when in a later chapter we consider the nature of the Spirit's witness. The question of spiritual infallibility will also arise. For the present it is sufficient to observe that the Holy Spirit's contemporary indwelling was accepted in principle by the more radical Puritans. What was new about Fox's message was, again, the assertion that this principle held in daily practice, that the Spirit which was in the Apostles not only could be, but was, in latter-day saints also, and was as much 'the Judg and Toutchstone' in them as in the Apostles.

So long as the Quakers sought to realize a true identity between the Spirit in the apostles, as manifested in the written word, and the Spirit in themselves, and so long as, whenever any discrepancy occurred, they gave the primacy to the Spirit in the apostles as regulative, they must be regarded as within the bounds of Puritanism. To give the primacy to the Spirit in the Word was but making explicit what was meant by giving the primacy to the Word. An entry in the

---

[1] J. Saltmarsh, *Sparkles of Glory*, p. 111.   [2] W. Erbury, *Testimony*, pp. 228 f.
[3] A. M., in S. Petto, *Roses from Sharon*, pp. 5 ff.

parish register of Hackness, Yorkshire, for September 12, 1653, records of the Quakers that 'they held out that that work which they had in them was not wrought by the Word, which I was sorry to heare, but they said they mayd use of the Word onely to try whether it were right or noe'.[1] So long as they did make use of it to try what was wrought in them, there was no genuine ground for being sorry.

Cause for sorrow arose from the Quakers' tendency to contrast and (as it seemed) even to oppose the Spirit in themselves to the Spirit in the Word, and to treat the former, not the latter, as the criterion. One chief charge against them was the charge which had already been brought against the Grindletonians, namely, that they held 'that their spirit is not to be tryed by the Scripture, but the Scripture by their spirit'.[2] The Associated Ministers of Cumberland and Westmorland, for instance, complained of the Quakers that 'the Scripture bindes not them, if not set on their hearts by a present impulse'.[3]

Examples of the kind of disputes which arose may be found in the records of the Baptist Church at Fen Stanton, Huntingdonshire. It should be noted that the first two of the following quotations date from before the arrival of James Parnell, who, so far as can be ascertained, was the first Quaker missionary to those parts,[4] and who is known to have disputed later at Fen Stanton:[5] the question was 'in the air'.

> Thomas Bagley asked whether a man might not have some manifestations of the Spirit above the scriptures, which question occasioned much discourse between us. At length they, with one consent, declaring that they had great manifestations of the Spirit of God . . . we replied again, that we did not know what was Godlike but by the holy scriptures, and we desired to know whether they would be tried by the scriptures. They answered, all with one consent, that they could not tell.

> they were resolved not now to try the spirits by the scriptures; the word, they said, they did not deny, which word is God himself; but as for the letter (which we call the word), they would not be guided by it.

> A maid named Isabel said, that the Spirit assured her she had Christ. It was demanded how she knew it to be a true spirit? She answered, by the effects and not by the scriptures; for she tried the Scriptures by the Spirit, and not the Spirit by the Scriptures.[6]

[1] *Hackness Parish Register*, in Yorkshire Parish Register Society Pubs., xxv, p. 73.

[2] E. Pagitt, *Heresiography* (1662 edn.), p. 115 (misprinted 145); the charge is consonant with the first of 'certaine erronious opinions gathered from the mouth of Bryerley and his hearers' printed from Rawl. MSS. 399.196 by T. Sippell, *Zur Vorgeschichte des Quäkertums*, p. 50, viz. that 'a motion riseing from the spiritt is more to be rested in, then the word it self'.

[3] Cf. B. Nightingale, *The Ejected of 1662 in Cumberland and Westmorland*, I. 101.

[4] Cf. *First Publishers of Truth*, ed. N. Penney, p. 129.   [5] Cf. *B.Q.*, p. 189.

[6] *Records of the Churches of Christ, gathered at Fenstanton, Warboys, and Hexham*, ed. E. B. Underhill (Hanserd Knollys Soc. Pubs., v), pp. 2, 8, 74. Such disputes give point to Baxter's warning

Such claims inevitably led to the further question, how men could discern God's Spirit within them from their own fancies. This subject we shall examine in the following chapter. So far as the relation between the Spirit and the Word is concerned, Quaker tendencies to dissociate the two were met with a fresh insistence upon their conjunction: 'he that would utterly separate the Spirit from the Word had as good burn his Bible'.[1] Thus Thomas Higgenson says:

> The Spirit and the Scriptures together ... are ... the perfect judge for ending all difference about spiritual matters, and the perfect rule for trial of all spirits and ways of religion: the Scriptures as the lantern, and the Spirit as the candle therein; ... either of these if set up as under without the other, brings forth a two-fold error, both perilous and hurtful.
>
> I. Imposing the letter of Scripture without the light of the Spirit, whether by churches or councils, may be an opposing the Scriptures against the Spirit, and sets up another dominion over the conscience, which is subject to Christ alone.
>
> II. Imposing anything for vision or spirit without liberty of appeal, or reference to Scripture, whether by an angel from heaven or an apostle, is a shaking men's minds from off the foundation of the apostles and prophets, Jesus Christ being the chief corner-stone. . . .[2]

With this may be compared the following passage from Richard Hollinworth:

> The Word is a Lantorn, a dark Lantorn (say some)[3] without the Spirit; but I am sure that Spirit is a going fire, a deluding Spirit that carries not, but contemns and confounds this Lanthorn. . . . Gods people are led by the Spirit, when they are led by the word inspired by the Spirit, and they are taught by God, when taught by his Book: No Spirit of Christ doth abstract any mans faith from the Word of God. . . . We are not warranted to expect or trust to Enthusiasms, or praeter-scriptural, much less contrascriptural Revelations;[4]

Baxter, in particular, with the passionate reasonableness characteristic of him, is never weary of reiterating 'concurrence' of Spirit and Word:

> There is an admirable, unsearchable concurrence of the Spirit, and his appointed means, and the will of man, in the procreation of the new

---

against 'the circle which the papists, falsely, charge upon protestants in general, but is the case but of these few, to wit, to prove by the Spirit that Scripture is God's word, and to prove by Scripture that this is God's Spirit, circularly': *Works,* xx. xxxiii.

[1] J. Owen, *op. cit.,* II. v. 4.   [2] T. Higgenson, *A Testimony to the true Jesus,* pp. 14 f.

[3] If this is a reference to the Quakers, the Quakers equally complain that 'ye presbuterians Called y Light Jack in ye Lantron & Willy-Wisp': MS. printed in *Journal* of Friends' Hist. Soc., XXIX. 62.

[4] R. Hollinworth, *The Holy Ghost on the Bench,* pp. 24 f.

creature, and in all the exercises of grace, as there is of male and female
in natural generation; and of the earth, the sun, the rain, the industry of
the gardener, and the seminal virtue of life and specification, in the
production of plants with their flowers and fruits. And as wise as it
would be to say, it is not the male but the female, or not the female
but the male that generateth; or to say, it is not the earth but the sun,
or not the sun but the rain, or not the rain but the seminal virtue, that
causeth plants with flowers and fruits; so wise is it to say, it is not the
Spirit but the word and means, or it is not the word and means but the
Spirit, or it is not the reason, and will and industry of man, but the
Spirit: or, if we have not wisdom enough to assign to each cause its
proper interest in the effect, that therefore we should separate what God
hath conjoined. . . .[1]

Should any discrepancy appear between the Spirit in the Word and
the Spirit in men's hearts, Baxter is sure which is to be preferred, and
ready to give reasons for his sureness.

We must not try the Scriptures by our most spiritual apprehensions,
but our apprehensions by the Scriptures: that is, we must prefer the
Spirit's inspiring the apostles to indite the Scriptures, before the Spirit's
illuminating of us to understand them, or before any present inspirations,
the former being the more perfect; because Christ gave the apostles
the Spirit to deliver us infallibly his own commands, and to indite a rule
for following ages; but he giveth us the Spirit but to understand and use
that rule aright. This trying the Spirit by the Scriptures, is not a setting
of the Scriptures above the Spirit itself; but is only a trying of the Spirit
by the Spirit; that is, the Spirit's operations in ourselves and his revelations to any pretenders now, by the Spirit's operations in the apostles,
and by their revelations recorded for our use. For they and not we are
called foundations of the church.[2]

Therefore, says Baxter elsewhere:

Interpret Scripture well, and you may interpret the Spirit's motions
easily. If any new duty be motioned to you, which Scripture com-
mandeth not, take such motions as not from God: (unless it were by
extraordinary, confirmed revelation).[3]

We may conclude the chapter with the following careful consideration of the matter by John Howe:

We speak not here of what God *can do*, but of *what he doth*. . . . Nor
do we speak of what he more rarely doth but of what he doth ordinarily,
or what his more usual course and way of procedure is in dealing with
the spirits of men. The supreme power binds not its own hands. We
may be sure the inward testimony of the Spirit never is opposite to

the outward testimony of his gospel which is the Spirit's testimony also; ... But we cannot be sure he never speaks nor suggests things to the spirits of men but by the external testimony, so as to make use of that as the means of informing them with what he hath to impart; nay, we know he sometimes hath imparted things—as to prophets and the sacred penmen—without any external means; and, no doubt, excited suitable affections in them, to the import of the things imparted and made known.

Nor do I believe it can ever be proved that he *never* doth immediately testify his own special love to holy souls without the intervention of some part of his external word, made use of as a present instrument to that purpose, or that he *always* doth it in the way of methodical reasoning therefrom. ... Nor is the matter of such moment that we need either be curious in inquiring or positive in determining about it; that principle being once supposed and firmly stuck to,—that he never says anything in this matter by his Spirit to the hearts of men repugnant to what the same Spirit hath said in his word; ... Hereby the most momentous danger in this matter is avoided; ... which being provided for,—as it is difficult, so it is not necessary, to determine whether the Spirit do always not only testify *according to* the external revelation, but *by it* also, and so only as to concur in the usual way of reasoning from it.[1]

These passages from Baxter and Howe may be taken as summing up the central position of Puritanism on this matter. The Spirit speaks in, by, or through the Word. Dissociation of the two is condemned. The Quaker tendency towards such dissociation, which, as we shall see, was no more than a tendency, was already implicit in Puritanism, nor only in radical Puritanism, as appears in the passage from Howe generally and in the final parenthesis of the passage from so judicious a writer as Baxter. Even so, though by some it may be admitted that the Spirit speaks in extraordinary cases without the written Word, it will still be 'according to' the Word, or, at the least, 'upon some Scriptural consideration'. The Apostles and not ourselves are the foundation stones.

[1] J. Howe, *Works*, ed. H. Rogers, II. 85 ff.; for Howe, cf. A. Gordon, in *D.N.B.*, *s.v.*

C

CHAPTER II

THE DISCERNING OF SPIRITS

SYNOPSIS OF ARGUMENT

i. Radical Puritan claim to contemporary indwelling of Holy Spirit led
   to question how to discern God's Spirit from men's fancies.
   Relation of Holy Spirit to reason
                                  conscience a prior considera-
                                  tion.

ii. Puritanism rooted in Renaissance: association of Spirit with reason:
                                  Sibbes, Cradock;
   Puritanism rooted in Reformation: association of Spirit with con-
   science: Sibbes,
         Fen Stanton.
   Puritan care not to identify Spirit with reason: Sterry, T. Goodwin;
                                  conscience: T. Goodwin.

iii. Radical Puritan association of Spirit with experimental perception
   analogous to sense perception: Sibbes, T. Goodwin, Hollinworth;
         especially in terms of light: Cradock, T. Goodwin, Owen;
   or analogous to intuitive reason: Owen, S. Petto, T. Goodwin.
   Fox's emphases carry forward those of radical Puritans: 'The light
   within' distinguished from reason and conscience.

iv. Difference between Puritans and Quakers over question how to discern
   God's Spirit from men's fancies.
   Possible criteria: (a) Scripture: accepted by Puritans,
                                  rejected by Quakers;
                     (b) Reason: J. Goodwin; Puritans chary of this;
                     (c) Authority of Church: rejected by Puritans:
                                  Sibbes, Sterry, Owen.
   Need for a criterion made more urgent by Quaker extravagances.

v. Fox's criteria: (a) a Christocentric and ethical ('that which shows a man
                                  evil'), counteracting rejection of Scripture as
                                  criterion;
                  (b) an ecclesiastical ('that which brings into unity'); this
                                  rejected by radical Quakers: W. Mucklow.

vi. Concluding quotations from Baxter:
   his attempt to synthetize spiritual and rational principles;
   later acknowledgement of primacy of witness of Spirit.

'Beloved, believe not every spirit, but try the spirits, whether they are of God' (1 *John* iv. 1).

'. . . to another, discerning of spirits' (1 *Cor.* xii. 10).

THE claim advanced by the more radical party within Puritanism that the Spirit which was in the apostles, as manifested in the written word, was also in themselves led inevitably, as already remarked, to the further question, how men could discern God's Spirit within them from their own fancies. Thus, in the disputes at Fen Stanton mentioned above:

> We then desired him, before he said any more, to prove what he had said. . . . 'He found it by experience,' he said. We desired him to prove it by the scriptures, for we would not be ruled by his fancy.[1]

The Associated Ministers of Cumberland and Westmorland complained, similarly, of the Quakers' 'setting up their Conceits and Experiences, as being of equal authority with the Scriptures'.[2] To pronounce the newly discovered authority '*their* Conceits'[3] was to beg the question; but to ask how men could *distinguish* God's Spirit from 'their Conceits' was an honest and necessary inquiry. Such an inquiry demanded a prior consideration of the questions, what was the relation of the Holy Spirit to reason and conscience; how, and to (or through) what in man, the Spirit spoke; and whether the physical senses had any analogue in spiritual perception.

Puritanism as a whole is rooted in the Renaissance as well as the Reformation. Such a distinction as that made by Dr. Freund in his study of toleration[4] between *im Denken der Renaissance wurzelnde Denker* and *im Denken der Reformation wurzelnde Denker* has its uses,[5] but with the Puritans it constantly breaks down. Milton and John Goodwin, for instance, whom Dr. Freund classes in the second category, may with equal propriety be classed in the first; and they are but the most distinguished exponents of what Professor Perry Miller has called 'the hidden rationalism' in Puritanism, 'in which the dialectic of Ramus has blended perfectly with the theology of Augustine and Calvin'.[6] Already in the sermons of John Preston, 'conversion is not prostration on the road to Damascus, but reason

---

[1] *Records of the Churches of Christ* (cf. *sup.*), p. 94.   [2] Cf. B. Nightingale, *op. cit.*, I. 101.

[3] It had been a charge equally against the Grindletonians that they tried the Scripture 'by *their* spirit' (cf. p. 30, *sup.*).

[4] Cf. M. Freund, *Die Idee der Toleranz im England der grossen Revolution* (*Deutsche Vierteljahrs-schrift f. Literaturwissenschaft u. Geistesgeschichte*, ed. P. Kluckhohn u. E. Rothacker, XII).

[5] Jeremy Taylor's *The Liberty of Prophesying*, e.g., is rightly classed in the Renaissance category, and breathes an entirely different air from Puritan writings: Taylor's *ganzes Wesen und Denken ist . . . von Skepsis und dem Gefühl*, 'dass wir nichts wissen können', durchtränkt (p. 44).

[6] P. Miller, *The New England Mind: the seventeenth century*, pp. 200, 162.

elevated';[1] and the collocation 'enlightened Protestantism and sound reason'[2] was a Puritan *sine qua non*. The natural tendency in Puritanism, therefore, was to associate the Holy Spirit in man with man's reason.

Sibbes, once again, presents the attitude which is normal before the matter has become controversial.

> The Spirit of God moveth according to our principles, it openeth our understandings to see that it is best to trust in God; it moveth so sweetly, as if it were an inbred principle, and all one with our own spirits.
>
> The Spirit of God is so wise an agent that he works upon the soul, preserving the principles of a man. It alters the judgment by presenting greater reasons, and further light than it saw before; . . . When the Spirit of God sets the will at liberty, a man doth that he doth with full advisement of reason; for though God work upon the will, it is with enlightening of the understanding at the same time; . . .
>
> The judgment of man enlightened by reason is above any creature; for reason is a beam of God, . . . Judgment is the spark of God. Nature is but God's candle. It is a light of the same light that grace is of, but inferior.[3]

Again, Cradock, who is fairly far to the left wing of the radical party in Puritanism, still refers to

> common reason, right naturall reason in us, which many of the duties of the New-Testament are grounded on. If you say; what is that? It is a light in the soule, that is a Relique of that light that was in Adam.[4]

In the introduction to Cradock's *Gospel-Holinesse* John Robotham[5] even asserts that 'reason considered in it's height & excellency is no other then Jesus Christ, and the spirit'.[6]

Being children of the Reformation, the Puritans are also acutely aware of the primacy of conscience. Despite his emphasis on *sola fides*, or rather dictating that emphasis, *Luthers Religion ist Gewissensreligion im ausgeprägtesten Sinne des Wortes*;[7] and from one angle the evolution of Puritanism may be seen as an increasing preoccupation with conscience, till the strain proved too great, and Antinomianism set in.[8] The Independent, says John Cook,[9] 'thinks all the delight in

---

[1] *Ib.*, p. 200; for Preston, cf. A. Gordon, in *D.N.B.*, *s.v.*

[2] Cf. R. Vaughan, *English Nonconformity*, p. 161.   [3] R. Sibbes, *Works*, I. 197; IV. 225, 234.

[4] W. Cradock, *Gospel-Libertie*, p. 117.   [5] Cf. *D.N.B.*, *s.v.*, as Robothom.

[6] W. Cradock, *Gospel-Holinesse*, 'To the Reader'.

[7] K. Holl, *Gesammelte Aufsätze zur Kirchengeschichte*, I. 35.

[8] Cf. T. Sippell, *opp. cit.*, esp. *Werdendes Quäkertum*, pp. 55 f.; Cradock says, 'I have known one eat but one meal in a week; and let them eat little or much, they defile their consciences. One while they must go so in their apparel with lace, and after that, lace damneth them': *Divine Drops Distilled*, p. 44.

[9] Cf. C. H. Firth, in *D.N.B.*, *s.v.*

this World without the liberty of his conscience, is a burthen intolerable' and 'reckons Liberty of Conscience to be Englands chiefest good'.[1] In politics, the place given to conscience was so great as to constitute, in Professor Woodhouse's phrase, 'a new phenomenon';[2] and its influence in politics followed directly from the attention it received in Puritan religion.

There was thus also a natural tendency in Puritanism to associate the Holy Spirit in man with man's conscience. Sibbes, for instance, defines conscience as 'an inferior light of the Spirit';[3] and the enthusiasts at Fen Stanton sometimes spoke of conscience as synonymous with the Spirit.

> They replied that the light in their consciences was the rule they desired to walk by. We granted that an enlightened conscience was a guide; but we demanded by what the conscience should be enlightened? They answered, 'Not by the scripture, for the conscience was above the scripture; and the scripture ought to be tried by it, and not that by the scripture'.[4]

This being so, it is remarkable how regularly the Puritans in general distinguish the Holy Spirit in man from man's reason and conscience, and insist that, though associated with both, the Spirit's working cannot satisfactorily be defined in terms of either. In a sermon preached before Parliament in 1645 Peter Sterry 'carefully distinguishes "reason" from "spirit" and lays particular stress on the superiority of "spirit" '[5]:

> The brute part of the world . . . is that which is acted by sense. Reason makes man. The spirit is the principle of a Saint.
> To seek out spirituall things by the s⟨c⟩ent and sagacity of reason: were to plough with an Oxe & an Asse. . . . You cannot reach the things of reason by the hand of sense. . . . You cannot understand spirituall things Rationally.
> Rationall and Spirituall convictions differ in their Perswasives, in their Principles.
> Some say, that all truths which come by revelation of the Spirit, may also be demonstrated by Reason. But if they be, they are then no more Divine, but humane truths; They lose their certainty, beauty, efficacy; . . . Spirituall truths discovered by demonstrations of Reason, are like the Mistresse in her Cook-maid's clothes.[6]

[1] J. Cook, *What the Independents would have*, pp. 13 f.; I have printed the substance of the pamphlet in *Transactions* of Congregational Hist. Soc., XIV. 1.
[2] A. S. P. Woodhouse, *Puritanism and Liberty*, p. [53].
[3] R. Sibbes, *Works*, v. 419.   [4] *Records of the Churches of Christ* (cf. sup.), p. 116.
[5] V. de S. Pinto, *P. Sterry*, p. 16: Professor Pinto points out that in this Sterry 'definitely separates himself from the rationalism of his Cambridge friends'.
[6] P. Sterry, *The Spirits Conviction of Sinne*, pp. 11 f., 16, 26 f.; cf. the following lines from

Thomas Goodwin says much the same:

> Reason indeed subserveth . . . but reason will never alone work out these mysteries.

> If we read the Scriptures, and to get the meaning of them, observe the connection of one thing with another by reason, yet there comes often a light of the Spirit beyond the height of reason, which, by that observation of the connection, seals up this to be the Holy Ghost's meaning; so as the Holy Ghost is to faith still his own interpreter. For else the Scripture were of private interpretation, which it is not, 2 Pet. i. 20. For such is *ratio humana* to the Spirit.

So, again, of conscience Goodwin says:

> Natural conscience sees very far and is as 'the candle . . .' Prov. xx. 27; but the Spirit's conviction goes and searcheth far beyond it.

Elsewhere, Goodwin remarks that

> Hierome, so long ago, should unluckily stumble on the very notion of the Quakers, . . . namely, that what light of God was in nature, or light of moral good in the conscience, was the grace of Christ, which is all one with what our Quakers' foundation is.[1]

'The very notion of the Quakers', which Goodwin attacks here, was their belief that to some degree the Holy Spirit was in every man, including the unconverted. This belief we shall examine in the last chapter; but it may be well to say at once that Goodwin was mistaken in supposing that, because they held this belief, the Quakers equated the Holy Spirit with conscience. Actually, as we shall see, they laid stress on the distinction already made between the Holy Spirit and conscience.

The radical Puritans, in particular, through their reaction alike against dead 'notions' and an over strict morality, sought to associate the Holy Spirit less with reason or conscience and more with a spiritual perception analogous to the physical perception of the senses and given in 'experience' as a whole. It was possible to avoid the charge of dependence upon something irrational by pointing out that reason has an intuitive aspect as well as a discursive.

Dante (*Paradiso*, xxiv. 91–96), which it is interesting to find Owen quoting in a Latin translation, as having been 'much affected' by them (*Divine Originall . . . of the Scriptures*, p. 97):

> La larga ploia
> dello Spirito Santo, ch' è diffusa
> in sulle vecchie e in sulle nuove cuoia,
> è sillogismo, che la m' ha conchiusa
> acutamente sì che in verso d' ella
> ogni dimostrazion mi pare ottusa.

Cf. also F. Rous, *Works*, p. 136: 'we want not the Glow-worm of demonstration'.

[1] T. Goodwin, *Works* (1861 edn.), IV. 304; VII. 65; X. 474; IV. 344. For Goodwin, cf. A. Gordon, in *D.N.B.*, *s.v.*

Sibbes already leads the way in this direction:

> A carnal man can never be a good divine, though he have never so much knowledge. An illiterate man of another calling may be a better divine than a great scholar. Why? Because the one hath only notional knowledge, discursive knowledge . . .
>
> It is a knowledge with a taste. . . . God giveth knowledge *per modum gustus*. When things are to us as in themselves, then things have a sweet relish.
>
> How do you know the word to be the word? It carrieth proof and evidence in itself. It is an evidence that the fire is hot to him that feeleth it, and that the sun shineth to him that looks on it; how much more doth the word . . . I am sure I felt it, it warmed my heart, and converted me.
>
> There is no other principle to prove the word, but experience from the working of it.
>
> Experience is the life of a Christian. What is all knowledge of Christ without experience . . .?[1]

All parties, really, are agreed about this: it is the essential Puritan emphasis. Hollinworth, for instance, uses the same analogies as the more radical Puritans:

> He that sees the Sun, knows it is bright and light; he that tastes honey, knows it is sweet.[2]

Owen says:

> He gives αἴσθησιν πνευματικὴν, a spirituall sense, a Tast of the things themselves upon the mind, Heart, and Conscience; when we have αἰσθητήρια γεγυμνασμένα, senses exercised to discerne such things.[3]

Similarly, Thomas Goodwin:

> God hath put into every creature a taste, and a discerning of what shall nourish it. . . . And as the senses in a man are suited to objects in the world, a man's eyes to colours, his ears to sounds, his stomach to meats, so hath God made the things of the gospel to suit the regenerate part, and the regenerate part to suit them. . . . in Phil⟨ippians⟩ i. 9 the knowledge of the saints it is called sense, . . . it is a judgment which ariseth from, or at least is joined with sense, a taste, a suitableness that the soul hath to the things revealed.
>
> The understanding, as made spiritual, is the palate of the soul.[4]

So, once more, Francis Rous:

> *Sensus non fallitur circa objectum*, . . . the Sun shines, or the Swan is white, because the unhindered sense hath apprehended it to be so.
>
> In one place we are told, That Christs love is pleasanter than wine;

---

[1] R. Sibbes, *Works*, III. 434; IV. 334 f., 363; II. 495; IV. 412.

[2] R. Hollinworth, *op. cit.*, p. 76.

[3] J. Owen, *Divine Originall*, p. 94; there is a biblical reference to *Heb.* v. 14 and perhaps to *Phil.* i. 9.   [4] T. Goodwin, *Works*, IV. 305 f.; VII. 143.

and in another, That the laws of God are pleasanter than Honey; . . .
By tasting the things themselves, God teacheth us to know what the
things are; and the more we know them, the more we shall love them;
and the more we love them, the more we shall taste them; and the more
we taste them, the more we shall know them. And thus shall we run on
in an endless circle of tasting, loving, and knowing, which grows still
greater, the more we round it.[1]

The simile of light, with or without mention of the sun, occurs
again and again in these writers,[2] and forms the link in their thought
between experience and intuitive reason. Thus Cradock, in a work
recommended by Robotham as 'the very experiments of his owne
soule, and the lively actings of the spirit of God within him', says:

> For as in natural things, you know, that by the same light whereby
> I see the Sun, by the same light I know that I see him: So there is in
> the very manifestation of God to the soule, it carries a witnesse in it self,
> it is so cleare, that when I have it, though I never had it before, and I
> cannot demonstratively speak a word what it is, yet I know as it is Gods
> sight, so I know as I see him.[3]

Thomas Goodwin, again, in a passage which deserves quoting *in
extenso*, makes the most of the simile:

> Suppose any one of the sons of men brought up in those *merae tenebrae*,
> mere darkness which were only nature's legacy, and on the sudden God
> should set up in the lantern of his brains the light of the greatest magni-
> tude that Plato or Socrates ever had, how would this man bless him-
> self . . . then let this man be carried forth into the open sky, and let
> any one shew him a full moon, walking in her greatest brightness, as
> Job speaks, Oh, how would he kiss his hand to it, and passionately cry
> out, Oh, this is light, this is day indeed; . . . anon when the day is
> approaching let him discover the twinkling stars to close up their lights
> and vanish, and the brightness to wash off by degrees from his so adored
> moon, which he verily took for the sun, and her face to grow pale and
> wan; and a far differing, stronger light to steal in by degrees, . . . till at
> last casting his eye to that quarter of heaven which is brightest, he

---

[1] F. Rous, *Works*, pp. 135, 623 f., with references to Pseudo-Dionysius, St. Bernard and
Gerson.

[2] The simile had a long literary tradition, springing from the Neo-Platonism of St. Augustine,
whose conversion came to him *in ictu trepidantis aspectus*, and who wrote of faith in terms of a
mentis obtutus (Patrologia Latina, ed. J.-P. Migne, XXXII. 745; XXXIII. 600). *Thomas bekämpft als
Aristoteliker jene Lichtmetaphysik scharf und sucht sie sogar aus Augustin hinwegzudeuten; but wieweit
auch im lateinischen Abendlande die Verbreitung dieser Lichtmetaphysik war, wo Augustin das Vor-
spiel zu ihrer mittelalterlichen Blüte gab, das hat die Forschung der letzen Jahre gezeigt:* C. Baeumker,
Der Platonismus im Mittelalter, pp. 19, 18; cf. *eund.*, *Witelo* (Beiträge zur Gesch. der Phil. der
Mittelalter, III. 2). There is evidence that the Lollards used the analogy of light in defence of
their biblicism; cf. R. Pecock, *The Book of Faith*, ed. J. L. Morison, pp. 166 ff.

[3] W. Cradock, *Gospel-Holinesse*, 'To the Reader', and p. 32.

discerns the body of the sun beginning to peep up above the horizon—
do but think with yourselves, upon the sight hereof, what this man
would say.[1]

The same analogy occurs constantly in Owen's writings:

Let the Sun arise in the firmament, and there is no need of Witnesses
to prove and confirme unto a seeing man that it is day. . . . Let the least
child bring a candle into a roome that before was darke, and it would be
a madnesse to go about to prove by substantiall Witnesses, men of
Gravity and Authority, that Light is brought in. Doth it not evince its
selfe, with an Assurance above all that can be obteined by any Testimony
whatever?[2]

Elsewhere, Owen describes how

we who were Darkness become Light in the Lord, or come to know
God in Christ savingly, looking into and discerning Spiritual Things
with a proper intuitive sight. . . .
The true Nature of Saving Illumination consists in this, that it gives
the Mind such a direct intuitive insight and prospect into Spiritual
Things, as that in their own Spiritual Nature they suit, please and
satisfie it.[3]

So also Samuel Petto says the Holy Spirit 'witnesseth not in a Discursive way, by deducing Conclusions from premises',[4] and Thomas
Goodwin describes 'the light of faith' as 'more intuitive'.[5]

From the foregoing passages it is sufficiently evident that when
George Fox distinguished 'fleshly knowledge'[6] from 'knowledge of
thee in the Spirit'; when he 'heard a voice which said, "There is one,
even Christ Jesus, that can speak to thy condition" . . . and this I
knew experimentally'; when he was disgusted because a man was
'nothinge but a notion⟨ist⟩', and because others 'begann with there logick
& syllogismes'; when, on the contrary, he was cheered by the sight
of 'a people had tasted of ye power of God'; and when, perceiving
that 'all must first know the voice crying in the wilderness, in their
hearts', he 'turned y^m to ye divine light of Christ & his spiritt . . .
with which light they might see there sinns & with ye same light
they might see there saviour Christ Jesus';[7] he was but carrying forward a line of development already well established within Puri-

---

[1] T. Goodwin, *Works*, VI. 256. [2] J. Owen, *Divine Originall*, pp. 72 f.
[3] *Id.*, Πνευματολογία, III. v. 54; ii. 16. [4] S. Petto, *The Voyce of the Spirit*, p. 26.
[5] T. Goodwin, *Works*, VII. 66.
[6] Cf. M. Llwyd to R. Baxter (1656): 'Neither shall men agree in God, till the fleshly mind
(that perks up in man's heart to judge of God's mind), bee mortified. (And in that the Quakers
say well as I thinke)': M. Llwyd, *Gweithiau*, ed. T. E. Ellis and J. H. Davies, II. 274.
[7] G. Fox, *Journal* (1901 edn.), I. 11, 33; *Journal*, ed. N. Penney, I. 18, 297, 20, 50.

tanism. 'Children of the Light', the name by which the Quakers originally called themselves,[1] is used by Rous as an appellation for spiritual Christians in general.[2]

Nor, from that part of Fox's message which we shall examine in the last chapter, that the light was in every man, or from his frequent use of the phrase 'the light in thy conscience', was there justification for the inference that by 'the light within' Fox meant conscience, in depreciation of the Holy Spirit. Both directly to John Tombes, and in the presence of Owen, both of whom later wrote against Quakerism,[3] Fox explicitly denied that the light within was 'a naturall light & a made light', and 'shewed him ye contrary & howe it was divine & spirituall from Christ...'[4] Dr. Sippell's definition of Quakerism as *in erster Linie Zeugnis; es ist der in Permanenz erklärte Gewissensappell an alle Menschen*[5] is acceptable only if taken in closest conjunction with his next sentence: *In Worten, Taten und äusseren Zeichen soll das, was der Geist Gottes sagt, ganz kompromisslos verkündet werden.*[6] For 'the light is thoroughly supernatural. It is not conscience, or the light of nature, or the light of reason.'[7] The attempts made by Owen and others to argue otherwise were misunderstandings, arising from their failure to consider what Fox meant rather than what they would have meant had they used his language.

Fox was thus largely at one with the Puritans, especially with the more radical Puritans, in holding the centrality of dependence on the Holy Spirit,[8] and in teaching that the Spirit was other than reason or conscience, and was mediated perceptively as light through experience as a whole. Where he and the Quakers differed from the Puritans was over the question, how a man can discern God's Spirit within him from his own fancies. This difference was in accord with that observed in the previous chapter over the relation between the Spirit and the Word.

[1] Cf. *B.Q.*, index, *s.v.* 'Children of the Light', and p. 182, n. 3, *inf.* Fox also says it was a nickname: *Journal*, ed. N. Penney, I. 389.
[2] Cf. F. Rous, *Works*, p. 134.
[3] Cf. J. Owen, *Pro Sacris Scripturis Adversus hujus temporis Fanaticos*; J. Tombes, *True Old Light exalted above pretended New Light.*
[4] G. Fox, *Journal*, ed. N. Penney, I. 275, 260.
[5] Cf. *ib.*, I. 337: 'to no other touchstone shall wee turne you, but into your owne consciences'.
[6] T. Sippell, *Werdendes Quäkertum*, p. 109.
[7] R. H. King, *George Fox and the Light Within, 1650–1660*, p. 57.
[8] Cf. R. H. King, *op. cit.*, p. 78: 'Broadly speaking, Fox's teaching was a re-emphasis on the belief in the Holy Ghost. He uses the term, Holy Ghost, quite often. . . . There is a general identification of the Holy Ghost with the light'; cf. p. 170, with references. Fox uses the word *Spirit* very much more than 'quite often'.

For 'trying the spirits', the primary 'Judg and Toutchstone' accepted by the Puritans was the Scriptures. Thus Sibbes says:

> The breath of the Spirit in us is suitable to the Spirit's breathing in the Scriptures; the same Spirit doth not breathe contrary motions.
>
> But there be, you will say, strong Illusions. True. Bring them therefore to some rules of discerning. Bring all your joy, and peace, and confidence to the word. They go both together. As a pair of indentures, one answers another.[1]

Owen similarly urges the necessity for Christians, 'that they diligently trye, examine and search into these things, by the safe and infallible Touchstone and Rule of the Word'.[2] This method of discerning, as we have seen, at least in its expression of 'the Word' *sans phrase*, the Quakers rejected.

A second possible criterion was reason. This commended itself to a mind like John Goodwin's:

> Unless these discoveries, which are pretended unto and held forth with the greatest confidence, shall commend themselves for truth unto the judgments and understandings of sober and judicious men, much versed and exercised in the Scriptures, either from their own light and evidence, or else shall be made out by light of argument and demonstration, whether from the Scriptures, or clear principles in reason, to be real truths . . . they are not to be looked upon as proceeding from any fulness of the Spirit in these men, but as the exertions and puttings forth of a spirit of vanity and delusion in men;[3]

Baxter, also, is always ready to give reason a real part to play in the discerning of spirits. In general, however, as we have observed, the Puritans were chary of testing God's Spirit by anything purely rational.

A third possible criterion was the authority of the Church, but this the Puritans rejected as papist. Thus Sibbes says,

> There is a great difference between us and our adversaries. . . . They say we must believe . . . because of the church. I say no. The church, we believe, hath a kind of working here, but that is in the last place. For God himself in his word, he is the chief. The inward arguments from the word itself, and from the Spirit they are the next. The church is the remotest witness, the remotest help of all.[4]

Owen, again, says,

> There is no need of Traditions, . . . no need of the Authority of any Churches . . .

[1] R. Sibbes, *Works*, v. 427, 441.
[2] J. Owen, Πνευματολογία, I. i. 31; cf. I. i. 22, quoted on p. 28, *sup*.
[3] J. Goodwin, Πλήρωμα τὸ πνευματικόν, p. 308.   [4] R. Sibbes, *Works*, III. 374.

A Church may beare up the light, it is not the light. It beares witnesse
to it, but kindles not one divine beame to further its discovery.[1]

So, also, Sterry says,

> The Papists . . . perswade us to receive the testimony, not of the
> Spirit, but of the Church, for a Touchstone of truth. . . . Thus the
> Church's Authority, not the Demonstration of the Holy Ghost, shall
> be the light of Faith to Truth. . . . But wee need no visible Judge on
> earth, to determine upon our consciences; what is Scripture; what is the
> essence of Scripture. We have an invisible Judge and Witnesse in our
> own breasts.[2]

In 1645, when Sterry preached this sermon, the question of discerning of spirits had not yet arisen with urgency. The early Puritans
did not allow what they believed to be the Holy Spirit's motions to
lead them into eccentric or fanatical sayings or behaviour. When,
later, the Quakers went naked 'for a sign'; when even Fox, who for
the most part had a 'sober bent of mind',[3] was betrayed into occasional extravagances;[4] most of all, when Nayler 'went to Bristol . . .
with a company . . . bowing, kneeling, and singing before him',[5] as
before the Messiah, the question became an immediate one. Nor, if
one is acquainted with some of the multitude of fanatics other than
Quakers who abounded at this time,[6] can one wonder that the
Puritans should have mistrusted what seemed to them, in the Quakers
also, nothing but the wildest whimsies.

The question of discernment was bound to arise in course of time
within Quakerism itself. 'A thoroughgoing radical of a conservative
type'[7] Fox has been termed, and it is interesting to observe the two
criteria which he formulated. They may be described as a Christocentric, with an ethical connotation, and, more surprisingly, an
ecclesiastical.

William Penn spoke for the first generation of Quakers as well as
his own, when he said, 'It is not our Way of Speaking to say the Light
within is the Rule of the Christian Religion; but that the Light of Christ
within us is the Rule of true Christians, so that it is not our Light
but Christ's Light that is our Rule';[8] and Fox never forgot the 'voice

---

[1] J. Owen, *Divine Originall*, pp. 44, 76.   [2] P. Sterry, *The Spirits Conviction of Sinne*, p. 28.
[3] *B.Q.*, p. 148; cf. p. 147 for a discussion of the subject.
[4] For Fox's rare 'mad or fanatical acts', cf. *P.G.F.*, p. 8, n. 2.   [5] *B.Q.*, p. 245.
[6] Cf., e.g. A. Gordon, in *D.N.B.*, *s.vv.* R. Crab, J. Robins, T. Tany, T. Tryon; C. H. Firth,
ib., *s.v.* A. Evans. Muggleton regarded the Quakers as 'but the very influence of John Robins'
witchcraft spirit': *Spiritual Epistles*, p. 57; cf. *eund.*, *Stream from the Tree of Life*, p. 36. *B.Q.*,
p. 253, n. 1, shows that A. Gordon, in *D.N.B.*, *s.v.* J. Nayler, is mistaken in identifying the
Robert Crab, who was arrested with Nayler at Bristol, with the fanatical Roger Crab.
[7] R. H. King, *op. cit.*, p. 37.   [8] W. Penn, *Works*, II. 812; cf. p. 17, n. 7, *sup.*

which said, "There is one, even Christ Jesus, that can speak to thy condition" '.[1] More than twenty years later a man told Fox, 'I perseive y^t you exalt Christ in all his offices as y^t I never heard so much before'.[2] His theoretic rejection of Scripture as a spiritual criterion was therefore largely counteracted by his association, in practice, of 'the light within' with Christ.

As far as I know, Fox never actually claims that the direct inspiration has revealed to him any religious beliefs, doctrines, or principles that he thinks are not recorded in the Bible. Certainly Fox never claims that the direct inspiration has revealed anything to him that supersedes New Testament teaching.[3]

Because he had Christ constantly before him, Fox's primary definition of the light within is 'that which shows a man evil'.[4] He was thus enabled to see that Nayler had 'runn out . . . Into Imaginations' and was 'out' and 'wronge',[5] and, on the whole, to protect the Society of Friends from an unbalanced fanaticism. In the Christocentric interpretation of Scripture which is implied in his adoption of a Christocentric criterion, and which is sometimes explicit,[6] Fox was in advance of his time.[7] The fact that the criterion was *eo ipso* also ethical provided something similar to part of what the Puritans meant by 'the witness of the Spirit', as we shall see in the next chapter.

Fox's other criterion of 'the light within' is that it is 'that which brings into unity and in which is unity'.[8] Fox had a mystical sense of 'unity with the creation',[9] but as a practical criterion the unity meant is rather unity among Friends, a unity so great as early to produce even a certain outward uniformity among them. In their initial stages, enthusiastic movements have always a warm group-consciousness, and Quakerism is no exception. 'Apart from a knowledge of this deep fellowship, there is no understanding of early Quakerism.'[10]

---

[1] G. Fox, *Journal* (1901 edn.), I. 11; quoted on pp. 8, 4 *sup*.

[2] *Id.*, *Journal*, ed. N. Penney, II. 194.

[3] R. H. King, *op. cit.*, p. 165. Some might consider Fox's disuse of the sacraments a supersession of New Testament teaching; but cf. ch. VI, *inf*.

[4] *Ib.*, p. 57; cf. the whole chapter. It is vital for Fox that 'with ye same light they might see there Saviour Christ Jesus': *Journal*, ed. N. Penney, I. 50.

[5] G. Fox, *Journal*, ed. N. Penney, I. 243 *f*.

[6] Cf. e.g., *ib.*, I. 151: 'Christ ends ye prophetts and ye first preisthoode & Moses . . . .

[7] Cf., however, J. Moffatt, *The Golden Book of John Owen*, p. 48: 'Owen displays comparatively little of that undue predilection for the Old Testament which often threw practical Puritanism out of gear . . . Owen's interests are in the New Testament. . . . In this and . . . in his supreme passion for Jesus Christ, he stands apart not merely from many of his own party but from the rational theologians . . .'; cf. also W. Cradock, *Gospel-Libertie*, p. 58: 'The greatest misery to an honest heart (next to an Old Testament spirit, that is the rise of all) . . .'.

[8] R. H. King, *op. cit.*, p. 108; cf. the whole chapter.   [9] Cf. *P.G.F.*, pp. 77 f.

[10] *Q.S.M.*, p. 114; cf. the whole chapter, esp. p. 120, n. 2, on 'the frequency in the seventeenth century of the words "one another" '.

'Friends have never stood for a bare individualistic principle of the "Inner Light" ': the Society has always existed 'to bear corporate witness to the principles and practices for which it stands'.[1]

This criterion of 'unity' is in effect a return to the New Testament criterion of κοινωνία, which, through its degeneration in institutionalized Christianity, had been abandoned by the Puritans with their rejection of the authority of the Church. In the first enthusiastic decades such a criterion might operate without difficulty; but it is piquant to find as early as 1673 a controversy arising within Quakerism in which 'Foxoman-unity' is condemned as seeking 'to deprive us of the Law of the Spirit and to bring in a tyrannical Government'.[2]

> What difference is there in these things between George Fox and the Papists? the one saith, No Liberty out of the Church; the other saith, No Liberty out of the Power.

> Moreover, as others before them set up the Scriptures above the Spirit, in having that to be the Tryal, Touch-stone, Standard of Doctrine, Worship, and of all Spirits; so do they greatly err in setting up the Body above the Spirit, in having the Spirit tryed by the Body; the one sayth, The Scripture is the Rule: but in truth, their Meanings they make the Rule: The other saith, The Spirit (and not the Scripture) is the Rule; but the Dictates of the Body they make the Rule.[3]

Here, in the re-erection of an ecclesiastical criterion, and in the objection to it expressed, in a sense 'the wheel is come full circle'.

We may conclude this chapter with some quotations from Baxter, who, as always, takes a central path, with a sympathy which remains judicious:

> The Spirit is not given to make our religion reasonable, but to make sinners reasonable, in habit and act, for the believing it. The Spirit, therefore, is not first any objective cause of our belief, unless you speak of the Spirit in the apostles or others, and not in men's selves, but it is the efficient cause; nor doth he cause us to believe by enthusiasm, or without reason, but he works on man as man, and causeth him to believe nothing but what is credible; . . .

> The rest have that immediate intuition of verities by the spirit within them, or by revelation, that it is above mere rational apprehension, and therefore they will not dispute, nor be moved by any arguments or Scriptures that you bring, affirming that ratiocination cannot prevail against their intuition.

---

[1] *Ib.*, pp. 171 f.; cf. I. Grubb, *The Quakers and Industry before 1800*, p. 29: 'In an Epistle in 1667 George Fox warns Friends that if any of them live unrighteously, the world will say, "The Quakers are not as they were" (*Epistles*, p. 251). So early . . . any deviation from the truth is detrimental to the good reputation of the Society as a whole.'

⟨W. Mucklow,⟩ *The Spirit of the Hat*, pp. 11, 18; W. C. Braithwaite, S.P.Q., p. 292, plausibly emends *Foxoman* to *Foxonian*.   [3] ⟨W. Mucklow,⟩ *op. cit.*, pp. 12, 21.

But

    Where is it that the Spirit giveth light, but into our own understandings; and how perceive we that light, but by the rational apprehensions and discourses of those understandings?

    By which you may see, that the Spirit and reason are not to be here disjoined, much less opposed. As reason sufficeth not without the Spirit, being dark and asleep; so the Spirit worketh not on the will but by the reason: he moveth not a man as a beast or stone, to do a thing he knoweth not why, but by illumination giveth him the soundest reason for the doing of it.

    I do, therefore, neither despise evidence as unnecessary, nor trust to it alone as the sufficient total cause of my belief; for if God's grace do not open mine eyes, and come down in power upon my will, and insinuate into it a sweet acquaintance with the things unseen, and a taste of their goodness to delight my soul, no reasons will serve to stablish and comfort me, however undeniable soever;

    the way to have the firmest belief of the Christian faith, is to draw near and taste, and try it, and lay bare the heart to receive the impression of it, and then, by the sense of its admirable effects, we shall know that which bare speculation could not discover. Though there must be a belief on other grounds first, so much as to let in the word unto the soul, and to cause us to submit our hearts to its operations, yet it is this experience that must strengthen it, and confirm it.[1]

In Baxter there is always an attempted synthesis, at once unique and 'ideally normal'[2] in Puritanism, of the rational and the spiritual principles, both of which were strongly marked in his own temperament; and, considering the vigour with which he controverted the Quakers for failing, as he believed, to test the movings of the Spirit by Scripture and by reason, it is striking to read his confession towards the end of his life that he was now

    much more Apprehensive than heretofore, of the Necessity of well Grounding Men in their Religion, and especially of the Witness of the indwelling Spirit: For I more sensibly perceive that the Spirit is the great Witness of Christ and Christianity to the World: And though the Folly of Fanaticks tempted me long to over-look the Strength of this Testimony of the Spirit, while they placed it in a certain internal Assertion, or enthusiastick Inspiration; yet now I see that the Holy Ghost in another manner is the Witness of Christ and his Agent in the world. . . .[3]

---

[1] R. Baxter, *Works*, xx. xxxii, 299 f., 147; iv. 294 f.; xviii. 297 f.; xx. 202.
[2] I borrow this useful phrase from R. M. Jones, introd. to *B.Q.*, xxxii.
[3] *R.B.*, i. 213 (4).

CHAPTER III

THE WITNESS OF THE SPIRIT

SYNOPSIS OF ARGUMENT

i. The witness of the Spirit may be studied in three spheres:
the intellectual
practical
evangelical.

ii. The mode of Spirit's indwelling a prior consideration:
The Spirit's personal indwelling denied by conservatives:
Hollinworth, Howe;
accepted by radicals: Goodwins, Petto.

iii. In intellectual sphere, are spiritual revelations granted, yielding infalli-
bility?
In practical sphere, are spiritual leadings granted, yielding perfectibility?
These queries answered in negative by conservatives: Owen, Baxter;
in affirmative in principle by radicals:
Brereley, Erbury;
in practice by Quakers:
Fox, Dewsbury.

iv. Quaker extravagance in language and action: consequent misunder-
standing.
Fox's attitude to Ranter claims in intellectual and practical spheres;
Other enthusiastic claims: Agnes Beaumont.
Baxter's caution.

v. In evangelical sphere, we may behave towards God with assurance and
reverent familiarity: Baxter, Forbes, Sibbes, Petto, Cradock,
Cromwell;
we must behave towards men with sanctification
and self-discipline: Hollinworth, Baxter, Owen, Sibbes.

vi. The witness of the Spirit in simple folk: Petto, Baxter, Howgill.

'The Spirit itself beareth witness with our spirit, that we are the children
of God' (*Rom.* viii. 16).[1]

'Who hath also sealed us, and given the earnest of the Spirit in our
hearts' (2 *Cor.* i. 22).

T HE passage from Baxter quoted at the end of the last chapter
brings us conveniently to another, more positive aspect of the
subject, closely related to that just considered. When, in a negative
way, by tests of elimination through the application of one or other

---

[1] With verse 26, quoted at the beginning of ch. iv, 'the greatest verses in the bible, very
good to "feed on", as Cromwell would have said': T. H. Green, *Works*, III. cviii f.

48

possible criterion, 'the discerning of spirits' has taken place, and it is decided that the Spirit of God is within men, it is natural to inquire further what the Spirit then says and what is His influence: in a word, to consider 'the witness of the Spirit'. For convenience, this witness may be studied in three spheres: the intellectual, the practical, and the evangelical. A logically prior consideration, however, is the mode of the Spirit's indwelling: is this personal and direct, granting what may properly be termed revelations and leadings, or is it indirect and metaphorical? and if the former, do such revelations and leadings yield infallibility and perfectibility?

About the mode of the Spirit's indwelling there is considerable discussion and difference of opinion. The conservative Hollinworth is sure that it is not personal:

> When I speak of the Spirit's being, or dwelling in a Saint: I mean not an essential or personal in-being or in-dwelling of the Spirit, as he is God, or the third Person of the Holy Trinity:
>
> This Scriptural phrase of in-being and in-dwelling, doth import only inwardness, meer relation and close union. Hence God is said to be in Christ, as well as Christ in God, and Saints are as well said to be in, and to dwell in Christ, and to be in the Spirit, as Christ or the holy Spirit are said to be, or dwell in them; and therefore this phrase doth no more evince personal inhabitation, on the one side then on the other.
>
> The Spirit by a Metonymy, may be said to dwell in us . . . when we partake of his Gifts and Graces, though these be not the Spirit it self; . . . as when we say the Sun comes into a house, we mean not the *body* of the Sun (for that abides in its own Orb) but the *Beams* of it;[1]

John Howe, again, is cautious:

> When we are cautioned not to 'quench the Spirit', how can that be understood of the eternal uncreated Spirit himself? And the very thing produced—not merely the productive influence—in the work of regeneration is expressly called by that name (as it is no strange thing for the effect to carry the name of its cause): 'That which is born of the Spirit is spirit'.[2]

The more radical Puritans, however, in their enthusiastic consciousness of the Holy Spirit's workings in their hearts, were not satisfied with such an explanation, and took the Apostle's words more literally, both John Goodwin and Petto drawing attention to Paul's emphatic expression:

> 'The Spirit itself,' or the Spirit himself, αὐτὸ τὸ πνεῦμα. The apostle by this emphatical expression, the Spirit himself, seemeth to imply that the

[1] R. Hollinworth, *The Holy Ghost on the Bench*, pp. 8, 10 f., with appropriate Scriptural references, here omitted.
[2] J. Howe, *Works*, ii. 80.

D

thing or act of which he speaketh is of a most worthy nature and import, of a sacred consequence . . .[1]

If it were onely τὸ πνεῦμα, The Spirit witnesseth—then it might be by a proxie, gifts and graces; but seeing it is αὐτὸ τὸ πνεῦμα, the Spirit himselfe, this argueth it to be a peculiar worke of the Spirit, requiring its own more immediate presence.[2]

Similarly, Thomas Goodwin says,

> Now for the manner of the indwelling of the Holy Ghost's person; it is no error to affirm that it is the same in us and the man Christ Jesus.[3]

Baxter has a characteristic passage on the point, in which he accepts the radical claim in principle, but safeguards it with rational qualifications:

> The Spirit itself is given to true believers, and not onely grace from the Spirit . . . the Spirit itself is present as the immediate Operator: not so immediate as to be without means, but so immediate as to be no distant agent, but by proximate attingency, not only *ratione virtutis*, but also *ratione suppositi*, performeth his operations;[4]

Resulting from this difference of opinion over the mode of the Holy Spirit's indwelling goes a difference over the effect of that indwelling, in both the intellectual and the practical spheres. Both Baxter and Owen are unwilling to grant to contemporaries the possibility of what may properly be termed revelations, yielding an infallibility such as was owned by the apostles. Of what he calls 'Objective Revelations', Owen says:

> Whether they contain Doctrines contrary unto that of the Scripture or additional thereunto, or seemingly confirmatory thereof, they are all universally to be rejected, the former being absolutely false, the latter useless. Neither have any of the Operations of the Spirit pleaded for the least respect unto them. For he having finished the whole Work of External Revelation, and closed it in the Scripture, his whole internal Spiritual Work is suited and commensurate thereunto.

Consequently, of the apostles he says:

> If any shall ask by what τεκμήρια or Infallible Tokens, they might know assuredly the Inspirations of the Holy Spirit, and be satisfied with such a perswasion as was not liable to mistake that they were not imposed upon? I must say plainly, That I cannot tell; for these are things whereof we have no Experience.[5]

---

[1] J. Goodwin, Πλήρωμα τὸ πνευματικόν, p. 448.
[2] S. Petto, *The Voyce of the Spirit*, p. 27.   [3] T. Goodwin, *Works*, VI. 66.
[4] R. Baxter, *Works*, XII. 209.
[5] J. Owen, Πνευματολογία, 'To the Readers' and II. i. 9.

Baxter puts it thus:

> There are two sorts of the Spirit's motions; the one is by extra-
> ordinary inspiration or impulse, as he moved the prophets and apostles,
> to reveal new laws, or precepts, or events, or to do some actions without
> respect to any other command than the inspiration itself. This Christians
> are not now to expect, because experience telleth us that it is ceased; or
> if any should pretend to it as not yet ceased, in the prediction of events,
> and direction in some things otherwise indifferent, yet it is most certain
> that it is ceased as to legislation; for the Spirit itself hath already given
> us those laws, which he hath declared to be perfect, and unchangeable
> till the end of the world. The other sort of the Spirit's working, is not
> to make new laws or duties, but to guide and quicken us in the doing of
> that which is our duty before by the laws already made. And these are the
> motions that all true Christians must now expect.[1]

Elsewhere, Baxter relates of James Berry (afterwards the Major-
General) how, 'when he had been a while most conversant with
those that in Religion thought the old Puritan ministers were dull,
self-conceited, Men of a lower form, and that new Light had declared
I know not what to be a higher attainment, his Mind, his Aim, his
Talk and all was altered accordingly'. Baxter comments on Berry's
'Being never well studied in the Body of Divinity or Controversie,
but taking his Light among the Sectaries, before the Light which
longer and patient Studies of Divinity should have prepossest him
with'.[2]

To the radical Puritans, however, such 'Studies of Divinity'
seemed merely 'notional' and of small weight in the balance, compared with their own experience of 'new Light'. This phrase,
indeed, became a term of mockery, Llwyd's congregation at Wrexham
being called 'New Lights'.[3] The enthusiasts, however, remained
unashamed:

> What is the new Moon then? Truly to me it is new Light. . . . Oh
> how terrible is this to the Pastors and Teachers to look for new Light . . .
> They cannot abide new Light.[4]

Even so, there is, until the beginning of Quakerism, the same kind

---

[1] R. Baxter, *Works*, IV. 294.

[2] *R.B.*, i. 83; for Berry cf. C. H. Firth, in *D.N.B.*, *s.v.*, and Sir J. Berry and S. G. Lee, *A Cromwellian Major-General*.

[3] Cf. M. Llwyd, *Gweithiau*, II. 299; Fox says Nathaniel Stephens, Rector of Fenny Drayton (cf. A. Gordon in *D.N.B.*, *s.v.*), told his relations, 'he was afraid of me, for going after new lights': *Journal* (1901 edn.), I. 8; cf. p. 152, *inf*.

[4] W. Erbury, *Testimony*, p. 83.

of caution as we observed in another connexion in the first chapter. Brereley, for instance, expresses himself thus:

> And yet there is a motive more than this,
> Which not by Nature, explicable is.
> And yet no dream, no fancie, nor temptation,
> Nor to be call'd in scorn New Revelation:

Nor, Antinomian though he is, will he do more than hope:

> Yea, even now I dare not say, but some
> May to good measure of perfection come.[1]

'He doubts the possibility of perfection in the saints on earth.'[2]

Similarly, those who were most conscious of 'dispensations', or stages, through which the truly spiritual must pass to ever higher attainments,[3] men such as Erbury and Saltmarsh, are careful not to lay claim to perfection or infallibility. John Webster's testimony to Erbury is:

> His spirit was still working up, to the highest pitch of attainments, though he were sensible of his present frailty, and could say with Paul, not as though I had already attained, or were already perfect, by reason whereof he did serve and groan under present bondage, and was as a servant in the house; yet there was a seed of freedom in his spirit which was not satisfied except with the highest enquiries. . . .[4]

With the Quakers the situation was different. As we have seen, Fox did not claim that the Holy Spirit had revealed anything to him which was not recorded in the Bible, or which superseded its teaching. He did claim, however, that things which were recorded in the Bible had been revealed to him independently. Thus, of his fundamental conviction 'that every man was enlightened by the divine light of Christ', he says,

> This I saw in the pure openings of the light, without the help of any man; neither did I then know where to find it in the Scriptures, though afterwards, searching the Scriptures, I found it.
>
> These things I did not see by the help of man, nor by the letter, though they are written in the letter, but I saw them in the light of the Lord Jesus Christ, and by his immediate Spirit and power, as did the holy men of God, by whom the Holy Scriptures were written.[5]

So, also, William Dewsbury says:

> The knowledge of eternal life I came not to by the letter of the Scripture, nor hearing men speak of the Name of God; I came to the

---

[1] R. Brereley, *Of True Christian Liberty*, pp. 15, 54. [2] A. Gordon, in *D.N.B.*, *s.v.*
[3] Cf. ch. VII, *inf.* [4] J. Webster, in W. Erbury, *Testimony*, introd.
[5] G. Fox, *Journal* (1901 edn.), I. 34 f., 36.

true knowledge of the Scripture, and the eternal rest . . . by the inspiration of the Spirit of Jesus Christ . . .:[1]

Parallel with this claim by the Quakers to 'an immediate consciousness . . . which penetrated to its object, as was then said, by revelation, as we should say, by intuition, without the intervention of any system of ideas',[2] went a claim to immediate leadings by the Holy Spirit in the sphere of practical activity. The way in which the Quaker emphasis was recognized as compatible with the contemporary *Weltanschauung*, but in fact went beyond it, is shown in a dispute Fox had at Swarthmore, in which Thomas Taylor, not yet convinced,

> did ingeniously confesse before Judge ffell y[t] hee never hearde ye voice of God nor Christ to sende him to any people but hee spoake his experiences, & ye experiences of ye saintes & preacht y[t]:

This was after another minister had

> burst out Into a passion & saide hee coulde speake his experiences as well as I: butt I tolde him experience was one thinge but to goe with a message & a worde from ye Lord as ye prophetts & ye Apostles had & did: & as I had donne to y[m] this was a nother thinge.[3]

From first to last Fox was sure of the Spirit's immediate guidance. Without embarrassment he could say,

> At this my spirit was greatly grieved, and the Lord, I found, was highly offended.[4]

His *Journal* is the best evidence of the sort of life to which such a conviction led, full as it is of 'openings', 'leadings', and waitings 'till I felt freedom from the Lord'. The following passage from a hostile source is a cameo of the working out of such dependence on the Spirit's leadings in a particular instance.

> Mr. Richard Stookes, Minister at Grayrigg,[5] told one of us[6] that discoursing with Fox at a meeting appointed, concerning his immediate Call: the said Fox affirmed he was called by a voice from heaven to Grayrigg; and at his affirming the same the simple deluded soules that were there with him affirmed they knew it to be true: he asked them whether they saw any vision, or heard any voice? They answered No, but all the account they gave of it was—That whereas he was walking

[1] W. Dewsbury, *Testimony*, p. 54; for Dewsbury cf. *D.N.B.*, *s.v.*
[2] T. H. Green, *Works*, III. 164, of Jesus and St. Paul.
[3] G. Fox, *Journal*, ed. N. Penney, I. 54 f.; quoted on p. 8, n. 4, *sup.*
[4] *Id., Journal* (1901 edn.), I. 447.
[5] A Baptist; cf. G. Fox, *Journal*, ed. N. Penney, I. 105, 416.
[6] 'W.C.' is printed here in the margin, i.e. William Cole, for whom cf. *C.R.*, *s.v.*

towards Firthbanke[1] suddenly he faced about and said he was commanded to go to Grayrigg.[2]

It is easy to see how such claims and behaviour could easily become extravagant, and, even without extravagance, would be misunderstood. The Quakers might distinguish between the earthly man and the spiritual man,[3] but, again, they might not;[4] in any case, their distinctions were neglected, and the furore aroused by the Nayler episode seemed to justify neglect. Had the authorities set eyes upon an early letter written to Fox by Margaret Fell and her family, they would but have been confirmed in their judgement that the Quakers, in addressing Messianic language to Fox,[5] were guilty of blasphemy:

> O thou bread of life, without which bread our souls will starve. O for evermore give us this bread . . .
> in thy presence is fullness of joy, and where thou dwells is pleasures for evermore . . .[6]

Even in an explanatory apologia published by Fox and others in 1653 occurs the sentence, 'he that hath the same spirit that raised up Jesus Christ is equal with God'.[7] One is bound to endorse Braithwaite's judgement that

> Fox's words, even in this answer, are open to misconception. . . . Fox, and others of the early Friends, had a vivid sense of personal union with their living Lord, but they coupled this experience of the indwelling Christ with a doctrine of perfection that betrayed them, during the first exhilaration of the experience, into extremes of identification with the Divine. They believed that inspiration gave infallibility, a belief that men have often held with respect to the writers of scripture, and they had to learn, with the help of some painful lessons, what we are learning to-day about the writers of scripture, that the inspired servant of God remains a man, liable to much of human error and weakness.[8]

Neither the Quakers nor their opponents had yet learned this. Their opponents considered Quaker claims necessarily to imply infallibility

---

[1] i.e. Firbank, Westmorland; B. Nightingale, *op. cit.*, II. 933 inaccurately prints *Forthbanke*.
[2] T. Weld *et al.*, *The Perfect Pharise*, p. 46.
[3] Cf., e.g., Nayler's query, when Fox was asked, 'Art thou equall with God': 'Dost thou aske him as a Creature or as Christ dwellinge in him': G. Fox, *Journal*, ed. N. Penney, I. 66.
[4] Cf., e.g., Fox's papers beginning 'To the world I clear my conscience, & to all people I speak to your conscience to be made manifest. I am the Light of the world . . .' and, to Cromwell, 'Have not I raised thee up and clothed thee with power and honour . . .': H. J. Cadbury, *Annual Catalogue of G. Fox's Papers*, p. 37, nos. 6, 89A, and 6, 96A, *s.a.* 1652.
[5] Cf. Appendix II, on the use of Messianic language in early Quakerism, p. 181, *inf.*
[6] Spence MSS. (Friends House), iii. 24; facsimile in J. Wilkinson, *Quakerism Examined*.
[7] G. Fox, in *Sauls Errand to Damascus*, p. 8.
[8] *B.Q.*, p. 109.

and moral perfection, *quod erat absurdum*, whether the Quakers themselves claimed these or not.[1]

Certainly the Quaker claims were accompanied by both an intense intuitive certitude and a sense of triumph over sin[2] which were something new, and which brought a powerful sense of release and integration to those who were 'convinced'. Karl Holl's question about Fox, *Ist es wohl zufällig, dass dieses Wort ⟨Gnade⟩, soweit ich sehe, im ganzen Journal nicht vorkommt?*[3] is not well founded[4]; but it is true that Fox does not use the accepted phraseology of grace, which he calls 'a tempting Customary Word'.[5] More than this, 'with all his sensitiveness of spirit, he never appears to have undergone any travail over his own sins . . . he seems never concerned about his own soul'.[6]

At the same time, Fox may be seen wrestling in his own way with the same problems, in his shrewd and unyielding opposition to the Ranters,[7] who 'had some kinde of meetinges but took tobacco: & drunk ale in y^m: & soe grew light and loose' ' & sunge & whistled & danced'. In the intellectual sphere,

> seeing they said they were God, I asked them, if they knew whether it would rain to-morrow? they said they could not tell. I told them, God could tell.

And in the practical sphere,

> One of them cryed all is ours & an other saide all was well: butt I replyed howe is all well when thou art soe peevish & envious & crabbed: for I saw hee was of a peevish nature.[8]

We see here how Fox would deal with a loose claim to infallibility or to the freedom from any moral code which tends to accompany the claim to moral perfection. It is not surprising if his contemporaries were not able to see it as clearly as we, and of Ranters 'said they was Quakers'.[9]

---

[1] As late as 1673 twenty-six Quakers in Cork, in a paper condemning Muggletonianism claimed 'an infallible discerning': cf. L. Muggleton, *Spiritual Epistles*, p. 379.

[2] 'The dominant note of Fox's life was the note of victory': *P.G.F.*, p. 155; cf. the whole section.

[3] K. Holl. *op. cit.*, I. 444, n. 5.   [4] Cf. *Journal* (1901 edn.), index, *s.v.* Grace.

[5] G. Fox, *Epistles*, ed. G. Whitehead, p. 6; Troeltsch perceives an emphasis on grace such as Luther's to be essentially of the 'Church-type': *op. cit.*, II. 481.

[6] R. M. Jones, introd. to *B.Q.*, pp. xxxii, xlii; cf., however, *Journal* (1901 edn.), I. 14: 'I was tempted again to despair, as if I had sinned against the Holy Ghost'. Cf. also E. Troeltsch, *op. cit.*, II. 748: in 'spiritual religion' (in the technical sense) 'the forgiveness of sins recedes into the background, and it is replaced by a direct experience of God and actual victory over sin . . .'.

[7] For the Ranters, cf. T. Sippell, *Werdendes Quäkertum*, ch. iv ('*Die Ranters*'); *Q.S.M.*, p. 136, n. 2.

[8] G. Fox, *Journal*, ed. N. Penney, I. 21, 152, 165; *Journal* (1901 edn.), I. 48.

[9] G. Fox, *Journal*, ed. N. Penney, II. 125.

Among the simpler folk who were not Quakers, the immediate leadings of the Holy Spirit were conceived mainly as suggesting and interpreting passages of Scripture to them:

> the Lord afforded me, a marvellous revelation of him selfe, on this manner. In the night, waking, I being very well, my understanding clearer than ever, Scriptures were cast in very thick, and without anything of my recollecting them, or study for them; and cleare interpretations came in with them. . . . Many Scriptures that were darke and mysticall, were made cleare to me, which before I knew nothing of, and the interpretations very spirituall.[1]

> As I was earnestly Crying to the Lord, with many teires, for his prsence, that blessed word darted in vpon my mind, 'ye righteous shall hold on their way . . .'[2]

Agnes Beaumont's narrative, from which this last passage is quoted, is full of examples of the way in which passages from Scripture 'would dart into my mind', 'Came suddainly vpon my mind' and 'would often run in my mind'. Such experiences, however, Baxter realized should not lightly be attributed to the immediate leadings of God's Spirit:

> it is an unsafe course which many such weak persons use, to think in their troubles that every text of Scripture which cometh into their minds or every conceit of their own is a special suggestion of the Spirit of God. You shall ordinarily hear them say, 'Such a text was brought to me, or was set upon my heart, and such a thing was set upon my mind,' when two to one, it was no otherwise brought unto them, nor set upon them, than any other ordinary thoughts are; and had no special or extraordinary operation of God in it at all. Though it is certain that every good thought which cometh into our minds, is some effect of the working of God's Spirit, . . .[3]

Upon this whole subject of spiritual revelations and leadings, Baxter has the following remarks:

> It is possible that God may make new revelations to particular persons about their particular duties, events, or matters of fact, in subordination to the Scripture, either by inspiration, vision, or apparition, or voice; for he hath not told us that he will never do such a thing. . . . Though such revelation and prophecy be possible, there is no certainty of it in general, nor any probability of it to any one individual person, much less a promise. And therefore to expect it, or pray for it, is but a presumptuous tempting of God. And all sober Christians should be the

---

[1] A. M., in S. Petto, *Roses from Sharon*, pp. 2, 4.
[2] A. Beaumont, *Narrative of Persecution*, ed. G. B. Harrison, p. 75, with ref. to *Job* xvii. 9.
[3] R. Baxter, *Works*, XII. 495 f.

more cautious of being deceived by their own imaginations, because certain experience telleth us, that most in our age that have pretended to prophecy, or to inspirations, or revelations, have been melancholy, crack-brained persons, near to madness, who have proved deluded in the end.

No person more fit for a Quaker, a Papist, or any sectary to work upon, than a troubled mind.[1]

In the foregoing pages we have concentrated on a consideration of the revelations and leadings of the Holy Spirit: of the Spirit's witness, that is, in the intellectual and practical spheres respectively. In this we have been following the line of Puritan interest and discussion, according as the personal indwelling of the Spirit Himself was believed or denied, and as the implications of this conviction were worked out in Puritan faith and experience. The witness of the Spirit in what we have termed the evangelical sphere has itself two aspects, the Godward and the manward. The implications of these will be drawn out more fully in the chapters on the Spirit and prayer, and on the life and fellowship of the Spirit, respectively.[2] Here, it may be sufficient to indicate how, essentially, this witness was regarded by the Puritans. This can be done the more briefly in that there was virtually no disagreement upon this subject. The witness of the Spirit is primarily 'that we are the children of God'. This means that towards God we may behave with the freedom and reverent familiarity of His children; and that towards one another we may behave with a sanctified moral character which has its origin in, and is similar to, His own. Baxter thus recommends Howe's *Blessedness of the Righteous*:

Here you have described to you the true 'witness of the Spirit'; not that of supposed internal voices, which *they* are usually most taken up with, who have the smallest knowledge and faith and love, and the greatest self-esteem or spiritual pride, with the strongest phantasies and passions: but the objective and the sealing testimony, the divine nature, the renewed image of God, whose children are known by being *like* to their Heavenly Father, even by being 'holy as he is holy'. This is the Spirit of adoption, by which we are inclined, by holy love to God and confidence in Him, 'to cry, Abba Father', and to fly unto Him: the Spirit of sanctification is thereby in us the Spirit of adoption; for both signify but the giving us that love to God which is the filial nature and our Father's image.[3]

[1] R. Baxter, *Works*, v. 556; xii. 500.   [2] Cf. chs, iv and ix, *inf*.
[3] R. Baxter, in J. Howe, *Works*, i. 11.

As early as 1616,[1] John Forbes wrote a treatise entitled *How a Christian man may discerne the testimonie of Gods spirit, from the testimonie of his owne spirit, in witnessing his Adoption*. In this he says we discern our election and adoption by God's presence with us, which in turn we discern by His work in us, working 'libertie . . . in the heart: making it free, and causing it to reioice, and making it confident towards God', in contrast with man's ignorance and blindness by nature, in which 'may he bee secure, because he is senselesse: but confident hee can not be, because he hath no knowledge'.[2] This is the line followed throughout Puritan writings on the subject. Sibbes, for instance, says,

> There is a great deal of familiarity in the spirit of adoption.
> A child needs not extrinsecal motives to please his father. . . . 'Where the Spirit of God is, there is freedom'; that is, a kind of natural freedom, not forced, not moved by any foreign extrinsecal motive.[3]

Petto, again, beseeches 'the Saints and people in and about Sandcrof',[4]

> rest not satisfied without a perswasion from the Spirit of Adoption that God is your Father. . . . Christ your spirituall Joseph (as with Reverence we may speake it) will be able to refraine no longer, he cannot but cry out, I am Joseph your Brother.[5]

How this may work out in practice Cradock's warm piety suggests in many passages like the following:

> A childe can command his father, and say, I must have a new coat, I must have a new book, or I must have a ball to play with: so a Saint can say, Father, there is a Covenant, thou art my Father, and I am thy childe, it cannot stand with thy Truth, thou wert not just if thou shouldest deny me any thing that is good: O this is a holy boldness![6]

Baxter would not express himself in such enthusiastic language, but the same spirit breathes in his testimony to his wife that 'for near these nineteen years that I have lived with her, I think I never heard her thrice speak a doubting word of her salvation, but oft of her hopeful perswasions, that we should live together in Heaven';[7] as also in Cromwell's words,

> The best of us are, God knows, poor weak saints; yet saints; if not sheep, yet lambs; and must be fed. We have daily bread, and shall have

[1] Not 1617, as in *D.N.B.*, *s.v.*   [2] *Op. cit.*, pp. 42 f., 47, 51.
[3] R. Sibbes, *Works*, I. 364; IV. 231.
[4] i.e. Sandcroft, *al.* South Elmham St. Cross, Suffolk.
[5] S. Petto, *The Voyce of the Spirit*, Epistle Dedicatory.
[6] W. Cradock, *Divine Drops Distilled*, pp. 57 f. (p. 57 is numbered p. 49).
[7] R. Baxter, *Breviate of Life of M. Baxter*, ed. J. T. Wilkinson, p. 128.

it, in despite of all enemies. There's enough in our Father's house, and He dispenseth it.[1]

On the Godward side, then, the witness of the Spirit is a sure faith in God and a ready, though reverent, familiarity in approach to Him, as of a child to his Father.

On the manward side, the Spirit of adoption, as Baxter puts it, becomes the Spirit of sanctification: what the Apostle calls 'the fruits of the Spirit' appear in several Puritan lists as the outward marks of the Spirit's witness 'that we are the children of God'. Hollinworth, for instance, includes goodness or holiness, truth, light, lowliness, liberty and unity among the properties of the Holy Spirit which appear also in the saints, 'not a Liberty *to* sin, but from *Sin* . . . *to* and *in* the service of God, and not *from* it'.[2] Baxter similarly mentions among ten marks 'how it may be known whether we have Christ's Spirit or not', not merely that 'the Spirit of Christ is from heaven, from God our Father, and leadeth us upward unto Him . . . making us cry Abba! Father! and working the heart by uniting love to God', but that 'the Spirit of Christ uniteth us to Christ, and one another by love, and is against hatred, division and abusing others, . . . is a spirit of holiness . . . inclineth to love, humility and meekness, and makes men stoop to each other for their good'.[3] Owen, again, spends two of the five books in his Πνευματολογία upon the Holy Spirit's 'Work in New Creation in Regeneration' and 'The Nature of Sanctification and Gospel Holiness'.

Schneckenburger has traced in detail the gradual reappearance in Reformed Protestantism of good works, no longer as securing salvation by merit, but as evidence of salvation already secured:

> *Da mit dem Vorhandensein des wahrem Glaubens im Subjekte die Seligkeit ihm unentreissbar zugehört, so könnte man zwar sagen, die Nothwendigkeit der Werke für die subjektive Glaubensgewissheit und für den wirklichen Seligkeits-genuss sei durchaus dieselbe. Dennoch findet ein Unterschied Statt, angedeutet schon darin, dass der Glaube das jus, die Werke die possessio salutis geben sollen . . .*[4]

To this English Puritanism was no exception. We have already mentioned Dr. Sippell's perception of the way in which *immer*

---

[1] O. Cromwell, *Letters and Speeches*, ed. T. Carlyle, Letter LXVIII; cf. Cromwell's dying prayer, *ib.*, *ad fin.*
[2] R. Hollinworth, *op. cit.*, chs. II and III.   [3] R. Baxter, *op. cit.*, pp. 71 ff.
[4] M. Schneckenburger, *op. cit.*, pp. 74 f.

präziser und strenger wurden die Forderungen der 'Praxis Pietatis', which for some resulted only in a *schwere Erschütterung der Heilsgewissheit*[1] and 'troubled minds' for Antinomians[2] and Quakers to 'work upon'. Yet many Puritans retained both quiet confidence in God and unforced piety towards men, untroubled by either intellectual doubts or moral problems. Self-discipline was needed by all. 'Where there is no conflict,' says Sibbes, 'there is no Spirit of Christ at all. . . . All spiritual graces are with conflict'. Yet

> Duties come from Christians as water out of a spring. They are natural, and not forced to issue, so far forth as they are spiritual.
> God's people are a voluntary people.[3]

With this in mind, it is good to find both the enthusiastic Petto and the judicious Baxter recognizing 'the witness of the Spirit' in simple folk, who neither understood fine-spun intellectual distinctions nor sought high-flown spiritual attainments, but who nevertheless were the real backbone of the Puritan movement.

> The rich mans window may be wider than the poore mans, and so the Sun may make his house more lightsome . . .: but the poore man may really injoy the beames of the Sun. . . . So the poorest Saint may know that the Spirit hath shined in his heart, as well as others, that are beholden to it, for brighter beames then he hath been acquainted with.[4]

> Thousands believe savingly, that have not wit enough to tell you truly what believing is; and many thousands have the Spirit that know not what the Spirit is. . . . I can give a truer description of any county in England, and distance of one town from another by my maps, though I know not the places, than most men that live in those counties can do, because they know but a smaller part of it; and yet they know their own homes better, and their knowledge is more sensible and experimental, and beneficial to them.[5]

They know their own homes better. Here, once more, is the essential Puritan emphasis, which includes all these writers in its circle, and

[1] T. Sippell, *Werdendes Quäkertum*, p. 55. Lewis Bayly's *Practice of Piety*, first published *c.* 1611, by 1630 was in its twenty-fifth edition, and had been translated into Welsh, French and German: cf. T. F. Tout, in *D.N.B., s.v.*

[2] For the place of Antinomianism in the sequence, cf. R. Baxter's revealing parenthesis, 'the Antinomians were commonly Independants': *R.B.*, i. 162; cf. p. 179, n. 4, *inf.*

[3] R. Sibbes, *Works*, I. 22; IV. 145, 221, 231.

[4] S. Petto, *The Voyce of the Spirit*, p. 53.

[5] R. Baxter, *Works*, XX. 189.

relates Baxter, despite his caution, to an enthusiastic Quaker such as Howgill, with his cry:

> return home to within: sweep your Houses all; the Groat is there; the little Leaven is there; the Grain of Mustard-seed you will see which the Kingdom of God is like; ... and here you will see your Teacher not removed into a Corner, but present, when you are upon your Beds, about your Labour, convincing, instructing, leading, correcting, judging, and giving Peace to all that love and follow Him.[1]

[1] F. Howgill, *Works*, pp. 70 f.; for Howgill, cf. *D.N.B., s.v.*

CHAPTER IV

THE SPIRIT AND PRAYER

SYNOPSIS OF ARGUMENT

i. Conviction of God's Fatherhood the foundation of prayer τῷ πνεύματι;
   rediscovery of conviction at Reformation;
   insistence of conviction among Puritans:
                   Sibbes, Hollinworth, Cradock, Sprigg.
ii. Prayer τῷ πνεύματι consequently *familiar*: Sibbes, Cradock.
iii. Typical systematic consideration of the subject: Forbes, Hollinworth.
iv. Radical Puritans' dislike of read prayers as 'stinted':
                   Barrow, Brownists, Cradock;
     preference for extempore prayer as more spiritual:
                   Erbury, Saltmarsh;
       silence, in which to pray inaudibly;
         out of which to pray vocally.
            in dependence on the Spirit's motions:
                   Seekers, Quakers.
v. Conservative Puritans' preference for read prayers:
                   Hollinworth, Featley.
   Middle party's acceptance of both read and extempore prayers as
     genuinely spiritual: Baxter's controversy with Owen.
vi. Similar development of thought over hymn-singing from books:
                   Featley, Baxter, M. Springett, Fox.

'the Spirit itself maketh intercession for us' (*Rom.* viii. 26).
'ye have received the Spirit of adoption, whereby we cry Abba, Father' (*Rom.* viii. 15).

THE first text quoted above is, it will be noted, from the verse preceding that from which was taken the first text quoted at the beginning of the last chapter. That text, furthermore, is associated with the second text quoted above in an essay on Puritanism by T. H. Green, who calls them 'the greatest verses in the bible, very good to "feed on", as Cromwell would have said'.[1] This will at once indicate the close connexion, alike in biblical and in Puritan religion, between the subjects of these two chapters, between 'the witness of the Spirit' and 'the Spirit and prayer'. It is in prayer, pre-eminently, that we see, taking effect, the Godward aspect of the Spirit's witness. That

[1] T. H. Green, *Works*, III. cviii f.; quoted on p. 48, n. 1, *sup.*

witness is 'that we are the children of God', and this means, as already remarked, that towards God we may behave with the freedom and reverent familiarity of His children. In a word, the foundation of prayer τῷ πνεύματι is the conviction of God's Fatherhood.

This conviction was, in fact, one of the major rediscoveries brought about by men's return to the Bible at the Reformation. Michelet's phrase, *Le moyen-âge a entièrement méprisé Dieu le Père*,[1] is no doubt as exaggerated as most generalizations; it is none the less true that 'one thing was the centre of all the life and all the teaching of the Reformers —that God was speaking to them as their reconciled Father, and that they were in direct communion with Him;'.[2] Dean Wace even suggests that 'the word which is perhaps most characteristic of the spirit fostered by the Reformers' teaching, especially in Germany, is the word *child*—the tender German word *Kind*— . .'.[3] It was inevitable that this changed attitude towards God should immediately influence both men's ways of prayer and their conceptions of prayer. In Melanchthon's correspondence there is a reference to Luther's manner of prayer which points the way: *Tanta reverentia petit aliquid ut cum Deo, tanta spe et fide ut cum patre et amico colloqui sentiat. Scio, aiebat, te patrem et Deum nostrum esse.*[4]

From the above considerations it would be strange if we did not find, what is in fact the case, that throughout Puritanism God's Fatherhood is a favourite and insistent theme. 'In a word,' says Sibbes, 'the word *Father* is an epitome of the whole gospel.'[5] Again, 'the whole world', he says in his address 'To the Reader' prefatory to Scudder's *Key of Heaven*, is 'not worth this one prerogative, that we can boldly call God Father'.[6] About this the Puritans of all parties are agreed.

> This Fatherhood is a good foundation of Faith and Prayer: Christ taught us to call God our Father; children cry Dad and Mam.[7]

So says Hollinworth, the Presbyterian and conservative; so, likewise, if more warmly, says Cradock, the Congregationalist and radical:

> it is ordinary with the Saints, that they have a little adoption, they can cry Abba father, a little, and low, and at sometimes: but there is a great

---

[1] J. Michelet, in G. Monod, *J. Michelet*, p. 375, as quoted by G. G. Coulton, *Five Centuries of Religion*, I. 138.
[2] H. Wace, *Principles of the Reformation*, p. 101.
[3] *Ib.*, p. 61; this may be illustrated by the fact that the theme of the Prodigal Son was treated by as many as twenty-seven German dramatists in the sixteenth century (cf. P. Smith, *The Age of the Reformation*, p. 696).
[4] V. Dietrich (1530), in *Corpus Reformatorum*, ed. Bretschneider & Bindseil, II. 159.
[5] R. Sibbes, *Works*, v. 25.   [6] *loc. cit., ad. init.*; for Henry Scudder, cf. *D.N.B.*, *s.v.*
[7] R. Hollinworth, *The Holy Ghost on the Bench*, p. 47.

deale of the spirit of bondage mingled with it, there are sometimes feares, secret whisperings in the heart. . . . Now in the New Testament we should labour for a full spirit of adoption. . . . If thou come below this, if thou call on God with feare, & canst not cry abba, abba, that is as much as daddie, daddie, as our babes use to say, if thou doe not come so high, thou art spoiled, and undone, desire God to teach you this lesson also.[1]

Joshua Sprigg,[2] a Congregationalist who represents the extreme radical position, and who goes so far as to alter the Pauline triad to 'one *Father*, one Lord, one Baptism', draws attention to the neglected (Johannine) saying of Jesus, 'I say not, that I will pray for you, for the Father himselfe loves you', and calls it 'the glory of our moderne Orthodox Divinity' 'that the Father himself loves us'.[3]

The bearing of this upon prayer is already evident and need not be laboured. Sibbes well represents the regular Puritan emphasis by his repeated use of the word *familiar*:

there is a great deal of familiarity in the spirit of adoption.
that 'Abba, Father,' it is a bold and familiar speech. . . . there is an inward kind of familiar boldness in the soul, whereby a Christian goes to God, as a child when he wants anything goes to his father. A child considers not his own worthiness or meanness, but goeth to his father familiarly and boldly: . . .
Take another man, in the time of extremity, he sinks; but take a child of God in extremity, yet he hath a spirit to go to God, and to cry Abba, Father; to go in a familiar manner to God. . . . That familiar boldness whereby we cry 'Abba, Father', it comes from sons. They only can cry so. This comes from the Spirit. If we be sons, then we have the Spirit, whereby we cry Abba, Father.[4]

Cradock says the same in his own way:

So a man that walks according to grace, he can go as a child, and speake loving, and plaine words to his Father, and get power over his sins, that all the howling, and roaring, and crying of another a whole Yeare together cannot doe.[5]

For examples of a more systematic consideration of the relation between the Holy Spirit and prayer, we may turn to Forbes and Hollinworth. Forbes, in his treatise upon the way by which God's

---

[1] W. Cradock, *Glad Tydings from Heaven*, pp. 40–3.
[2] Baxter calls Sprigg 'the chief of' Vane's 'more open disciples' (*R.B.*, i. 119). In 1656 Sprigg headed a deputation pleading for Nayler's release; cf. C. H. Firth, in *D.N.B.*, *s.v.*
[3] J. Sprigg, *A Testimony to Approaching Glory*, pp. 127, 37 and Preface.
[4] R. Sibbes, *Works*, I. 364; III. 456 f.; IV. 232 f.
[5] W. Cradock, *Gospel-Holinesse*, p. 279; cf. *eund.*, *Divine Drops Distilled*, pp. 57 f. (quoted on p. 58, *sup.*)

Spirit within men may be discerned from their own fancies, says that we may discern 'his voyce in us', 'when the spirit within us, speaketh to God for us', in three ways:—(*a*) 'when we by the spirit, call upon God as our Father'. Prayer must be 'made unto God', which 'cannot be without the Spirit: because we have no entrance nor accesse to God in Christ, but by the spirit'. (*b*) Prayer must be 'made in the Name of Christ', and 'we can not pray in the Name of Christ, except we acknowledge God his Father, and in him our Father; which we can never doe, except we be taught by the spirit'. (*c*) Prayer must be 'made according to the will of God', and this also cannot be done 'but by the spirit'. 'The babling of hypocrits, is no prayer: seeing it proceedes not from the spirit.'[1]

Hollinworth's chapter on 'The Spirit of Prayer', without being less biblical in intent, is more scholastic in manner. The subject is described in two main sections, negative and positive. Consideration of the former of these may be postponed momentarily, as arising out of a controversy yet to be noticed. Positively, Hollinworth describes the work of the Holy Spirit in prayer as (*a*) in regard to the person: (i) enlightening; (ii) enlivening; (iii) enlarging 'the soul with faith and love to God, only Sons can call God Father'; (*b*) in regard to the prayer: (i) exciting; (ii) discovering; (iii) bringing 'to our remembrance the savory and suitable phrases and passages of holy Writ, especially the precious Promises . . . Promises and Prayers are like figures of 6. and of 9. the very same figure, only the Promises like the figure of 9. do bend downward, and Prayers like the figure 6. do point upward'; (iv) exciting graces of prayer: 'our hearts (saith one) are dead and dull, and lye like a Log in a Ditch, and though we toil and tug with them, we cannot lift them up, but συναντι-λαμβάνεται'; (v) enlarging our affections 'with sighs and groans'; (vi) restraining our tongue.[2]

In this last-mentioned work of the Holy Spirit may perhaps be seen the influence of Hollinworth's conservative reaction to contemporary over-enthusiastic utterances in prayer; but not only so, for in the following chapter on the difference between the gift of prayer and the Spirit of prayer, he gives full value to silent prayer:

> The Spirit of Prayer may be found in silent Ejaculations. . . . when a man cannot speak, the Spirit may pray. . . . their affections are too big for their expressions. . . . words are but the outside of Prayer. . . . the Father hath compassion on his sick Child, though it cannot speak articu-

---

[1] J. Forbes, *op. cit.*, pp. 60–3.   [2] R. Hollinworth, *op. cit.*, ch. v.

E

lately, nor speak at all, but only sighs, groans, looks upon his Father, and then his Bowels yearn.[1]

The same acceptance of the reality and value of στεναγμοὶ ἀλαλήτοι is to be found in Cradock:

> How many thousand prayers doth God put into thy heart that it is impossible for thee to utter with thy mouth?[2]

On the principle of prayer τῷ πνεύματι as a familiar communion with the Father, immediate and not necessarily dependent upon words, the conservative and the radical, it may be observed, are still agreed. It is over the putting of the principle into practice, over the outward manner of prayer's expression, that disagreement arises.

The more radical Puritans, acutely conscious of the working of the Holy Spirit, immediately, in their hearts, increasingly felt there to be no place in worship for liturgies or read prayers. By a people who could come to God boldly and familiarly, as children to their Father, such set forms of address were no longer required. These became for them, in fact, a positive hindrance to spiritual freedom of access to God, and were regarded by them, therefore, as sinful, in that they quenched the Spirit within, which 'itself maketh intercession for us'. The point at issue had been expressed already with vehemence by early Separatists such as Barrow:

> May such old written rotten stuffe be called praier, the odours of the Saintes, burnt with that heauenly fire of the Altar, the liuely graces of the spirit &c. May reading be said ⟨to be⟩ praying?[3]

The worship of some Separatists about 1588 is described thus in depositions:

> In yᵉ prayer one speketh, & the rest doe grone, or sob, or sigh, as if they woulde wringe out teares, but say not after him that prayeth. Their prayer is extemporall. . . . They teach that all stinted prayers & red service is but babling in the Lords sight & hath neyther promises of blessing nor edification, for that they are but Cushyns for such idell Priests and Atheists as have not the Spirit of God;[4]

Ephraim Pagitt complains similarly of the Brownists, that

> They pretend set prayers to be a device of Man, a muzling of the spirit, a nurse of idleness, and a means to neglect the graces of God that are in them; whereas they pretend extemporary Prayers to be the work

---

[1] *Ib.*, ch. vi.   [2] W. Cradock, *Divine Drops Distilled*, p. 169.
[3] H. Barrow, *Discoverie of the False Church*, p. 65.
[4] Cf. H. M. Dexter, *The Congregationalism of the Last Three Hundred Years*, p. 257.

of the Spirit; whereas rather thereby they muzzle the spirit of the people, being tyed to the *extempore* and crude prayers of the Ministers.[1]

With the sudden uprush of Independency in the 1640's, such a conviction of the wrongfulness of what were called, almost as a technical term, *stinted* prayers, became no longer characteristic merely of a few eccentric Separatists. In 'Fairfax's (or rather Cromwell's) Army'[2] Baxter found the men 'sometimes against Forms of Prayer' and 'sometimes against Set-times of Prayer, and against the tying of our Selves to any Duty before the Spirit move us'.[3] Cradock thus passionately expresses the growing conviction that to use a liturgy had been wrong:

> And for Prayer, when it may be the poore Ministers soule was full of groanes, & sighs, & he would have rejoyced to have poured out his soule to the Lord, he was tied to an old Service-Booke, & must read that till he grieved the Spirit of God, and dried up his owne spirit as a chip, that he could not pray if he would;[4]

In some cases, this antipathy to formal prayer extended even to the customary use of the Lord's Prayer. *Man gab sich viel Mühe, zu beweisen, dass das Vaterunser von Christus nur als Beispiel, nicht als Vorschrift eines Gebetes gemeint sei.*[5] Milton, writing *De Cultu Externo*, in the sub-section headed *auctore sancto spiritu*, says that the Lord's Prayer is

> *documentum potius quam formula precandi ab apostolis olim aut nunc ab ecclesiis verbatim recitanda: unde perspicitur quam nihil opus sint in ecclesia Liturgiae; cum auctores adjutoresque precum nostrarum divinos, non humanos, habeamus.*[6]

Baillie says regretfully of the Independents that 'at London their p⟨r⟩actise is constantly to forget the Lords Prayer'.[7]

The more extreme the radicalism, the more insistence we find that that prayer only is spiritual which is dependent on the immediate movings of the Holy Spirit. Erbury, for instance, praises the

---

[1] E. Pagitt, *Heresiography* (1662 edn.), pp. 82 f.
[2] R. Baxter, *Account* . . . (printed in his *Catholick Communion Defended against both Extreams, ad fin.*), p. 26.
[3] *R.B.*, i. 77.
[4] W. Cradock, *Glad Tydings from Heaven*, p. 29.
[5] H. Weingarten, *Die Revolutionskirchen Englands*, p. 29.
[6] J. Milton, *De doctrina christiana*, ed. C. R. Sumner, p. 416.
[7] R. Baillie, *Dissuasive from the Errours of the Time*, p. 119; for examples of omission, cf. *D.N.B.*, *s.v.* C. Feake; *C.R.*, *s.vv.* R. Herring, R. Lancaster. Baxter, on the contrary, describes the Lord's Prayer as 'doubtless . . . the most perfect method for universal Prayer or holy desires, that can be possibly invented': *R.B.*, ii. 173.

Fifth Monarchist, Christopher Feake,[1] for speaking 'to the purpose'

> That the Saints should now return to their old spirit of Prayer in Gospel-times, which was not in loose requests, and long confessions of sin, but in short breathings out their present desires to God, with abundance of fervency and faith to obtain. . . . the spirit of Prayer in Gospel-times was more in Spirit, lesse in the Form.[2]

Saltmarsh, again, after remarking that

> prayer is rather a work of the Spirit than of any form, and . . . no set form ought to be put upon the Spirit of God, but what it freely breathes and speaks, and all constant speakings to God in this (as they call) a conceived way, or impremeditate, or extemporary way is taken commonly amongst Christians for prayer in the Spirit,

adds the caveat that extemporary prayer is worse than formal prayer, if it is 'more properly the flowings and breathings of reason, and the strength of man's wit, and memory and affections'. True, spiritual prayer is 'an immediate, proper, and spiritual act of the Spirit of God in the Saints'.[3]

The extent to which such radical convictions prevailed is indicated by the number of 'Seeker' groups, which were found by George Fox and others on their travels and were caught up by them into the organized Quaker movement. At Wigton, Cumberland, for instance, 'A few People were Gathered together from ye publique worship of ye Nation, & oftentimes sat together in Silence'. At Ross-on-Wye, Herefordshire, some 'did often before meet together by ymselves, & would many times sitt in silence'.[4]   At Kendal, Westmorland, 'there was a seeking People, who met often together, sometimes sitting in Silence, other times in Religious Conferences, and often in fervent Prayer'.[5] At Bristol was a group which

> sat down sometimes in silence; and as any found a Concern on their Spirits, and Inclination in their Hearts, they Kneeled down, and sought the Lord; so that sometimes, before the day ended, there might be Twenty of us might pray, Men and Women and sometimes Children spake a few words in Prayer;[6]

Such silent worship was clearly spiritual in the strictest sense, and depended on the conviction of the centrality, in worship, of prayer.[7]

---

[1] Cf. A. Gordon, in *D.N.B.*, *s.v.*   [2] W. Erbury, *Testimony*, pp. 44 f.
[3] J. Saltmarsh, *Sparkles of Glory*, p. 143 ff.
[4] *First Publishers of Truth*, ed. N. Penney, pp. 52, 124.
[5] J. Tomkins, *Piety Promoted*, III. 199.
[6] C. Marshall, *Sion's Travellers Comforted*, Journal, *ad init.*
[7] It could also have an eschatological significance; cf. M. Llwyd, *Gweithiau*, I. 216: 'let him watch in silence, for the day is dawning'.

Others might regard the ritual acts of the priest, or the reading and preaching of Scripture, as worship's climax; for these men worship was essentially prayer,[1] and in the silence the prayers of those present might be made severally, yet together, without the intervention of prearranged, set forms, or, equally, any might pray vocally '*out of the silence* (not as an inlay clumsily inserted in it)',[2] as in the silence moved by God's Spirit so to do, and only as so moved. 'I could not pray in man's will',[3] says Fox. Edward Burrough thus expresses the ideal of this silent waiting upon the Spirit, which in Quaker worship was accepted from the beginning as normal:

> We met together often, and waited upon the Lord in pure silence, from our own words, and all mens words, and hearkned to the voice of the Lord, and felt his word in our hearts, to burn up and beat down all that was contrary to God, and we obeyed the Light of Christ in us, and followed the motions of the Lords pure spirit . . .[4]

One can see how in unbalanced minds the development outlined above might lead to the notion that silence in worship was, in itself, superior to vocal prayer. In Quakerism such an exaggeration did not arise until the eighteenth century, when '*for years together* many meetings were held wholly in silence'[5] except on rare occasions. The germ of it, nevertheless, may be perceived in Fox's phrase of Francis Howgill that 'hee saw they had noe need of words: for they was all sitting doune under there teacher Christ Jesus'.[6] As early as 1650, in fact, Cradock lamented

> there is a people that throw away the ordinance of prayer, and they professe to live immediately upon God without ordinances, without prayer, and without all the rest. I do not know what their perfections may be, therefore I cannot judge; but this I know as far as ever I had experience, that the chiefest way of communion with God is spirituall prayer.[7]

Cradock himself perceived that, on the contrary, the outcome of such dependence on the Holy Spirit's motions in prayer should be not, through the practice of silence, a gradual cessation from vocal prayer and finally from prayer entirely, but rather a freedom for

---

[1] Penn says of Fox (introd. to G. Fox, *Journal*, 1901 edn., I. xlvii f.) that 'above all he excelled in prayer. . . . The most awful, living, reverent frame I ever felt or beheld, I must say, was his in prayer'.

[2] *Q.S.M.*, p. 104.   [3] G. Fox, *Journal* (1901 edn.), I. 24.

[4] E. Burrough, in G. Fox, *The Great Mistery of the Great Whore*, 'To the Reader'; for Burrough, cf. *D.N.B.*, *s.v.*

[5] *Q.S.M.*, p. 254.   [6] G. Fox, *Journal*, ed. N. Penney, I. 137.

[7] W. Cradock, *Divine Drops Distilled*, pp. 86 f.; cf. L. Muggleton, *Spiritual Epistles*, p. 23: 'this worship of the Spirit, which is now [1660], hath no visible forms of worship at all belonging to it, neither is there any necessity for any public meetings at all'.

increasingly frequent prayer, without undue attention to the time, manner or place.

> I have observed that souls that are far from God, they must always go upon their knees, but a soul that is neer can pray standing, or walking, or talking, as that good man that you read of in the Book of Ezra, he can pray with his hat on, he can pray in his bed, or where you will, when he is in communion with God.[1]

In the development traced in the last few paragraphs we have been following a line which ran on through radical Puritanism into Quakerism. It is not to be supposed that the development represents Puritanism as a whole, although Puritanism as a whole can be understood best when seen in relation to such a development. All Puritans, in their thought about prayer, give a large place, as we saw, to the Fatherhood of God as apprehended through the witness of the Holy Spirit within; but Puritans of the conservative and middle parties stop at various points along the line traced above, the middle party being sympathetic to extempore prayer but still allowing read prayer to be genuinely spiritual, the conservatives preferring read prayer and resolutely declining to allow it to be in any way unspiritual.

The arguments used are of much the same type as those which we have seen used before. A Presbyterian like Hollinworth, since, as we have noticed, he regards the indwelling of the Holy Spirit as no more than a metonymy, approaches the question from a conservative position, and in his chapter on the Spirit of prayer puts the negative aspect first.

> The Holy Ghost doth not immediately inspire the Method, Matter, words of Prayer; as he inspired the holy men of God in their Prophesying & Penning of holy Scriptures.

> The Spirit is not in our prayers properly, the person praying or petitioning; that is below the High and Holy Spirit of God: . . . the Spirit is said to pray, as we say Solomon builded the House, yet he was a Magistrate, a King, not a Mason or Carpenter; he directed how to build.

Consequently,

> The help of the Spirit of God doth not prohibit, evacuate or invalidate other helps; . . . our Saviour saith not, Ye have the Spirit, Therefore you need not to be taught, nor saith he, John was to blame to teach them to pray, nor . . . I will send my Spirit to teach you, and in the mean time I will not help you; but he teacheth them again, giving them hence, a special rule of direction.[2]

---

[1] *Ib.*, p. 58; the reference to *Ezra* is probably for *Neh.* ii. 4 f.; the liberty to 'pray with his hat on' is interesting in view of the controversy within Quakerism over this subject in later years (cf. p. 46, *sup.*). 　　　　[2] R. Hollinworth, *op. cit.*, ch. v.

Again, the old claim is made that the Spirit's working in the apostles was extraordinary; as in a work against the Baptists by Daniel Featley,[1] one of the moderate Anglicans who sat in the Westminster Assembly. Featley also relies on the assumption that a prayer genuinely dependent upon the Holy Spirit's motions would be perfect, so that 'they who pray *extempore*' 'pray not by the Spirit . . . for then they could not be out, which they are often'.[2]

It is over this question of prayer τῷ πνεύματι that the dividing line comes between Baxter and Owen, both of the middle party. That Baxter in no way undervalued extempore prayer is clear from passages such as the following:

> God did not deny their prayers, though they were *without book*, and such as some deride as extemporate. I was not with them in any of these, but laymen that were humble praying persons only.[3]

Baxter, however, is not blind to the danger that such prayer may be 'with Disorder and Repetitions and unfit Expressions', and remarks that

> old Mr. Ash[4] hath often told us, that this was the Mind of the old Nonconformists, and that he hath often heard some weak Ministers so disorderly in Prayer, especially in Baptism and the Lord's Supper, that he could have wish'd that they would rather use the Common-Prayer.[5]

Baxter himself, whose 'conscience was a subtle and complex one',[6] also 'always took the Faults of the Common Prayer to be chiefly Disorder and Defectiveness'; but he never regarded it as 'a Worship which a Christian might not lawfully join in, when he had not Liberty and Ability for better',[7] and in 1660 he did his utmost, though unavailingly, to help in revising the Prayer Book. To the end of his life he remained obedient to his principle,

> I separate from none of them further than they separate from Christ. I mentally separate from the Sin that is in their Worship, and as far as I can in my own.[8]

Accordingly, he went to the Parish Church, or to 'the privater Minister and Worship', whichever was 'most spiritual, powerful and profitable' in the place where he happened to be; and in each case he would go occasionally to the worship which he did not regularly

---

[1] Cf. *D.N.B.*, *s.v.*   [2] D. Featley, *The Dipper Dipt* (1651 edn.), p. 164.
[3] R. Baxter, *Breviate of Life of M. Baxter*, ed. J. T. Wilkinson, p. 74.
[4] i.e. Simeon Ashe; cf. *D.N.B.*, *s.v.*   [5] R.B., ii. 174.   [6] *D.N.B.*, *s.v.*
[7] R.B., ii. 174; cf. i. 29.
[8] R. Baxter, *Unnecessary Separating disowned* (printed in his *Catholick Communion Defended*, *ad fin.*), p. 15.

attend, 'yea, tho it were to one that is against Infant-Baptism by mistake', that he might not seem to disown either communion.[1]

The Congregationalists, however, were 'against a Liturgy as such',[2] and in this Owen was true to type. The manuscript of a work by Owen, entitled *Twelve Arguments against any Conformity to Worship not of Divine Institution*, which was not published till 1720, fell into Baxter's hands and was answered by him in advance. Owen's second argument is that liturgical worship 'was in its first contrivance, and hath been in its continuance, an Invention and Engine to defeat, or render useless the Promise of Christ unto his Church, of sending the holy Spirit in all Ages to enable it unto the due discharge and performance of all Divine Worship in its Assemblies'. To this Baxter replies that liturgical worship was, rather, 'to be a help subordinate to the Spirit's help, to those that have it but in part; as Spectacles to dark Sights, and Sermon Notes to weak Memories. . . . I can truly say, that Forms are oft a help to me:'

> It is a great Error to think, that the Gifts and Graces of the holy Spirit may not be exercised, if we use the same words, or if they be prescribed.
> I doubt you lay too much on words; . . . Words must be used and weighed; but the main work is heart work, and God knoweth the meaning of the Spirit, when we have but groans, which we canot express, and cry but Abba, Father.[3]

Such a remark as the last shows how close spiritually Baxter and Owen in fact were. Baxter evidently found it hard to understand how Owen could be so passionately 'against all Liturgies, and for Separation from them when yet he was of late years of more complying mildness, and sweetness, and peaceableness, than ever before'.[4] The explanation is to be found, in Owen's case, less, perhaps, in an enthusiastic consciousness of the Holy Spirit's workings within, such as the more radical Puritans claimed, than in an acute reaction to the evils of past days, when the Holy Spirit's

> gifts and graces were not only decried, but almost excluded from the public worship of the church, by the imposition of an operose form of service, to be read by the minister; which to do is neither a peculiar gift of the Holy Ghost to any, nor of the ministry at all. . . . The name of the Spirit was grown a term of reproach. To plead for, or pretend to pray by, the Spirit, was enough to render a man the object of scorn and reproach from all sorts of men, from the pulpit to the stage.[5] . . . The

[1] *Ib.*, p. 11.   [2] *R.B.*, ii. 172.   [3] R. Baxter, *Account* (cf. *sup.*), pp. 19 ff.
[4] *Ib.*, postscript.
[5] For a conspectus of sarcastic stage references to extempore prayer and Puritan worship generally, cf. E. N. S. Thompson, *The Controversy between the Puritans and the Stage* (Yale Studies in English, xx), II. ii.

Lord grant there be nothing of this cursed leaven still remaining amongst us! Some bleatings of ill importance are sometimes heard.[1]

It was his horror of this 'silencing, destroying, banishing, men whose ministry was accompanied with the evidence and demonstration of the Spirit'[2] which made Owen's Nonconformity of a more Separatist type than Baxter's. Owen, however, refrained, as did the Congregationalists generally, from taking the further step of waiting in silence for the Holy Spirit's leadings into prayer.

It remains to describe, more briefly, the similar but not wholly parallel ·development with regard to hymn-singing. A regular weapon in the conservatives' armoury was that, if all read prayer was to be omitted from worship, so no less must be all hymn-singing from books, *quod erat absurdum*. Featley, for instance, says:

> we are as well to sing by the Spirit as to pray by the Spirit. . . . But a man may sing by the Spirit, and yet sing pricksong.[3]

Baxter, again, argues that 'Our common use of singing Psalms and Hymns, is the use of stinted imposed forms',[4] so that forms in prayer also must be permissible. Some of the radical Puritans rejected the analogy, regarding hymns primarily as edifying,[5] and many Puritan versions of the Psalms were produced, that by the Congregationalist Francis Rous being approved by the Westminster Assembly, authorized by Parliament, and still popular in Scotland.[6] Other radical Puritans accepted the analogy, and disused hymn-singing from books. Objection to the practice was one of the reasons for the Separatist movement at Amsterdam led by John Smyth,[7] and among both General and Particular Baptists hymn-singing from books was not in use till the end of the century, when its gradual introduction caused much concern and several secessions.[8] The Congregationalist 'Mr. Faldo at Barnet was fain many years to Preach to a people that excluded singing Psalms',[9] and at Wrexham Morgan Llwyd's congregation came to 'disowne singing of Psalms in mixt Assemblyes'.[10] We

[1] J. Owen, *Works*, II. 255 f. [2] *Ibid.* [3] D. Featley, *op. cit.*, p. 164.
[4] R. Baxter, *op. cit.*, p. 4. [5] Cf. J. Robinson, *Works*, III. 21 f.
[6] Cf. *D.N.B.*, *s.v.* For a tune used in the Congregational church at Amsterdam, cf. H. M. Dexter, *op. cit.*, p. 333, n. 162.
[7] Cf. J. Smyth, *Works*, ed. W. T. Whitley, I. 273; for Smyth, cf. *D.N.B.*, *s.v.*, as Smith.
[8] Cf. A. Taylor, *History of English General Baptists*, I. 424 ff.; H. W. Robinson, *Life and Faith of Baptists*, p. 51; A. Gordon, in *D.N.B.*, *s.vv.* C. Feake and B. Keach: 'The practice of conjoint singing . . . was condemned by the London general baptist association in 1689 as a "carnal formality".'
[9] R. Baxter, *op. cit.*, p. 33; for John Faldo, cf. *D.N.B.*, *s.v.*
[10] P. Henry, *Diaries and Letters*, ed. M. H. Lee, p. 55.

noticed earlier the passage in which Mary Springett describes how she
and her husband

> tore out of our Bibles the common prayer, the form of prayer, and
> also the singing psalms, as being the inventions of vain poets, not being
> written for that use. We found that songs of praise must spring from
> the same source as prayers did; so we could not use any one's songs or
> prayers.[1]

It is not difficult to see how here, also, a line of development leads
to the complete disuse in Quaker worship of hymn-singing from
books. Fox regarded his mission as being

> to bring them off from all the world's fellowships, and prayings,
> and singings, which stood in forms without power; that their fellowship
> might be in the Holy Ghost, and in the Eternal Spirit of God; that they
> might pray in the Holy Ghost, and sing in the Spirit . . .[2]

That Fox had no personal objection to singing is clear from the
occasion during his imprisonment at Carlisle, when 'I was made to
singe in ye Lords power', and, on the gaoler's fetching a fiddler, 'I
was moved in ye everlastinge power of ye Lord God to singe: & my
voice droned yᵐ'.[3] Nor is it true to say that 'Fox excluded singing in
Meeting'.[4] Singing τῷ πνεύματι was permissible, and there were
occasions in Quaker worship when, as at the Munster Province
Meetings in 1669,

> Yᵉ power of yᵉ Lord was soe great, yᵗ friends in the power, & spiritt
> of yᵉ Lord brake out into singeing many together with an Audable
> voice, makeing mellody in their hearts; . . .[5]

From early days, however, there were some Quakers who opposed
hymn-singing, even when without books, and the liberty for this
practice remained but little used.[6]

---

[1] M. Penington, *Experiences*, ed. N. Penney, p. 26, quoted on p. 19 *sup.*; cf. the disuse
of hymn-singing *before* they became Quakers recorded by W. Dewsbury, *Testimony*, p. 47;
L. Howard, *Love and Truth in Plainness Manifested*, p. 6.

[2] G. Fox, *Journal* (1901 edn.), I. 37.   [3] *Id.*, *Journal*, ed. N. Penney, I. 126.

[4] G. K. Lewis, 'Puritan Singing in the Seventeenth Century', in *Friends' Quarterly Examiner*,
LIII. 171.

[5] G. Fox, *Journal*, ed. N. Penney, II. 141 (this reference should be added to the Index, *s.v.*
'Singing', *q.v.* for other references); cf. the approval by Yearly Meeting in 1675 of 'reverent
singing' (*S.P.Q.*, p. 300).

[6] Cf. N. Penney, *ib.*, I. 442.

CHAPTER V

THE SPIRIT AND PROPHESYING

SYNOPSIS OF ARGUMENT

i. Nature and origin of 'prophesying' in Puritanism:
Northampton, Norwich.

ii. Practice of 'prophesying' and lay preaching among Separatists and Independents: Robinson, S. Simpson, Petto.

iii. Presbyterian objection to lay preaching as ecclesiastically out of order:
Hollinworth, T. Hall, Baxter;
and as extempore and uneducated.

iv. Reading of sermons introduced by Puritans, but extempore preaching also practised: Brereley, Bunyan, Baxter.
Relation of Holy Spirit to education:
Cradock, Baxter, T. Goodwin, Cromwell.

v. Fox der 'Prophet' κατ' ἐξοχήν der Zeit.
Quaker worship a development from 'prophesying':
Fox, Dewsbury, Burrough.

vi. 'Prophesying' and lay preaching by women.
Precedents for women's ministry in Quakerism.

'Would God that all the Lord's people were prophets' (*Num.* xi. 29).
'Ye may all prophesy one by one' (1 *Cor.* xiv. 31).

IN closest conjunction with the development traced in the last chapter is the line of thought and conviction to be found in Puritanism about a similar subject, namely, the relation between the Holy Spirit and 'prophesying'. 'Prophesyings' are defined by John Goodwin as 'the opening and interpreting the word of God by a proper gift of the Spirit for the work',[1] but this definition does not sufficiently differentiate the activity from that of preaching. More illuminating is Baillie's description of the Independents:

> About prophesying after Sermon, they are at a full agreement, permitting to any private man of the flock, or to any stranger whom they take to be gifted, publickly to expound and apply the Scripture, to pray and blesse the people.[2]

'Prophesying', that is to say, was an activity of biblical exegesis, coupled with personal testimony and exhortation, after the preacher

[1] J. Goodwin, Πλήρωμα τὸ πνευματικόν, p. 348.
[2] R. Baillie, *Dissuasive from the Errours of the Time*, p. 118.

75

'had donn his stuffe',[1] and was open to all. Its *provenance* was the New Testament, where such 'prophesying' seems to have been a regular feature of Christian worship, and it reappeared with the rediscovery of the New Testament at the Reformation. The phrase used of those who were regarded as suited for the exercise, 'gifted brethren', points to its essentially charismatic nature. Its possibility, in the sixteenth and seventeenth centuries, as in the first century, was dependent upon a conviction of the presence and activity of the Holy Spirit in men's hearts.

In England, 'prophesyings' 'had their origin'[2] in 1571, at All Saints' Church in Northampton, a town then showing as great a liking for Puritanism as previously it had shown for the Lollard movement. In 'the orders and dealings in the Churches of Northampton established and sett up, by the consent of the Bysshop of Peterborough . . . 5 June 1571', section twelve reads:

> There is on euery other Satterdaye, and nowe euery Satterdaie from IX to XI of the clocke in the mornynge, an exercise of the mynisters bothe of Towne and countrye about the interpretacon of scriptures, the mynisters speaking one after another doth handell some texte, and the same openly amonge the people;[3]

In another Puritan stronghold, Norwich, 'prophesyings' began four years later, during a short period when the see was vacant, and were held at Christ Church on Mondays, also from nine to eleven. The first speaker was not to exceed three-quarters of an hour, and the others present were to speake in order, as they sat, 'and if they meane not to speake to signifie it by some like gesture, as by putting on their hatt, and so referring it to him that sitteth next'. Speakers were urged to

> be carefull to keepe them to the text; . . . having alwaies a speciall care to rippe up the text, to shew the sense of the Holy Ghost, and briefly, pithily, and plainly to observe such things as afterward may be well applied, and more at large handled in preaching, concerning either doctrine or manners.[4]

It will be observed that in these early days 'prophesyings' were a merely clerical exercise, hardly more than an extension of the usefulness of preaching by giving liberty to 'any godly-learned Brother to

---

[1] G. Fox, *Journal*, ed. N. Penney, II. 32.
[2] R. M. Serjeantson and W. R. D. Adkins, in *Victoria County History of Northamptonshire*, II. 43.
[3] *Records of the Borough of Northampton*, II (ed. J. C. Cox), 386 f., *q.v.*, for the rules of 'prophesying' in full. The 'Bysshop' was Edmund Scambler.
[4] Cf. J. Browne, *History of Congregationalism . . . in Norfolk and Suffolk*, pp. 18 ff.

lay forth any fruitfull matter revealed unto him out of the text'; and that they were essentially expositions of Scripture. Even so, they were frowned on by Queen Elizabeth, and, despite support for them from several leaders in Church and State,[1] archiepiscopal authority was used for their suppression. It was such treatment which caused Puritans to despair, and created Separatism, in which, from the first, 'prophesyings' were accepted as a natural and regular part of the worship of God.

In the Congregational churches 'prophesying' thus came to be practised partly through the Separatist strain in their ancestry; but not only so. John Robinson refers twice to the Synod held at Emden in 1571 (the year in which the exercise arose in England), at which it was decreed 'that in all churches, . . . the order of prophecy should be observed . . . and that into this fellowship, to wit of prophets, should be admitted not only the ministers, but also . . . of the very common people (*ex ipsa plebe*)'; in fact, Robinson claims 'prophesying' as 'the practice of all reformed churches'.[2] The work in which he makes this claim, *The Peoples Plea for the Exercise of Prophecy, against Mr. John Yates*[3] *his Monopolie* (1618), is the *locus classicus* for an early discussion of the subject. Yates' arguments turn largely upon the assumption, with which we are familiar, that all biblical prophesyings were 'extraordinary'; speaking with tongues has ceased, so has prophesying. Robinson retorts:

> To imagine extraordinary & miraculous things, without good evidence, is extraordinary licentiousness and presumption.
>
> The Scriptures are to be extended as largely, and to as common use as may be, neither is anything in them to be accounted extraordinary, save that which cannot possibly be ordinary.
>
> To yield you without further dispute, that revelation & interpretation were, viz. only, the immediate work of the Spirit, were in us, more courtesy than wisdom.[4]

Elsewhere Robinson sums up as 'excellent ends attainable only by this means' of 'prophesying':—the preservation of purity of doctrine; the clear shining of the light of truth, 'as by the beating together of two stones'; the conversion of outsiders; and familiarity and goodwill between ministers and people.[5]

---

[1] e.g., Grindal, Sandys, Burghley, Knollys, Mildmay (cf. *D.N.B.*, *s.vv.*).

[2] J. Robinson, *Works*, III. 334, 55.

[3] Cf. *D.N.B.*, *s.v.*; Robinson may have been drawn into controversy with Yates through Yates' curacy at St. Andrew's, Norwich, where Robinson had ministered previously (cf. C. Burrage, *New Facts concerning J. Robinson*).

[4] J. Robinson, *Works*, III. 319, 305.   [5] *Ib.* III. 55.

It is not difficult to see how this conviction of the right not only of ministers but of all, *ex ipsa plebe*, to 'prophesy' would develop into the conviction that not only ordained pastors but laymen might also preach in the more formal sense. The development may be perceived at work in the case of Sidrach Simpson,[1] one of the 'Dissenting Brethren' in the Westminster Assembly. In 1639 Simpson left a Congregational church at Rotterdam and founded a separate congregation, partly because he 'stood for the Ordinance of prophesying',[2] 'after the Brownists way',[3] during worship on Sundays, which was not favoured by those who ministered there; later it was complained that some of the members of this separate congregation, 'not Officers of the Church, nor Ecclesiasticall persons, do publikely Preach in Master Cans Pulpit at Amsterdam',[4] Canne being a Brownist;[5] and in 1647 we find Simpson publishing a Διατριβὴ . . . *the Iudgement of the Reformed Churches . . . concerning . . . Preaching by those who are not Ordained.* This was but one in a stream of works for or against lay preaching which poured from the press between 1641 and 1652; after this date, as Quakerism became the major subject of controversy, the stream gradually dried up. The practice of lay preaching was greatly stimulated by enthusiasts in Cromwell's army; 'great Preachers they were,'[6] says Baxter, reproachfully, of the soldiers. 'Look at Colonel Fleetwood's regiment,' writes another, 'what a cluster of preaching officers and troops there is!'[7]

Throughout the Commonwealth period the question whether lay preachers, or 'gifted brethren', should be encouraged in worship was a chief source of strife between the Congregationalists and the Presbyterians, whose 'Principle was not to hear a man not bred up at ye university, and not Ordained'.[8] In Lancashire, the dispute raged with especial fierceness.

Hollin[g]worth, Harrison, Gee, all the presbyterian controversialists, exhausted their stores of logic and learning in proving the negative of this question. Their arguments, however logical and learned, produced little impression upon the Independents. The reply was always ready: Why are brethren gifted, if they are not to use their gifts? Many a lay brother could preach quite as long and as loud as a presbyterian parson.

[1] Cf. A. Gordon, in *D.N.B.*, *s.v.*   [2] T. Edwards, *Antapologia*, p. 142.
[3] R. Baillie, *op. cit.*, p. 76.   [4] ⟨A. Forbes⟩, *An Anatomy of Independency*, p. 24.
[5] As successor to Henry Ainsworth; cf. *D.N.B.*, *s.vv.*   [6] *R.B.*, i. 77.
[7] *Manchester's Quarrel with Cromwell* (Camden Soc., N.S., xii), p. 72.
[8] E. Terrill, *Records of a Church of Christ meeting in Broadmead, Bristol* (Bunyan Library, xiv), ed. N. Haycroft, p. 98.

Why should he not use the gift of the Spirit? Why should he quench the Holy Ghost?[1]

A late example of this reply is *The Preacher sent: or, A Vindication of the liberty of Publick Preaching, By some men not Ordained* (1658), by Petto, John Martin and Frederick Woodal,[2] all East Anglian Congregational ministers and holding livings.

> Every man . . . to whomsoever the Spirit hath afforded a gift, either wisely to speak, and apply Gospel truths to the souls of others . . . or understandingly to give an exposition of the Scriptures, every man that hath such gifts, it belongeth to his place and calling, to use those gifts . . . else he crosseth the end of the Spirit.

The authors instance Apollos as one who 'being fervent in spirit, spake and taught diligently the things of the Lord', and who was not ordained nor yet extraordinarily gifted, since those to whom he preached had not so much as heard whether there were any Holy Ghost. Preaching in itself, they argue, 'is not an act of Office; but preaching in such a manner, or under such a relation'; and it is not preaching *ex officio* but preaching *ex dono* for which they plead.[3]

On the other side, Hollinworth has a chapter on the Spirit of Prophecy in his *Holy Ghost on the Bench*. His arguments are much the same as were Yates' forty years earlier. The prophecy of *Joel* ii. 28, he claims, was fulfilled at Pentecost.

> And, if the Prophecy was fulfilled at this time (as doubtless it was) it is enough. . . . it is too much when a Prophesie is fulfilled once, to expect it should be fulfilled again; or because it was fulfilled in one Age, therefore to expect it shall be fulfilled in every Age.
>
> Indeed it were to be wished that all the Lords people were Prophets, but not that they may Prophesie till they be Prophets, and may lawfully do it: Now the word Prophet always imports a distinct Order, Office and Calling from others; . . .
>
> This Prophesie is not rightly and regularly fulfilled, in the Preaching of uncalled and ungifted men; For First, As they have no lawful ordinary Call . . . so they have not any extraordinary Call, above what many others have, which are as gifted as well as they . . .
>
> The Spirit of God gave the Apostles ἀποφθέγγ⟨γ⟩εσθαι, to speak apothegms, Acts ii. 4, wise and weighty sentences, not many words to little purpose, as phrantick, phantastick men do . . .[4]

<hr>

[1] R. Halley, *Lancashire: its Puritanism and Nonconformity* (1872 edn.), p. 308; for John Harrison and Edward Gee, cf. *D.N.B.*, *s.vv.*
[2] For Martin, cf. J. Browne, *History of Congregationalism . . . in Norfolk and Suffolk*, p. 343, and *C.R.*, p. 555; for Woodal, cf. *C.R.*, *s.v.*, as Woodall.
[3] *Op. cit.*, pp. 48, 66–73, 87, 116.   [4] *Op. cit.*, pp. 61 ff., 67.

Another Presbyterian antagonist was Thomas Hall, who, after a public dispute at Henley-in-Arden, Warwickshire, published *The Pulpit Guarded With XVII Arguments* (1651).[1] In this Hall, like Hollinworth, disposes of whatever biblical examples of lay preaching might be adduced, as extraordinary. 'The sons of the prophets' he rules out as 'Ministers *virtualiter, inchoative & dispositive, licet non actualiter & realiter'*. In '*Ecclesia constituenda*, . . . where no Ordination can be had, gifted persons (in such extraordinary cases) may preach'; but in *Ecclesia constituta* no one, however gifted, may preach without a call, which is either immediate and extraordinary, such as the prophets, apostles and evangelists had, or else mediate and ordinary, such as the pastors and teachers had and still must have. If gifted brethren may preach, why may not women? and why may they not also baptize? The calling of the ministry is a distinct calling, and its work exceeding weighty and laborious; lay preaching springs from pride and conceit, was invented by Socinians, Anabaptists and Arminians, and breeds disorder, error and confusion. To his interlocutor's objection, 'I am a saint, I and my fraternity are high attainers, . . . the spirituall people', Hall retorts, like Campion before him, 'what? Saints?'.[2]

The chief ground of objection here to lay preaching was that it was ecclesiastically out of order. A fundamental conviction is that

> God is the God of order; . . . God hath appointed Orders in his Church. . . . His Canon is, Let all things be done in order.[3]

What the Lancashire Presbyterians particularly disliked was the interference of itinerant 'gifted brethren', who, not content to 'prophesy' within their own congregation, would enter strangers' pulpits, sometimes with the encouragement of their own ministers.[4] Baxter, who had as sympathetic an understanding of the ideal which occasioned lay preaching as he had of the convictions which gave rise to extempore prayer, was yet also concerned for church order, and in this largely agreed with the Presbyterians. Though, therefore, in exceptional circumstances, '(as if a layman were cast on the Indian shore and converted thousands, who could have no other ordination:) . . . upon the people's reception and consent, that man will

---

[1] The date is misprinted 1561 in *D.N.B.*, *s.v.*
[2] *Op. cit.*, pp. 4 f., 1, 43 and Arguments 5, 3, 11–15.
[3] R. Hollinworth, *op. cit.*, p. 16.
[4] Cf. R. Halley, *op. cit.*, p. 309; cf. pp. 322 f., for the 'Accommodation' between Presbyterians and Congregationalists on this subject in 1659.

be a true pastor', yet 'the regular way of entrance appointed by Christ to make a person capable, is the said election and ordination'.

That which is proper to the ministers or pastors of the church is, 1. To make a stated office of it . . .; and not to do it occasionally only, or sometimes, or on the bye; . . . (though they [particular churches] may sometimes permit a layman when there is cause to teach them 'pro tempore').[1]

The other chief ground of objection to lay preaching, and an objection which with Baxter probably weighed more heavily, arose out of the tendency of 'gifted brethren' to preach, as they prayed, extempore. The 'gifted brethren' claimed the ability to preach thus as their 'gift' from the Holy Spirit. Their opponents retorted that they preached thus because they were uneducated, which in fact very many of them were. This raises the whole question of the relation of the Holy Spirit to education. Before we consider this, it may be well to examine the tradition in the delivery of sermons at this time.

From Fisher[2] to Donne, almost all great preachers preached without book. William Perkins, in his *Art of Prophesying*, first published in 1592, can still speak of 'the received custom for preachers to speak by heart (*memoriter*) before the people'.[3]

It appears to have been the Puritans who, in their emphasis on the centrality of the sermon in worship, introduced the custom of reading sermons. A letter is extant from the Duke of Monmouth to the Vice-Chancellor and University of Cambridge, in which is signified Charles II's 'pleasure, that the said practice [of reading sermons], which took beginning with the disorders of the late times, be wholly laid aside; and that the foresaid preachers deliver their sermons, both in Latin and English, by memory, or without book'.[4] Baxter may be taken to be representative of much Puritan preaching, when he says, 'Never since I was twenty years old, did I ever learn and say without the Book, the words of one Prayer, or one Sermon, since I preacht';[5] and it was probably in reaction to the method used during the period when 'the pulpit had been the great stronghold of puritanism' that Tillotson, who regained it as 'a powerful agency for weaning men from puritan ideas', at first ' "had always written every word" and "us'd to get it by heart" ' and only later for personal reasons set a new fashion of reading sermons.[6]

[1] R. Baxter, *Works*, v. 278 f., 399 f.
[2] For Fisher's influence in the revival of preaching, cf. E. A. Benians, *John Fisher*, pp. 14, 25.
[3] F. E. Hutchinson, in *Cambridge History of English Literature*, IV. 226.
[4] Cf. *Notes and Queries*, July 5, 1851, p. 9.
[5] R. Baxter, *Account* (*ut sup.*), p. 20; cf. Llwyd's comment on unacceptable preachers, *Gweithiau*, I. 190: 'they write their sermons, but only for reward from men'.
[6] A. Gordon, in *D.N.B.*, *s.v.*

F

At the same time, the introduction of 'prophesying', an exercise of an extempore nature, was bound to influence preaching generally. We noticed earlier the minister who told George Fox that 'he spoke his experiences, & ye experiences of ye saintes & preacht yt';[1] and we find Brereley writing

> Accordingly things are to hearers brought,
> As they before are in the speakers wrought:
> For what man gives another of a store
> Which himself hath not in some sort before?
> A cause why such whose heart and tongue agree,
> So wondrous powerful in their preaching be,
> And those who teach not by experience so,
> So little profit by their preaching do.[2]

For this type of preaching, Bunyan's 'preaching what I felt, what I smartingly did feel',[3] an extempore delivery was almost essential. The amount of memorizing which preceded delivery would vary with the preacher. With a man like Owen, whose sermons 'were written out afterwards, in part from memory',[4] or like Howe, who, 'we have every reason to believe, . . . addressed these weighty and closely-packed discourses to his people *extempore*',[5] there was probably a considerable degree of memorizing. With an enthusiast like Llwyd, the case would be more as was complained of Thomas Horrockes, 'yt he comes not to them with a sermon out of a booke, but with that which the Lord hath spoken to him'.[6] By many this extempore preaching, such as became increasingly familiar through 'prophesyings', was preferred, and Baxter, for all that his own practice was otherwise, understands and can pithily express the reason why:

> there is . . . among the most of the Religious serious people of these Countreys . . . a greater inclination to a rational convincing earnest way of Preaching and Prayers, than to the written Form of Words which are to be read in Churches. And they are greatly taken with a Preacher that speaketh to them in a familiar natural Language, and exhorteth them as if

---

[1] G. Fox, *Journal*, ed. N. Penney, I. 55; quoted on p. 53, *sup.*

[2] R. Brereley, *Of True Christian Liberty*, p. 38.

[3] J. Bunyan, *Grace Abounding*, § 276; quoted on p. 8, *sup.*

[4] J. Moffatt, *The Golden Book of J. Owen*, p. 78.

[5] R. F. Horton, *J. Howe*, pp. 22 f.; cf. G. D. Henderson, *Religious Life in seventeenth century Scotland*, p. 197: 'Sermons in Scotland were not read . . . opinion in Scotland did not tolerate manuscript. There was of course careful preparation. . . . while the subject for the day was carefully meditated, and the sermon planned, something of the treatment depended upon the moment. Extemporaneous preaching was not unknown'.

[6] State Papers, Domestic, Charles II, 99.7 quoted by T. W. Davids, *Annals of Evangelical Nonconformity in . . . Essex*, p. 425; for Horrockes, cf. *C.R.*, *s.v.*

it were for their Lives; when another that readeth or saith a few composed
Words in a reading Tone, they hear almost as a Boy that is saying his
Lesson: . . .[1]

In a word, with these people, earnestness, in dependence upon the
Holy Spirit's assistance, counted for more than education. As Baxter
himself says elsewhere, 'the Transcript of the Heart hath the greatest
force on the Hearts of others'.[2]

We noticed earlier how chary the Puritans were of relating the
work of God's Spirit in man too closely to man's reason. In radical
Puritanism this caution found natural expression in suspicion of, and
even in attacks on, learning. Thus, Brereley says,

> Its not brain knowledge that doth make men free,
> But where Gods Sp'rit is, there is liberty.[3]

So, also, Cradock complains,

> it may be he hath Greek and Latine, and not Hebrew,[4] though he be
> full of the Holy Ghost, and yet the people must be starved.

> There are many men, I [ay], and many Professors, that doe not love to
> heare a man in a few modest words to commend the spirit of God: but
> all must be by studie, and reading, and learning, and for the spirit of
> God it is a plaine meere Cypher, and there is an end. But my life on it
> (if I had a hundred I would say so) they shal be beholding to the spirit of
> God, and extoll him before they be taught spiritually; they shall be
> willing to lay downe all their learning (as I have seen a learned godly
> man of late) even with the Plow-boy.[5]

Of Sidrach Simpson, again, whose defence of 'prophesying' and lay
preaching we noticed earlier, it was complained that 'he sett up the
spiritt of God against humane learning';[6] and Saltmarsh remarks, what
Fox (the same year)[7] regarded as an independent 'opening', 'Surely
it is not an University, a Cambridge or Oxford, a Pulpit and Black
gowne or Cloak, makes one a true Minister of Jesus Christ'.[8] Dell

[1] *R.B.*, i. 49.   [2] *Ib.*, i. 157.   [3] R. Brereley, *op. cit.*, p. 55.
[4] Cf. O. Cromwell, *Letters and Speeches*, ed. T. Carlyle, Speech XIII: 'If any man could
understand Latin and Greek, he was sure to be admitted; as if he spake Welsh; which in those
days went for Hebrew with a good many'. It is curious to compare the last remark with
G. Fox, *Journal*, ed. N. Penney, II. 106: 'hee came to dispute & spoake Hebrew to mee and I
spoake in Welch to him'.
[5] W. Cradock, *Divine Drops Distilled*, p. 205; *Gospel-Holinesse*, pp. 306 f.
[6] Cf. *Original Letters*, ed. J. Nickolls, p. 82.
[7] A. Gordon, in *D.N.B.*, *s.v.*, says Saltmarsh 'anticipates' Fox, but this seems incapable of
proof. For recognition of Saltmarsh as a forerunner of Quakerism, cf. J. Locke's entry in his
diary *s.d.* Oct. 5, 1685, in Lord King, *Life of Locke* (1830 edn.), I. 309 f.: 'Concerning the beginning of the Quakers, all I can learn from B. Furly is, that John Saltmarsh, who had been
Fairfax's chaplain, and a member of the Church of England, was the first that began to be
scrupulous of the hat, and using common language, in 1649' (Saltmarsh actually died in 1647).
[8] J. Saltmarsh, *The Divine Right of Presbyterie*, p. 22; cf. G. Fox, *Journal* (1901 edn.), I. 7.

also attacked the practice of 'making universities the fountains of the ministry . . . For human learning hath its place and use among human things, but hath no place nor use in Christ's Kingdom'.[1]

Such attacks on learning did not make it easier for the men of the middle party to be in sympathy with lay preaching. 'Education', says Baxter, 'is God's ordinary way for the Conveyance of his Grace, and ought no more to be set in opposition to the Spirit, than the preaching of the Word;'.[2] Elsewhere Baxter says:

> if we give to reason, memory, study, books, methods, forms, &c., but their proper place in subordination to Christ and to his Spirit, they are so far from being quenchers of the Spirit, that they are necessary in their places, and such means as we must use, if ever we will·expect the Spirit's help.
>
> He that hath both the Spirit of sanctification, and acquired gifts of knowledge together, is the complete Christian, and likely to know much more, than he that hath either of these alone.[3]

Thomas Goodwin, also, remarks judiciously:

> Whereas some men are for preaching only *extempore*, and without study, Paul bids Timothy meditate and study . . .
>
> Neither can they be said to preach *extempore*, or what is at that present revealed, for they preach those things which their thoughts and speeches have been exercised in before. So as ordinarily the extemporariness is in respect of memory, for it is what comes to their memories of notions again and again meditated upon.[4]

Once again, however, such detached judiciousness and comprehensive moderation proved no match for the radicals' enthusiasm: when the harvest was plenteous, but the labourers few, those who were convinced of the Spirit's immediate help could not stay for reasons either ecclesiastical or academic. Saltmarsh protests that, by the Declaration by Parliament (1647) against preaching without ordination,

> the infinitely abounding spirit of God, which blows when and where it listeth, and ministers in Christians according to the gift, and prophesies according to the will of the Almighty God . . . is made subject to the Laws and Ordinances of men . . . to outward ceremonies, as Ordination, &c. God must not speak till man give him leave; not teach nor Preach, but whom man allows, and approves, and ordains.[5]

---

[1] W. Dell, *Select Works*, pp. 583 f.; cf. pp. 355 f.   [2] *R.B.*, i. 6 (3).
[3] R. Baxter, *Works*, v. 567; xx. 179.   [4] T. Goodwin, *Works*, xi. 378 f.
[5] J. Saltmarsh, *Sparkles of Glory*, p.v; cf. E. Chillinden (for whom cf. C. H. Firth, in *D.N.B.*, s.v., as Chillenden), *Preaching Without Ordination* (1647), To the National Synod or Assembly: 'take heede to your selves what ye intend as touching the suppressing of preaching the Gospel by the breathing of the Spirit of God in the hearts of his people (though not ordained by your humane Ordination)'.

The need for preachers, of whatever kind, so long as they had the Spirit, is eloquently voiced by Cradock, in his joy that 'the Gospel is run over the Mountaines between Brecknockshire & Monmouthshire, as the fire in the thatch':

> They have no Ministers: but some of the wisest say, there are about 800 godly people, and they goe from one to another. They have no Ministers, it is true, if they had, they would honour them, and blesse God for them; & shall we raile at such, & say they are Tub-Preachers, and they were never at the University? Let us fall downe, and honour God.[1]

Cromwell, who held that in the ministry 'The true Succession is through the Spirit given in its measure. The Spirit is given for that use, To make proper Speakers-forth of God's eternal Truth; and that's right Succession', is probably the only Chancellor of the University of Oxford who has expressed satisfaction that the undergraduates 'instead of studying Books, study their own hearts'. Cromwell speaks for radical Puritanism generally on this subject, when he addresses the Scottish Presbyterians thus:

> you say, You have just cause to regret that men of Civil employments should usurp the calling and employment of the Ministry; to the scandal of the Reformed Kirks. Are you troubled that Christ is preached? Is preaching so exclusively your function? . . . Though an Approbation from men hath order in it, and may do well; yet he that hath no better warrant than that, hath none at all. I hope He that ascended up on high may give His gifts to whom He pleases: and if those gifts be the seal.of Mission, be not envious though Eldad and Medad prophesy. You know who bids us covet earnestly the best gifts, but chiefly that we may prophesy; . . . Approbation is an act of conveniency in respect of order; not of necessity, to give faculty to preach the Gospel.[2]

With such support from Cromwell and from others in high position, it was natural that the practice of 'prophesying' and lay preaching should prosper and increase. There is no need to retrace in detail the development through the Seeker movement which reached its logical conclusion in Quakerism. In radical Puritanism the ministers practised extempore prayer and preaching, and encouraged both in the laity; but a separated Ministry, 'as helpers of, not lords over, God's people',[3] remained. In Quakerism the separated[4]

---

[1] W. Cradock, *Glad Tydings from Heaven*, p. 50; L. Seaman had published a work entitled *Tub-Preachers overturned, or Independency to be abhor'd, as destructive to the Ministery, Church and Commonwealth.*

[2] O. Cromwell, *Letters and Speeches*, ed. T. Carlyle, Speeches I & v, and Letter CXLVIII. 'Approbation' here means 'ordination'; the 'Triers' for the approbation of public preachers, among whom were Owen, T. Goodwin, Cradock and Sterry, were not appointed till later.

[3] *Ib.*, Letter CXLVIII.   [4] The ministry was retained, but not a separated ministry.

ministry was entirely abandoned, and the speaking in meeting became not only as extempore, but as lay, as the praying. The force of Fox's personality and convictions—'as to man he was an original, being no man's copy'[1]—undoubtedly gave to the movement which he led a specific form which without him it would not have had. He could at times be silent, as when 'I sate of a hey stacke: & spoake nothinge for some houres: for I was to famish y^m from words';[2] but more often he *spoke* for some hours, with what effect can be judged from his own naïve record, justifying Kattenbusch's description of him as *der 'Prophet' κατ' ἐξοχήν der Zeit*.[3]

When all is said, Fox was still 'of his time', and in the type of worship which he encouraged, as in much else, it is clear that he was irrigating a channel already made, in this case the channel of 'prophesying' $τ\hat{ω}$ $πνεύματι$. When he writes,

> lett it be your Joy to heare or see y^e Springs of life breake foıth in any . . . such as are Tender, if they should be moved to bubble forth[4] a few words & speake in y^e seed & lambs power suffer & beare y^t that is y^e Tender, & if they should goe beyond their measure beare it in ye meeting for peace sake & order . . .[5]

or when Dewsbury writes,

> And thou faithful Babe, though thou stutter and stammer forth a few words in the dread of the Lord, they are accepted;[6]

or when Burrough writes,

> We received often the pouring down of the spirit upon us and the gift of Gods holy eternal Spirit as in the dayes of old, and our hearts were made glad, and our tongues loosed, and our mouths opened . . .[7]

it is not difficult to see the tradition in which they stood. This tradition made it possible for them to bear witness in Congregational and Baptist services, as at Leominster, Herefordshire, where

> som of them, hereing yt aman Caled A quaker was to be at the Meeting, did Conclud yt they shoud not suffer him to speake, but one of ye Meeting Tould them that was ffrom abad spirit to Judg amans testimony before they had heard him speake, and Contrary to ye Order

---

[1] W. Penn, introd. to G. Fox, *Journal* (1901 edn.), I. xlvi.
[2] G. Fox, *Journal*, ed. N. Penney, I. 28.
[3] F. Kattenbusch, in A. Hauck, *Realencyclopädie*, XXIV. 490; cf. W. Penn, introd. to G. Fox, *Journal* (1901 edn.), I. xlvii: 'He had an extraordinary gift in opening the Scriptures'.
[4] Llwyd, also, speaks of the 'spring . . . within, seeking to burst forth': *Gweithiau*, I. 227.
[5] G. Fox, *Journal*, ed. N. Penney, I. 222; I follow Ellwood in twice emending y^e to *they*.
[6] W. Dewsbury, *Testimony*, p. 185.
[7] E. Burrough, in G. Fox, *The Great Mistery of the Great Whore*, 'To the Reader'.

of ye Church of Christ, and ye Constitusion of that Meeting, which was yt All might speake Theyr Experiences of ye Work of Salvation or of any mesure of it Wrought in them[1]

or as in one of Vavasor Powell's[2] congregations in Montgomeryshire, where, when two Quaker women came 'in the time of their breaking of their Bread' and 'opened their Mouths in the Name of the Lord', 'the Independent Elders stood still, and gave the Women leave to speak', only after a second interruption ordering their removal, and then 'none was very ready to do it'.[3] Unfortunately the Quakers also followed the tradition in attacking learning and study, and it is impossible not to feel some sympathy with Baxter's retort,

> When the lazy fit overtaketh Ministers, they are ready to preach without study as well as you do.
> I use notes as much as any man, when I take pains; and as little as any man, when I am lazy, or busie, and have not leisure to prepare.[4]

The Quakers' abandonment of a separated ministry was accompanied by the abandonment of a purely male ministry. 'It was clear to them that neither a separated clergy nor a privileged sex was to monopolize any of the gifts of the Spirit.' 'The equality of men and women in spiritual privilege and responsibility has always been one of the glories of Quakerism.'[5] 'What, are all true Christians Priests?' Fox asks rhetorically; 'Yes: What, are Women Priests? Yes, Women Priests.'[6] 'The first Quaker preacher after Fox was a woman', Elizabeth Hooton,[7] who was probably also Fox's first convert; and 'women were the first to preach the principles of Quakerism in London, in the English universities, and in the American Colonies', as also in Dublin and Cork.[8] There had been certainly nothing previously like equality *on this scale*. Nevertheless, the Quakers were still following the practice of the more radical Puritans in their 'prophesyings'. Presbyterians such as Hall might regard the preaching of women as a *reductio ad absurdum*, but Robinson had drawn attention to the preaching of the woman of Samaria.[9] Baillie quotes Bastwick and Prynne for evidence that 'our London Independents exceed all

---

[1] *First Publishers of Truth*, ed. N. Penney, pp. 116 f.; cf. pp. 134, 142.
[2] Cf. A. Gordon, in *D.N.B.*, *s.v.*   [3] R. Davies, *Account* (1710 edn.), pp. 99 f.
[4] R. Baxter, *The Quakers Catechism*, p. 20; *id.*, *One Sheet for the Ministry*, pp. 13 f.; 'having once left his Notes behind him,' Baxter proved 'wonderful at Extemporate Preaching', explaining afterwards 'that he thought it very needful for a Minister to have a Body of Divinity in his head': M. Sylvester, *Elisha's Cry After Elijah's God* (printed in *R.B.*, *ad fin.*), p. 17.
[5] *S.P.Q.*, pp. 270 f.   [6] G. Fox, *Epistles*, p. 244.
[7] Cf. *D.N.B.*, *s.v.*, as Hooten; E. Manners, *E. Hooton*.
[8] N. Penney, in his edition of G. Fox, *Journal*, II. 463 f., 470.
[9] J. Robinson, *Works*, III. 317.

their Brethren, who of late begin to give unto women power of debating in the face of the Congregation', with 'liberty of preaching, prophesying, speaking in their Congregations',[1] and John Rogers devotes a chapter in his *Ohel or Bethshemesh* to the defence of women's spiritual liberties.[2] John Bramhall, Bishop of Derry, complains to Laud, 'I have had Anababtisticall prophetesses runne gaddinge upp and downe'.[3] The Duchess of Newcastle later tells sarcastically how

> The pure lady, or Lady Puritan, is so godly, as to follow all those ministers she thinks are called and chosen by the Holy Spirit . . . first, the minister expounds the Scripture, and then the women-hearers expound the sermon; . . . [4]

Dorothy Osborne refers to 'the woman at Somerset House',[5] probably Anna Trapnel, author of *A Legacy of Saints*, a Fifth Monarchist woman preacher who was arrested in 1654.[6] 'Doomsday' Sedgwick received his sobriquet from adopting the eschatological prophecies of a woman at Swaffham Prior, Cambridgeshire.[7] Sir Bulstrode Whitelock mentions a woman's preaching several times at York.[8] Another notable woman was Katherine Chidley, author of the *Ivstification of the Indepandant Chvrches of Christ* (1641), 'as fine a piece of controversial criticism as that age produced', who was a main instrument in gathering the Congregational church at Bury St. Edmunds, Suffolk.[9] Nor should the considerable part played in the religious development of New England by Anne Hutchinson be forgotten.[10]

For the ministry of women in Quaker worship there was thus plenty of precedent, though never before had the extent of their ministry been comparable. Even in Quaker worship at first, 'there was a strong general objection to women preachers, and the ministers

---

[1] R. Baillie, *op. cit.*, pp. 111, 140 f.

[2] *Op. cit.*, II. viii. (printed in E. Rogers, *Life and Opinions of a Fifth-Monarchy-Man*, p. 68); for Rogers, cf. *D.N.B.*, *s.v.*

[3] J. Bramhall, in State Papers, Ireland, vol. 254, quoted by W. E. Collins, in *Typical English Churchmen*, 1st ser., ed. W. E. Collins, p. 95 (printed in modified form in *Cal. Stat. Pap.*, Ireland Chas. I, 1633–1647, ed. R. P. Mahaffy, p. 182).

[4] M. Cavendish, *Sociable Letters*, 'The Lady Puritan'.

[5] D. Osborne, *Letters*, ed. E. A. Parry, Letter 59.

[6] Cf. L. F. Brown, *Baptists and Fifth Monarchy Men*, p. 49; T. Richards, *Religious Developments in Wales, 1654–1662*, p. 217; J. Smith, *Descriptive Cat. of Friends' Books*, *s.v.*

[7] Cf. A. Gordon, in *D.N.B.*, *s.v.* W. Sedgwick.

[8] B. Whitelock, *Memorials*, *s.d.* Aug. 8, 1649.

[9] J. Browne, *op. cit.*, p. 393; cf. p. 450 for another woman writer, Elizabeth Warren, whose book the licenser recommends with the words, 'Vpon my handmaids will I powre out of my spirit'.

[10] Other references to women's preaching are collected by R. Barclay, *Inner Life of the Religious Societies of the Commonwealth*, pp. 155 ff.; cf. also T. Edwards, *Gangraena*, ii. 31 f. for the woman-preacher, Mrs. Attoway. For Anne Hutchinson, cf. *D.N.B.*, *s.v.*

strongly caution Fox against employing them too freely',[1] while the place allowed to women in Quaker business meetings developed much more slowly.[2] By the majority of the Puritans the new liberty was deemed unbiblical and therefore wrong. Fox and other Quaker leaders did their utmost to justify women's ministry from Scripture, which was not a difficult task but in any case, on their own principles, was ultimately not necessary, if the practice were supported by the Light of Christ within. As Fox says, in summing up,

> And if there was no Scripture for our Men and Womens meetings, Christ is sufficient.[3]

It was this underlying principle of dependence upon God's Spirit, if necessary even without Scriptural precedent, rather than their actual practice, which differentiated Quaker worship from what had preceded it. It is the same principle which appears even more evidently in the Quaker disuse of the sacraments. To this subject of the Spirit and the ordinances we now may turn.

[1] R. Barclay, *The Inner Life of the Religious Societies of the Commonwealth*, p. 344; objection to women preachers was vocal in Cornwall and Devon (cf. *B.Q.*, p. 238, n. 1).
[2] Cf. *S.P.Q.*, ch. x.   [3] G. Fox, *Epistles*, p. 388.

CHAPTER VI

THE SPIRIT AND THE ORDINANCES

SYNOPSIS OF ARGUMENT

i. General Puritan acceptance of baptism and Lord's Supper as specific
means of grace, equally with the Word:
Sibbes, Hollinworth, Baxter.
ii. Warning against undue reliance on ordinances: Sibbes, J. Jones.
Reason for this.
iii. Weakening in importance attached to ordinances:
(*a*) Ordinances not to be observed without pastor, but not necessary to *esse* of Church:
Barrow, Brownists, Robinson.
(*b*)   not to be observed except *in coetu fidelium*:
J. Cotton.
Congregational Commonwealth incumbents.
(*c*)   not observed because of personal scruple:
J. Knowles, H. Vane.
(*d*) Baptism in conventional sense disused by Baptists;
its sacramental character lost by Congregationalists;
mutual tolerance between Baptists and Congregationalists:
J. Cook, Bunyan, V. Powell, Cradock.
(*e*) Lord's Supper observable without pastor:
J. Smyth, K. Chidley, Milton.
iv. Unsettlement over ordinances: Cradock, Llwyd.
v. Depreciation of ordinances: Dell, Saltmarsh, Erbury.
vi. Disuse of ordinances by Quakers: Fox's arguments; Fox's use of sacramental language;
dependent on new 'liberty of the Spirit'.

'he shall baptize you with the Holy Ghost' (*Mark* i. 8).
'we . . . have been all made to drink into[1] one Spirit' (1 *Cor.* xii. 13).

THE convictions of the Puritans about the relation between the
Holy Spirit and the sacraments, or, as they preferred to call them,
the ordinances,[2] are best studied in closest conjunction with their
convictions about the relation between the Spirit and the Word.[3]

---

[1] This, the Authorized, Version (rendering the assimilated reading, εἰς ἓν πνεῦμα) is the
version which the Puritans use.
[2] *Sacrament* is not a biblical term; *ordinance* is biblical, but is not applied by biblical writers to
baptism or the Lord's Supper.
[3] Cf. ch. I, *sup.*

Their fundamental belief was that God's Spirit had elected two specific means by which to work upon men's hearts: the Word and the ordinances. Those who would know the Spirit's work and witness within must attend carefully upon both means of salvation, God's chosen tools or instruments. Sibbes thus lays down the general principle:

> Attend upon the ordinances of God, the communion of saints, &c., and the Spirit of God will slide into our souls in the use of holy means. There is no man but he finds experience of it.
>
> Will the Spirit work when we neglect the ordinance? it is but a pretence. . . . holiness comes from the Spirit, and the Spirit will work by his own ordinances.
>
> The Spirit must go with the ordinances, as the arteries go together with the veins.[1]
>
> The ordinance is the grand conduit that conveyeth all Spirit.[2]

Hollinworth says much the same:

> Indeed the Spirit of God hath sometimes wrought *without*, or *above* the Word and Ordinances; yet it never wrought *against* them . . .
>
> The Spirit of God witnesseth *in* ordinances, or at least *not without* them . . . God indeed doth not tye his own hand, but ours: God can feed with Manna, but will not, when men may plough and sow.[3]

Baxter uses the same analogy:

> Neglect not those means which the Spirit hath appointed you to use. . . . Though your ploughing and sowing will not give you a plentiful harvest without the sun, and rain, and the blessing of God, yet these will not do it neither, unless you plough and sow.[4]

This is the regular, central Puritan teaching on the subject. Yet Sibbes thinks it wise to say also:

> shut out of your hearts too much relying on any outward thing.
>
> Trust not in the sacraments above their place . . . the papists . . . attribute too much to the sacraments, as some others do too little. They attribute a presence there. They make it an idol. . . . Oh, there is I know not what presence. . . . there is grace *by* them, though not *in* them.[5]

This warning brings us to what was always a problem for Puritan thought, though one may doubt how far it was consciously seen to be so. Religiously, the Puritan movement was a movement towards

---

[1] Sibbes uses the same image of the relation between the Spirit and the Word; cf. p. 23, *sup.*

[2] R. Sibbes, *Works*, IV. 215, 229; II. 240; IV. 295, 372.

[3] R. Hollinworth, *The Holy Ghost on the Bench*, pp. 35, 84.

[4] R. Baxter, *Works*, II. 197.   [5] R. Sibbes, *Works*, IV. 295; III. 134.

immediacy, towards direct communion with God through His Holy Spirit, in independence of all outward and creaturely aids, and could be 'content with nothing short of absolutes';[1] yet were not the ordinances, in a sense, outward and creaturely aids? Again, ecclesiastically, the Puritan movement was rooted in a repudiation of the sacerdotal system, was a violent reaction against everything savouring of papistry; and the sacraments had been the hinge of the priesthood's power, the very badge of the popish religion. In relation to the sacraments there thus remained in many Puritans' minds something of an unresolved tension, such a tension as that described in an appreciation of one in whom, although he was no Puritan, the Puritan influence of his earliest years[2] was never wholly eradicated, Cardinal Newman:

> He loved to seek everywhere for symbols of the divine, which would at once assure him of the Eternal Presence, and help him to gain more conscious access to it; yet he had the genuine mystic's feeling that all means were inadequate, and so divisive; as mediative they held the spirit out of the immediate Presence, and not only shaded but obscured its glory. . . . what he wanted was to stand face to face with God himself. . . .[3]

Such a passage helps to explain and to justify Troeltsch's dictum that 'sooner or later . . . the sect always criticizes the sacramental idea' and 'replaces the ecclesiastical doctrine of the sacraments by the Primitive Christian doctrine of the Spirit and by "enthusiasm" '.[4] Few things, in fact, were more deeply rooted in Puritan conviction than that men were called to love the world with 'weaned affections';[5] and the conviction was bound to influence the attitude taken even towards the very means of grace, towards the ordinances themselves. Cromwell's brother-in-law, John Jones, says much the same as Sibbes:

> the Lord keepe us close in the sure word of truth in our walkeings that the ordinances of Christ which are as soe many Spirituall Buoys, to Direct us in the right Channell, may not be esteemed nugatory and of noe force nor advance above theire due Latitude, as the Papists doe . . .[6]

---

[1] P. Miller, *The New England Mind: the seventeenth century*, p. 45.

[2] Cf. J. H. Newman, *Apologia pro vita sua, ad init.*

[3] A. M. Fairbairn, *Catholicism: Roman and Anglican*, p. 299; for a qualification of this, so far as Newman was concerned, cf. his phrase in W. Ward, *Life of Newman*, II. 277: 'If you had *experience*, how would it be faith?'

[4] E. Troeltsch, *op. cit.*, I. 339, 342.   [5] Cf. P. Miller, *op. cit.*, p. 42.

[6] J. Jones, in *Transactions* of Lancashire and Cheshire Historical Society, New Series (1861), I. 213; for Jones, 'the first Welshman to take a conspicuous and pre-eminent place in the political sphere in Great Britain' (T. E. Ellis, introd. to M. Llwyd, *Gweithiau*, II. xi), cf. C. H. Firth, in *D.N.B., s.v.*

With the religious and psychological background thus appraised, we may proceed to consider the actual development in the faith and practice of those radical Puritans whose characteristic was their emphasis on the doctrine of the Holy Spirit. We may begin by remarking Barrow's dislike of 'that traditional word [i.e. sacrament], which engendreth strife rather then godly edifying' and his assertion that 'many thowsands that neuer attained ye symbole of the supper, yet do feed of that body & blood of Christ by faith vnto eternall life'. He says, furthermore, that those gathered in Christ's name 'are to be esteemed an holy Church, . . . although they haue as yet obteined to haue neither a ministerie nor sacramentes among them: alwaies provided, that this be not by any default or negligence in them'.[1] This may well have reference to the Separatist congregation in London to which Barrow bequeathed property, for it was confessed by one of its members, 'who never missed y^r meetings of a year and a half', that 'he never saw any ministration of the sacrament'. The reason for this was almost certainly that at that time the congregation had not yet 'attained' a pastor, Francis Johnson not being chosen till later.[2] Barrow, it may therefore be argued, would have accepted the thirty-fourth section of the Brownists' *True Confession of the Faith* (1596), which runs: 'no sacraments are to be administered until pastors or teachers be ordained in their offices'. John Robinson held to this policy in Holland;[3] and, when the Pilgrim Fathers could not persuade William Brewster, their ruling elder, to accept the pastoral office, on Robinson's explicit advice[4] they remained for nine years without observing the sacrament: they 'were constrained to live without the supply of that office'.[5]

Their doctrine was so far orthodox. The fact remains, since both Separatists and Pilgrim Fathers did 'live without' the ordinances, that, however desirable in their eyes, the ordinances were already considered not essential for the possibility of Christian life or for the being of a church. This is, indeed, openly proclaimed. Sacraments, says Barrow, 'are not a perpetual Mark of the Church'.[6] Robinson explicitly denies that the preaching of the word and the administra-

[1] H. Barrow, *Discoverie of the False Church*, pp. 116, 236, 34.
[2] Cf. H. M. Dexter, *op. cit.*, pp. 265 (with n. 52), 267.
[3] Cf. J. Robinson, *Works*, II. 130.   [4] Cf. A. Young, *Chronicle of the Pilgrims*, p. 477.
[5] W. Hubbard, *General History of New England* (Massachusetts Hist. Soc., 1815), p. 97. Similarly, the Baptist Church at Broadmead, Bristol, which was formed by covenant in 1640, did not observe the ordinance of the Lord's Supper until 1642, when this was administered by Cradock, then minister of the exiled Llanvaches Congregational church which temporarily joined Broadmead; and again in 1670-1 for a year 'did not break bread' while without a pastor: E. Terrill, *Broadmead Records* (cf. *sup.*), pp. 25, 68; cf. p. 186.
[6] H. Barrow, *loc. cit.*

tion of the sacraments are the marks of the true church and stresses instead 'the gifts of the Spirit of Christ'.[1] John Cook, also, in his pamphlet, *What the Independents would have*, argues that word and sacraments are not the church's constitution.[2]

There is a further point. A distinguishing tenet which the Congregationalists inherited from the Separatists was 'That the Sacraments, being seales of Gods covenant, ought to be administred only to the faithful, and Baptisme to their seed or those vnder their governement'.[3] Not only a pastor, that is to say, but a genuine *coetus fidelium*, was a *sine qua non*. Thus John Cotton[4] declined to baptize the child added to his family in mid-Atlantic and called Seaborn, because there was 'no settled congregation' in the ship;[5] and some of the Congregational ministers who held livings during the Commonwealth[6] were so strict in administering the sacrament only to the members of a church gathered by covenant that they did not administer it at all. At Altham, Lancashire, for instance, Thomas Jollie was accused of 'refusing the Lords Supper to all the parishioners except three families, and the baptizing of our children'. A note in the parish register at Northbourne, Kent, records that Richard Lane baptized no children.[7] At Hambledon, Buckinghamshire, Walker relates that Henry Goodeare 'never Administred the sacrament'.[8] In 1658 Thomas Palmer, of Aston-on-Trent, Derbyshire, and other ministers, despite a petition signed by the mayor of Boston and many ministers, were actually prosecuted at the Lincoln Assizes for refusing the sacrament to parishioners.[9] When Baxter went to live at Acton in 1661, after 'two able Independents', Philip Nye and Thomas Elford,[10] 'had been the setled Ministers',

> there remained but two Women in all the Town, and Parish, whom they had admitted to the Sacrament (whereof One was a Lady that by alienation from them turned Quaker, and was their great Patroness . . .)[11]

---

[1] J. Robinson, *Works*, III. 428 f.; cf. W. Erbury, *Testimony*, p. 272: 'The Gospel-Order was in these three things . . . the manifestation of the Spirit . . . A Ministry of the Spirit . . . the administration of the Spirit . . .'.

[2] pp. 4 f.

[3] ⟨F. Johnson and H. Ainsworth,⟩ *Defence of . . . Brovvnists*, ⟨1604⟩, p. 38.

[4] Cf. A. Gordon in *D.N.B.*, suppt., *s.v.*

[5] J. Winthrop, *History of New England 1630–1649* (1853 edn.), I. 131.

[6] Cf. G. F. Nuttall, 'Congregational Commonwealth Incumbents', in *Transactions of Congregational Historical Society*, XIV. 3, pp. 155 foll.

[7] Cf. *C.R.*, *s.vv.*   [8] J. Walker, *Sufferings of the Clergy*, *s.loco.*

[9] Cf. *C.R.*, *s.v.*, and p. 11; cf. p. 313 for R. Lancaster, of Amport, Hampshire, an Antinomian who did not administer the Lord's Supper. For the widespread controversy which arose over this subject, cf. *D.N.B.*, *s.v.* Sir William Morice.   [10] Cf. *C.R.*, *s.vv.*

[11] *R.B.*, iii. 106, cf. 143. For Fox's founding 'a meetinge in ye feildes neere Ackton', cf. G. Fox, *Journal*, ed. N. Penney, I. 170. For another example of 'alienation', when 'A strange Mayd',

until Baxter recovered her. It is true that this non-observance of the sacraments through lack of suitable recipients, as through lack of an ordained pastor, was owing to strict doctrine, not to loose doctrine; but its unintentional effect, and not only at Acton, was undoubtedly to weaken the indispensability which men formerly attributed to the sacraments.

Sometimes also the observance of the Lord's Supper was hindered by scruples concerning the right posture for receiving the sacrament. In their antipathy to papistry, the Puritans followed a tradition originated by Zwingli of not kneeling at the table but standing, or else receiving the sacrament in the pew.[1] This tradition, which had been supported by Bishop Hooper and others,[2] was still being defended in the early seventeenth century,[3] but met with no sympathy from Laud, who suspended several clergy because they gave the sacrament to 'non-Kneelants'.[4] Some radical Puritans remained so determined not to kneel that they preferred to go without the sacrament altogether. Thus the Congregational John Knowles,[5] who was a Lecturer[6] at Colchester, Essex, 'forsook lecture and town and all, rather than he would receive the communion',[7] and shortly after emigrated to America. Sir Henry Vane the younger, also, after abstaining from the Sacrament for two years,[8] went 'into New England for conscience' sake', partly because 'none of our ministers would give him the sacrament standing'.[9]

Again, the abandonment by the Baptists of the affusion of infants for the immersion of believers (generally adult) at baptism was owing to strict doctrine, not to loose doctrine; but it meant, in effect, a neglect of what had always been regarded, and by most men was still

to whom, when she spoke 'in Conference', the Presbyterian Philip Henry made no reply, 'not approving of her speaking', 'is since turn'd Quaker', cf. P. Henry, *Diaries and Letters*, ed. M. H. Lee, p. 45.

[1] For Zwingli's first evangelical observance of the Lord's Supper, at Zürich at Easter 1525, cf. M. D'Aubigné, *History of the Reformation* (1846 edn.), pp. 406 f.

[2] Cf. J. Hooper, *Early Writings* (Parker Soc.), p. 536: 'sitting, in mine opinion, were best'. For other references, cf. Parker Soc. *General Index*, p. 735 (j); and cf. *An Admonition to the Parliament* (1571), i. 4 (in *Puritan Manifestoes*, Ch. Hist. Soc., lxxii, ed. W. H. Frere and C. E. Douglas, p. 24): 'in receavying it now sitting accordyng to the example of Chryst, we signifye rest, that is, a ful finishing thorow Chryst of al the ceremonial law . . .'.

[3] Cf. H. M. Dexter, *op. cit.*, bibliographical appendix, nos. 475, 494.

[4] A number of cases are collected by 'A Romish Recusant', *Life of Archbishop Laud*, pp. 220 f.

[5] Cf. A. Gordon, in *D.N.B.*, *s.v.*; to be distinguished from John Knowles, the anti-Trinitarian, for whom also cf. A. Gordon, in *D.N.B.*, *s.v.*

[6] Lectureships 'sprung from a desire to promote spiritual edification by means extraneous to the old parochial system, and . . . practically anticipated . . . the principles of voluntaryism': J. Stoughton, *Religion in England*, i. 46.

[7] W. Laud, *Works*, ed. W. Scott and W. Bliss, v. 348.

[8] Cf. T. Wentworth, Earl of Strafford, *Letters and Despatches*, ed. W. Knowler, i. 463.

[9] *Calendar of State Papers, Domestic*, Charles I, 1635, ed. J. Bruce, p. 385.

regarded, as the ordinance of baptism, and it did much to weaken the sacramental idea. In Congregationalism, 'the covenant idea became more controlling than in Anabaptism', and Congregationalists continued to sprinkle infants; but just because 'they were baptized long before they believed, and the Church was composed only of believers', baptism 'evidently meant primarily that believers took a pledge to bring up all those dependent on them in the admonition of the Lord. It thus lost all sacramental character'.[1]   This seems strong language; but John Rogers explicitly distinguishes the Independents from the Presbyterians as affirming 'that the children of the faithful that are holy are holy before Baptism'.[2]

Furthermore, there is much evidence of sympathy between Baptists and Congregationalists, which suggests an increasing readiness on both sides to count the 'shadowish or figurative ordinances . . . not the fundamentals of our Christianity, nor grounds or rules to communion with saints'.[3] 'That ever any of the London-Independents did cast out of their Churches any man or woman for Anabaptism, Antinomianism or any other Errour,' Baillie complains, 'we never heard';[4] and the Congregational John Cook approvingly admits of adult immersion that 'possibly that may bee a truth, which for want of light hee conceiveth to bee an errour; if it be an errour, it is a very harmlesse one, resting there . . .'.[5] At Newton Ferrers, Devon, John Hill, who 'never administered the sacrament', also 'had an Anabaptist to preach for him'; and at Yelden, Bedfordshire, Dell, who was accused of 'neglecting for the past twelve years the due administration of the sacraments', was also charged with 'allowing one Bunyon of Bedford, a tinker, to speak in his pulpit on . . . Christmas Day'.[6] Bunyan is generally claimed as a Baptist, but he did not insist on immersion, or indeed on baptism with water at all. He says explicitly:

> I do not plead for a despising of baptism, but a bearing with our brother that cannot do with it for want of light. . . . The best of baptism he hath . . . he is baptized by that one Spirit; he hath the heart of water baptism; the signification thereof; he wanteth only the outward shew.[7]

Nor was such tolerance, which in Bunyan's neighbourhood is pre-

---

[1] A. C. McGiffert, *Protestant Thought before Kant*, pp. 135 f.
[2] J. Rogers, *Ohel or Bethshemesh*, p. 466.
[3] J. Bunyan, *Works*, ed. H. Stebbing, I. 425.
[4] R. Baillie, *Dissuasive from the Errours of the Time*, p. 93.
[5] J. Cook, *What the Independents would have*, p. 8.   [6] Cf. *C.R.*, *s.vv.*
[7] J. Bunyan, *Works*, I. 430; cf. his 'Differences in Judgment about Water Baptism No Bar to Communion', *ib.*, pp. 436 foll.

served to this day,[1] unique. Baptists and Independents worshipped together in Bristol between 1642 and July 1643,[2] and also in the church to which Llwyd ministered at Wrexham.[3] Vavasor Powell was baptized in 1655, but earlier he had written that 'outward partaking of Ordinances is one of the least things in Religion',[4] and three years later he was invited to attend the Savoy Conference of Congregationalists and did attend. Robert Brown was another Baptist who did not renounce infant baptism,[5] and Henry Jessey yet another who 'did not, however, make baptism a term of communion'.[6] Cradock, once more, held that 'difference of opinion' about baptism 'should not hinder ... mutual receiving each other to fellowship and communion, who are in fellowship with God and Jesus Christ';[7] and from the Congregational side John Jones shows as great a tolerance as Bunyan, when a Colonel in the Irish army underwent baptism:

> let noe man despise his brother that hath not attained to his light, or withdraw his communion with him, because he submitts not his judgm[t] to him, the comunion and fellowship of saints in the ordinances of X[t] is one of the most principall parts of the S'[ts] privilidges and enjoyment in the fflesh, and the greatest Tirany that can be exercised upon any member of X[t] is to debar him from those Privilidges and enjoym[ts] upon the acc[t] of being different in judgm[t] or upon any account for which our heavenly father will not keepe him out of heaven, ...[8]

Weingarten thus hardly exaggerates, though his choice of a predicate might be happier, when he says that *der ganzen enthusiastischen Partei gilt die Kindertaufe als etwas Indifferentes*.[9]

In the person of John Smyth the Baptists were the first to query the rule that only ordained pastors might administer the Lord's Supper:

> It may be questioned whither the Church may not as well administer the Seales of the Covenant before they have Officers as Pray, Prophesy, Elect Officers and the rest ...[10]

---

[1] In Bedfordshire and also in Huntingdonshire the Baptist and Congregational churches are associated in a single Union, both infant and believers' baptism being permitted in some of the churches, among which is that to which Bunyan himself ministered at Bedford, now called Bunyan Meeting; cf. *Church Book of Bunyan Meeting, Bedford*, ed. G. B. Harrison.

[2] E. Terrill, *Broadmead Records* (cf. *sup.*), p. 25; as late as 1674 this church was still only 'most parte Baptized' (p. 92).

[3] Cf. M. Llwyd, *Gweithiau*, II. 1.

[4] V. Powell, *Spirituall Experiences*, as quoted by T. Richards, *The Puritan Movement in Wales*, p. 210.

[5] Cf. *C.R., s.v.*   [6] A. Gordon in *D.N.B., s.v.*

[7] W. Cradock, *The Saints Fulnesse of Joy*, p. 28.

[8] J. Jones, in *Transactions* of Lancashire and Cheshire Hist. Soc., N.S., (1861) I. 216.

[9] H. Weingarten, *Die Revolutionskirchen Englands*, p. 105.

[10] J. Smyth, *Works*, II. 419 f.

G

For the radical Congregationalists Katharine Chidley says,

> Yet that they must want the word preached, or Sacraments administred, till they have Pastors and Teacher⟨s⟩ in Office, is yet to be proved.[1]

Milton, to whom 'the sacraments are not absolutely indispensable', agrees with this:

> we nowhere read in Scripture of the Lord's Supper being distributed to the first Christians by an appointed minister . . . I know no reason therefore why ministers refuse to permit the celebration of the Lord's Supper, except where they themselves are allowed to administer it.[2]

We see here the lay aspect of Puritanism showing itself clearly. With the repudiation of sacerdotal claims and practice, the ordinances are on an equal level with preaching. Preaching is no longer confined to the ordained; why should the administration of the sacraments be so? It is, in fact, the church which administers, the ministers only distribute. For Thomas Hall the consequences of prophesying, that women might preach, and that 'gifted brethren' might administer the ordinances, had been *argumenta ad absurdum*.[3] By the radical Puritans the latter consequence, no less than the former, came in time to be accepted.

The considerations of the last few paragraphs are sufficient to show the progressive weakening in the sacraments' hold over many Puritans. They represent paths followed with varying purposes, and covering different types of mental country, but all converging towards a diminution of the importance which formerly had been attributed to the ordinances. In a work published in 1650, when the Quaker movement was quite unknown in the South of England, Cradock already laments that 'the devil . . . hath brought us from repetition of the word, & from singing of Psalms, & many from baptizing the infants of the godly, and divers from the Supper of the Lord, and from hearing the word of God preached . . .'.[4] An example of unsettlement over the ordinances we find at Wrexham, in the Congregational church to which Llwyd ministered. In 1652 Llwyd writes

> But now the bryers are come up
> and thorns and thistles tall
> therefore with Christ they do not sup
> in ordinances all.[5]

---

[1] K. Chidley, *The Ivstification of the Independant Chvrches of Christ*, p. 8.
[2] J. Milton, *Works* (Bohn edn.), IV. 417 f.   [3] Cf. p. 80, *sup.*
[4] W. Cradock, *Divine Drops Distilled*, p. 147.   [5] M. Llwyd, *Gweithiau*, I. 89.

This was twelve months before two members of this church were despatched northwards, 'to try us', as Fox puts it, '& see what a manner of people wee was'.[1] In the glowing terms with which both Cradock and Llwyd describe the immediacy of their spiritual communion with God there is little or no mention of the ordinances; but personally, in practice, they both held to sacramental observance. In them, as in most radical Puritans, the relative depreciation of the ordinances is only implicit, and must be felt from their tone[2] or deduced *a silentio*.

Dell, Saltmarsh and Erbury go farther, and have a definitely depreciatory attitude, for which they can give reasons. Dell says succinctly, 'Christ's baptism put an end to John's water-baptism, and Spirit-baptism to creature-baptism'.[3] Saltmarsh says,

> I believe, that as the Lord did suffer the Law of Ceremonies to die out by degrees, and to be worn out by the ministration of the Gospel, so he did that part of John's Ministery, by washing, by the Baptism of Christ, of his Spirit.
> The Baptism of the Holy Ghost or Gifts, is that Baptism which is said to be more properly Christ's ministration, He shall baptise you with the Holy Ghost and with fire.[4]

Even Saltmarsh says little explicitly of the Lord's Supper. Erbury is bolder:

> the Lord's Ordinance . . . is the Spirit's presence and power from on high; this was the first Gospel-Ordinance, the Baptism of the Spirit and of Fire; . . . in breaking of bread, they drank into one Spirit . . . all outward Ordinances of the Gospel were but the Ordinances of man, though appointed by God, the appearance and power of the Spirit was the Ordinance of God.
> Why should Ordinances continue, and not the gifts? Why should Baptism, and breaking of Bread abide more then than the Baptism of the Spirit, and all those gifts, seeing the Spirit was given to abide with them for ever?[5]

As a popular preacher, Erbury was exceptional, but he *was* a popular preacher; and, even without such preaching, simply as the result of independent 'searching the Scriptures', families like the Hutchinsons and the Springetts, as we saw earlier, were being brought to an entire disuse of the ordinances. The Seekers, again, were meeting without

---

[1] G. Fox, *Journal*, ed. N. Penney, I. 141.
[2] Cf. M. Llwyd, *Gweithiau*, I. 306 f.: 'be not thou a mocker and scorner' of 'Ordinances and institutions': 'instead of vilifying of outward things (as the manner of some is) seek after the Christ who is hid through all these'.
[3] W. Dell, *Select Works*, p. 391.   [4] J. Saltmarsh, *Sparkles of Glory*, pp. 21, 28.
[5] W. Erbury, *Testimony*, pp. 55, 303.

separated ministers, as the earlier Separatists had met, but with this difference, that the Seekers do not appear to have regretted, as the Separatists had regretted, the consequent lack of any sacramental observance in their worship.

It should be clear by now that, when Fox and the Quakers from the beginning disused the ordinances, there was considerable precedent within Puritanism for their behaviour. What was new, in this sphere as in other spheres, was that they disused the ordinances openly, deliberately and systematically, and offered explicit reasons for their doing so. One may surmise that the disuse of the ordinances would have appeared in Puritanism, for the psychological reasons suggested above, much sooner, had there not appeared inexpugnable evidence in Scripture for their dominical institution, and consequently for the moral necessity of their observance. The freer attitude to Scripture which marked Quakerism was required before any pronouncedly or permanently negative attitude to the ordinances could be adopted. Even so, Fox remains most anxious to justify the Quaker position by Scripture. 'The Priests of the World', he says, profess Christ, but 'act those things he forbids'.

> As first sprinkling of Infants, and telling People they Baptize them into the Faith, into the Church, which there is no Scripture for; but the Baptism by the Spirit into one Body, this we own; . . . And they tell People of a Sacrament, for which there is no Scripture; that we do deny, and them, but the Supper of the Lord we own: The Bread that we break is the Communion of the Body of Christ, the Cup we drink is the Communion of the Blood of Christ, all made to drink into one Spirit.
>
> There is not a Word in all the Scripture to hold up the Practice of Sprinkling Infants, nor the Word Sacrament . . .
>
> if hee meant ye one baptisme with ye spiritt Into one body y^t wee owned but to throwe a litle water in a childes face & say they was baptised or cristned there was noe scripture: for y^t.[1]

Elsewhere we find Fox arguing with a Jesuit that Christ's words 'This is my body' are to be interpreted in the same metaphorical sense as His words 'I am the vine & ye doore & rocke of Ages'; and stressing the phraseology of 'as oft as you take it': 'hee doth not say yee shall take it always'. Reaching deeper is such an appeal as this:

> For after yee have eaten in ye remenbrans of his death then yee must come Into his death & dye with him if yee will live with him as ye

---

[1] G. Fox, *Gospel-Truth Demonstrated*, ed. G. Whitehead *et al.*, p. 24; *Epistles*, p. 57; *Journal*, ed. N. Penney, II. 129.

Apostles did: & y^t is a neerer & a further state to be in ye fellowshippe with him in his death then to take bread & wine in remenbrans of his death.[1]

We see here the desire for immediacy and the ethical concern, both so characteristic of Puritan piety, together in fine fusion.

It would, however, be mistaken to suppose that this negative attitude to the ordinances implied any lack of the richly devotional sense which is the claim of conventional sacramentalists. Fox can often be found speaking with joy of a company 'feedinge with his eternall & heavenly foode';[2] and there is an early Epistle by him, which well suggests the biblical fulness with which he could make sacramental language his own.

> Dear Friends, Mind the stedfast Guide in the Lord, where we do all meet in the Eternal Spirit, in Oneness, all being Baptised by it into one Body, having one Food, the Eternal Bread of Life, which the Immortal feed upon, and all made to drink into one Spirit, which is the Cup of the Communion of the Blood of our Lord Jesus Christ, which makes Perfect, and Redeems from all that is Vain, Fleshly and Earthly, up to God, who is Holy, Pure, Spiritual and Eternal.[3]

The startling words here are, 'which makes Perfect'. One almost expects Fox to go on to claim the fulfilment of the prophecy, 'when that which is perfect is come, then that which is in part shall be done away', and in the Quaker disuse of the ordinances some such claim is in fact implicit. It is this sense of perfection or completion, of a new age in the Spirit, with fresh light and with freedom for new practice, which, present as it is throughout radical Puritanism, becomes most noticeable in Quakerism, and pre-eminently noticeable in the Quaker disuse of the ordinances. On this subject of the liberty of the Spirit we have already touched lightly from time to time; we must examine it now more closely.

---

[1] G. Fox, *Journal*, ed. N. Penney, I. 325, 253 f.; his argument (p. 325) 'if this breade & this cuppe was Christs body . . . then how can Christ bee with a body in heaven' is turned against the Quakers by Muggleton, *Spiritual Epistles*, p. 117: 'I say that same flesh and bone is now living in heaven above the stars, and not as the Quakers do vainly imagine him to be, all diffused into spirits, and so he is gotten into them; . . .'.
[2] G. Fox, *Journal*, ed. N. Penney, I. 262.   [3] G. Fox, *Epistles*, p. 26.

CHAPTER VII

THE LIBERTY OF THE SPIRIT

SYNOPSIS OF ARGUMENT

i. History composed of change and continuity:
  In Middle Ages sense of continuity predominant;
  At Reformation sense of change predominant, bringing
           new historic sense.
ii. Combination in Puritanism of new historic sense with
           religious enthusiasm.
  Sense of 'halcyon days': Brereley, Cradock, Milton, Sibbes, Sprigg.
iii. Radical Puritans' conviction of 'the age of the Spirit':
           Saltmarsh, Erbury, J. Salmon.
  Possible relation to Joachism.
iv. Consequent 'principle of mutability': Smyth, Robinson, Llwyd;
       passage through dispensations and forms:
           Cradock, J. Rogers, Sprigg, Quakers.
v. Combination in Puritanism of this dynamic principle with eschato-
       logical consciousness, Millenarianism (Chiliasm), Fifth Monarchism:
           Muggleton, Milton, Llwyd.
  Quakerism as *wesentlich vergeistigter Chiliasmus*.
vi. Consequent principle of tolerance: Robinson, Milton, Llwyd, Rous.
  Cromwell's tolerance.
  Cromwell's religious establishment.

'where the Spirit of the Lord is, there is liberty' (2 *Cor.* iii. 17).
'The wind bloweth where it listeth . . . : so is every one that is born
of the Spirit' (*John* iii. 8).

IN the last chapter we traced a gradual weakening in the importance
attached in radical Puritanism to the sacraments, until in Quakerism
they ceased entirely to be observed. It is not possible to understand
this disuse of something which in historic and orthodox Christianity
has been considered of quite primary importance, nor indeed many
other Puritan tendencies, of which this is only the most startling,
unless we realize that many Puritans believed themselves to be living
in a remarkable age, a new age, perhaps the last age, and that their
conception of history was quite different from any conception to
which we are accustomed to-day.

To-day we should say that history, as process, is composed of two
elements, of change and continuity. In the last hundred years the

element of change has received a degree of attention previously without parallel. In the Middle Ages this element received no attention: history, then, *was* continuity, one might almost say was sameness. Just as the Church was universal geographically, very much the same monastic ground-plan being visible and very much the same Latin service being audible in every country in Western Christendom, so the Church was universal temporally and straddled history. Men believed themselves spiritually one with the men of bygone ages in a way which might be called anachronistic, were not the application of such a thought-form itself an anachronism: Dante and Vergil (even Vergil, despite his paganism) are embraced in a single society. The Church, moreover, by its very claim to be *semper eadem* and to possess 'the faith . . . once delivered unto the saints', cut the ground from under the feet of any who sought to inquire into the differences between past and present, and to ask how things had altered and developed. When George Fox envelops the past centuries in the single, naïve condemnation, 'the Apostasy since the Apostles days', the condemnation is of his own day, but the enveloping is not: it is, as it were, the mediaeval lack of the historic sense grown cynical and turned in upon itself.

Only with the break-up of the Middle Ages which was effected by the Reformation does a sense of history, as we understand this to-day, begin to emerge, the historical use of *saeculum* in the sense of 'century', for instance, being coined by 'religious controvertists of the Reformation time, who found it a convenient framework within which to set the results of their researches into the history of the Early Church'.[1] We can see the dawn in Erasmus, with his phrases, *Albertus habuit suum seculum, Gerson suum*, and *Scripsere suo seculo*.[2] The names of Machiavelli and Guicciardini are sufficient to remind us of the part contributed earlier, and more specifically by the Renaissance, to the new historical sense on its secular side; but it is not until the seventeenth century that in the religious sphere the new perception spreads throughout Europe, and Roman Catholics like Petavius and Bossuet in France join with Protestants like Vossius in Holland and John Forbes in Scotland[3] in the study of what we now call Church History.

[1] G. M. Young, *Daylight and Champaign*, p. 167; the earliest instance in the *Oxford English Dictionary* of the use of *century* in the now accepted sense is, significantly, from the works of the Millenarian Joseph Mead (cf. p. 109, n. 3, *inf.*).

[2] *Erasmi Epistolae (ut sup.)*, Epp. 1581.590; 1334.916; cf. G. F. Nuttall, 'History and Church History', in *Congregational Quarterly*, xix. 125 foll.

[3] The words in the title of the Protestant Forbes' *Instructiones Historicae-Theologicae* (1645, the year after the publication of Petavius' first volume), *vario rerum statu*, may be compared with the word *variations* in the title of the Roman Catholic Bossuet's *Histoire* (1688).

In this country, where Protestantism had taken firm hold, keen interest was felt in the Lollard movement, and, by deriving true Christianity through the Lollards and Waldenses, men such as George and Robert Abbot sought to carry forward John Foxe's work of providing Protestantism with an historical background, making it a movement as ancient as the Church of Rome.[1]

This consciousness of change, this new historic sense, happened to reach its acutest stage in the very decades which saw an outbreak and rapid increase of religious enthusiasm. It is customary for enthusiasts to find it bliss to be alive—Erasmus in 1517 thought that he could see beginning *aureum quoddam saeculum*[2]—but among the radical Puritans 'halcyon days' seems to have been a catchword. We saw Brereley use it;[3] so does Cradock;[4] so does John Rogers, the Fifth Monarchist.[5] Sibbes says of 'these latter times' that 'in the reformation of religion, after our recovery out of popery, there is a second spring of the gospel' through 'the revelation of Christ by the Spirit, which hath the Spirit accompanying it'.[6] Sprigg reminds his readers 'what a spirit of prayer was powred forth upon the people of God in this Kingdome some 6 or 7 yeares past'.[7] Milton refers to his own day as the 'age of ages wherein God is manifestly come down among us to do some remarkable good'.[8] We noticed earlier similar references to the assurance felt by others that they were living in an age altogether different from those which had gone before, an age in which they might justly expect 'new light' from the Holy Spirit.

For increasingly it was borne in upon the radical Puritans that the age in which they lived was 'the age of the Spirit'. It is probable that this issued simply from their own insistence on the centrality of the doctrine of the Holy Spirit, combined with the current reawakening of an historic sense. It is much less likely that it depended on any rediscovery of earlier Joachite ideas, although the similarity of tone is sometimes striking.[9] Joachism had not been unknown on the Con-

---

[1] Cf. *D.N.B.*, *s.vv.*; on this aspect of Foxe's *Actes and Monuments*, cf. also H. Massingham, *s.v.*, in *The Great Tudors*, ed. K. Garvin, pp. 383 f.

[2] *Erasmi Epistolae* (cf. *sup.*), Ep. 541.8; Erasmus returns to the phrase somewhat wistfully in 1531, Ep. 2452.33.

[3] Cf. p. 25, *sup.*   [4] Cf. W. Cradock, *Divine Drops Distilled*, 'To the Reader'.

[5] Cf. J. Rogers, *Ohel or Bethshemesh*, p. 32.   [6] R. Sibbes, *Works*, IV. 302 f.

[7] J. Sprigg, *A Testimony to Approaching Glory*, 'To the Reader'.

[8] J. Milton, *Works* (Bohn edn.), III. 69; cf. also O. Cromwell, *Letters and Speeches*, ed. T. Carlyle, Speech XI: 'the Halcyon Days of Peace'; E. Terrill, *Broadmead Records* (cf. *sup.*), p. 33: 'those Halcyon days of Prosperity, liberty, and Peace'.

[9] Cf., e.g., M. Llwyd, *Gweithiau*, I. 196: 'Why do you come in the late afternoon and not in the morning with your news? Because it is towards the end of the world that the everlasting gospel is to be preached'; cf. II. 251 (quoted on pp. 109 f., *inf.*). The Quakers also refer to 'the everlasting gospel' (cf., e.g., G. Fox, *Journal*, ed. N. Penney, II. 27), but this proves rather that they had read *Rev.* xiv. 6 than that they had read Joachim (cf. p. 16, n. 13, *sup.*).

tinent, it is true: Karl Holl quotes Münzer as saying, *Ir sollt auch wissen, das sie dise lere dem Apt Joachim zuschreiben und heissen sie ein ewiges euangelion in grossem spott. Bei mir ist das getzewgnis Abatis Joachim gross.*[1] Occasional references to Joachim can also be found in English sixteenth-century writers.[2] Joachim's works, however, were not translated into English, so far as is known, and there is no evidence of any study of him. Dr. Sippell's assurance must be considered unjustified, therefore, when he says of Saltmarsh, *können wir leicht feststellen, aus welchen Quellen seine neue Weisheit geschöpft ist . . . die Lehre von den aufeinanderfolgenden Offenbarungsstufen von Joachim von Fiore.*[3] Alexander Gordon says simply that Saltmarsh's work is 'remarkable for its assertion of the progressive element in divine knowledge'.[4] Weingarten, also, is more cautious in remarking of Joseph Salmon's[5] *Grundgedanken* only that they *erinnern in merkwürdiger Weise an die Weissagungen Joachim's von Floris, und an seine drei Weltperioden.*[6] Without further inquiry into its origins, we may proceed to notice the teaching of these men, and also of Erbury, with whom 'the age of the Spirit', in contrast with all forms which have been outlived, is a favourite subject.

Their teaching may be summed up in the following sentence from Salmon:

> this power (which is God) comes forth and offers itself in a diversity of appearance, and still (by a divine progresse in the affairs of the earth) moves from one to another; from one dispensation to another, from one party to another; hereby accomplishing his eternally decreed designe in and upon the Creature. This is manifest in all dispensations, civil and spirituall.

Salmon draws out the distinction between 'the Jewish ceremonies', 'the Son' and the necessity for God to 'move hence also'; but he is not really interested in the Holy Spirit. He has a political *arrière-pensée*, and proceeds to make a similar distinction 'in Civil or outward dispensations', where God dwells first in an 'absolute and arbitrary Monarchy', then in Parliament and lastly, Salmon claims, in the army.[7]

---

[1] Cf. K. Holl, *Gesammelte Aufsätze zur Kirchengeschichte*, i. 425, n. 3.
[2] Bishops Bale and Jewel, e.g., mention Joachim in their works.
[3] T. Sippell, *Werdendes Quäkertum*, pp. 88 f.　　[4] A. Gordon, in *D.N.B., s.v.*
[5] Dr. Sippell is probably right in reckoning Salmon, whose *A Rout, a Rout* (1649) he reprints in *Werdendes Quäkertum*, pp. 187 foll., as among the 'Ranters of the sober kind' (*ib.* p. 95); Salmon may have been influenced by his meeting with Fox (cf. G. Fox, *Journal*, 1901 edn., i. 48).
[6] H. Weingarten, *Die Revolutionskirchen Englands*, p. 97.
[7] J. Salmon, *op. cit.*, pp. 9, 11 foll.

Saltmarsh and Erbury give more attention to the nature of the third dispensation as the age of the Spirit. Saltmarsh says:

> The Christian passes through several ages and dispensations; as Christ was in the world, so is every Christian; he was made under the Law, under Circumcision, under Baptism, and the Supper of bread and wine, and then crucified all that flesh he walked in under those dispensations, and entered into glory . . . and the great and excellent design of God in all these things, is only to lead out his people, Church, or Disciples from age to age, from faith to faith, from glory to glory, from letter to letter, from ordinance to ordinance, from flesh to flesh, and so to Spirit, and so to more Spirit, and at length into all Spirit. . . . And for Disciples to stay longer in any ministration than the Lord or the life and the Spirit of Christ is in it, is as if Lot should tarry in Sodom, Israel with the ark when God was departed, the Jews in the Temple when the Veil was rent . . .[1]

Erbury's way of stating the same conviction is as follows:

> God under the Law and to the Fathers before, was known, as the Father. In the Gospel God was known, as the Son; or the knowledg of the Son was peculiar to the Gospel-dispensation. The third will be pure Spirit, when nothing but Spirit and power shall appear, when God shall be all in all: . . .
>
> you know the appearances of God, from the beginning, have been more and more spirituall . . . In the Gospel, the presence of the Lord, and his power, was more spiritual, in inward and eternal things; . . . Therefore the third dispensation . . . will be more spirituall yet; for though Christ was in the days of his flesh, yet he was not full come, till the Spirit was sent; therefore this second coming will be more in the Spirit yet; . . .

Erbury also observes 'four great steps of Gods glorious appearance in mens preaching', in which Sibbes is put on the second step, 'both the famous Goodwins' on the third, and 'the fourth step which some have attained to' is 'holding forth Christ in the Spirit, as Mr. William Sedgwick, Mr. Sterrie, Mr. Sprig, and others . . .'[2]

Similar conceptions, expressed in language less chronological in interest, are characteristic of radical Puritanism generally. In connexion with the doctrine of the Holy Spirit, 'forms' and 'dispensations' and 'attainments' are words in all these men's mouths: in one way and another there is a keen sense of fuller freedom in the new 'age of the Spirit'. Baillie, for instance, complains that, although, on account of the Dissenting Brethren's opposition in the Westminster Assembly, 'it was found meet to put them to declare their mind positive what they would be at', yet 'Every day this moneth we have been expecting

---

[1] J. Saltmarsh, *Sparkles of Glory*, pp. 49–53.   [2] W. Erbury, *Testimony*, pp. 66, 248, 68 f.

their positive tenets, but as yet we have heard nothing of them; ...'.¹
In a work published in the same year (1645) he says, 'It is not easie to
set down with assurance the Independents positions, both because
they have to this day declined to declare positively their minds; as
also because of their principle of mutability, whereby they professe
their readinesse to change any of their present Tenets';² and quotes
the Dissenting Brethren's explicitly claimed 'reserve . . . to alter and
retract'.³ This bold 'principle of mutability' was always a trouble
to those who had no understanding of its spiritual basis; but it was
laid down as early as 1609-10 by John Smyth and John Robinson.
'Wee are inconstant in erroer:' says Smyth; 'my earnest desire is,
that my last writing may . . . be taken as my present judgment'.⁴
'If God have caused a further truth like a light in a darke place to
shine in our hearts,' says Robinson, 'should we still have mingled
that light with darknesse, contrarie to the Lords owne practice?'.⁵
So, again, in later years, Llwyd says, 'its better be wavering in some
things all the dayes of his life, and still to seek, though called unstable
in judgement, then sit down too soon, or be seated and settled in a
false or imperfect opinion, . . .'.⁶

Cradock is among those who, conscious of new-found spiritual
freedom, is always, so to speak, tugging at the leash:

> It is base to tie a son as much as a servant. So we being now to be
> sonnes, truly and really, the Lord hath given us a larger liberty.
>
> What an abominable thing it is to tie the sonnes of God that are not
> babies, now under tutors, with paltrie things, when the Spirit of God in
> the least Saint is better able to determine than all the Bishops.
>
> our main reformation is in pulling down, and not in setting up: for
> we have a world of institutions set up that will never hold: . . . but when
> a man can say, this is Christ crucified, & Christ pouring out of his
> spirit, . . . this is the maine that will hold.⁷

John Rogers is another who can wax eloquent on the subject, as when
he thus addresses Cromwell:

> Some compare Queen Elizabeth to a sluttish Housewife, who swept
> the house, but left the dust behinde the door: But now you, you (my

---

¹ R. Baillie, *Letters* (Bannatyne Club Pubs. 73b), II. 266 f., 271.
² *Id.*, *Dissuasive from the Errours of the Time*, p. 101.
³ T. Goodwin *et al.*, *Apologeticall Narration*, p. 11; as late as 1688 Baxter complains that 'Independents greatly differ among themselves': *R.B.*, App., p. 69.
⁴ J. Smyth, *Works*, I. 271.
⁵ J. Robinson, *Answer to a Censorious Epistle*, known only as printed by J. Hall, in *Apologie against Brownists*, p. 602; Hall treats the claim with the usual scorn: 'What? so true and glorious a light of God, and neuer seene till now?' (p. 603).
⁶ M. Llwyd, *Gweithiau*, II. 236; cf. also *Puritanism and Liberty*, ed. A. S. P. Woodhouse, p. [46], n. 1.
⁷ W. Cradock, *Gospel-Libertie*, pp. 18, 48; *Divine Drops Distilled*, p. 212.

Lord) have swept the whole House indeed. . . . O then! Set not aside the Broom now! (For new brooms sweep clean!)

This is an old trick of the Devil, to keep down truth from further discovery.

The spiritual man makes speed . . . ; And at the end of one forme, takes up another, and so speeds through that into another, till he comes at his journies end, and then he hath done with all.

Now, I say, that Church members may live lesse in the letter, and more in the life, lesse in the forme, and more in the faith, as good proficients in the Spirit, . . . I have undertaken this taske, in this Tract.

The Forme dyes as it grows . . . But the Spirit and Power, lives as the Form and appearance dyes daily![1]

Sprigg, again, is one who is eager to lay aside all forms:

every forme hath weaknesse in it, & therefore you cannot rest in the knowing God in a forme.

formes are but helpes, but God doth by formes bring us to know himselfe without a forme;[2]

When this was the spirit of the time, it becomes less surprising that what others had preached and desired, the Quakers at last carried into practice, and, in their eager penetration to immediate communion with God, seeking to lay aside all outward forms, entirely disused the ordinances of baptism and the Lord's Supper.[3] In their application of the principle by such disuse only a few would agree with them, but the principle which they applied was familiar to all, and by many was accepted as a sound and spiritual principle.

Accompanying this dynamic principle of pressing on, through and beyond all outward and imprisoning forms, to attain to the full liberty of the Holy Spirit, was a powerful eschatological consciousness. Religious enthusiasm, working over the prophecies in *Daniel* and *Revelation*, and conscious of contemporary religious revival, has issued in eschatological convictions at other periods also. Puritan eschatology combined such convictions with the further belief, based on the tone of references to the Holy Spirit such as they found in *Joel*, *Acts* and Paul's Epistles, that the last age had come, or was at hand, for the reason that it was 'the age of the Spirit'. Precisely when the end

---

[1] J. Rogers, *op. cit.*, pp. 15, 9, 46, 66.
[2] J. Sprigg, *op. cit.*, pp. 56, 60.
[3] By Joachim, also, 'the teaching of Christ and the Apostles on the Sacraments is considered, implicitly and explicitly, as transitory, as representing that passage from the *significantia* to the *significata* which Joachim signalizes at every stage of his demonstration': P. D. Alphandéry, in *Encyclopaedia Britannica* (11th edn.), *s.v.*

was to be was a subject admitting difference of opinion, but it would not be long delayed. In Llwyd's words (1648):

> fifty goes big, or fifty sixe
> or sixty five some say
> But within mans age, hope to see
> all old things flung away.[1]

These convictions first became popular through John Archer's *The Personall Reigne of Christ Vpon Earth*[2] and Robert Maton's *Israel's Redemption* (later reissued as *Christ's Personall Reigne on Earth*), both published originally in 1642;[3] the latter work was 'taken up by the independents and baptists' and was in wide circulation in Rotterdam within two years of its appearance.[4] They spread with extraordinary rapidity in Puritan circles, so that, by the time of the Commonwealth, 'the idea of a speedy approach of our Lord's millennial reign was very widely diffused among all classes of religionists'.[5] It is most noticeable in the extremists who, from their prophecies and demands, became known as the Fifth-Monarchy-Men.[6] It is also the *raison d'être* of Muggletonianism, since Muggleton conceived his 'Commission of the Spirit' not only as succeeding those of Moses and of Christ, but as the last.[7] It infuses Milton's *Areopagitica* (1644):

> We reckon more than five months yet to harvest; there need not be five weeks; had we but eyes to lift up, the fields are white already. . . . For now the time seems come, wherein Moses the great prophet may sit in heaven rejoicing to see that memorable and glorious wish of his fulfilled, when not only our seventy Elders, but all the Lord's people, are become prophets.[8]

Llwyd writes thus to his cousin, John Price, in 1652:

> I am persuaded y^t . . . you may probably live to see more blessednes then ever our fathers thought any of their posterity should be made to vnderstand. . . . God . . . moveth three tymes (for he is three). Two motions are past in ye creation of this vniverse and incarnation of y^e

---

[1] M. Llwyd, *Gweithiau*, I. 22; for a reason why the year 1656 was selected, cf. I. 198: 'But from the beginning of the world to the flood there were 1656 years: wherefore I advise you (O eagle) to watch, for it comes near'. 1666 was also considered a possible year; cf. G. Fox, *Journal*, ed. N. Penney, II. 12.

[2] This work is wrongly attributed to John Aucher, in *D.N.B.*, *s.v.*; the 'correction' by T. Sippell, *William Dells Programm* (cf. p. 12, n. 7, *sup.*), p. 6, n. 2, is erroneous.

[3] These works were preceded by the *Clavis Apocalyptica* of Joseph (not Henry, as J. Stoughton, *Religion in England*, II. 59) Mead, which was published in 1627 but not translated into English (as *The Key of the Revelation*, by R. More) till 1643; but this 'expressly rejects a terrestrial reign of Christ': A. Gordon, in *D.N.B.*, *s.v.*

[4] Cf. *D.N.B.*, *s.vv.* R. Maton and A. Petrie.   [5] A. Gordon, in *D.N.B.*, *s.v.* C. Feake.

[6] *Fifth*, because Christ's rule was to follow the Assyrian, Persian, Greek and Roman: cf. *Dan.* vii.

[7] Cf. L. Muggleton, *Spiritual Epistles*, pp. 35* f. (printed after p. 38), 462.

[8] J. Milton, *Areopagitica* (Everyman edn.), pp. 32 f.

word, the third is at hand in yᵉ fiery consumption of heaven and earth
and in yᵗ all shall be shutt vp in their eternall Dwellings.¹

Even Owen and Thomas Goodwin 'delivered sermons with an unmistakable millenarian flavour, so much so that two of the latter's
expositions were pirated (September 1654 and May 1655) and
published by Livewell Chapman, in the interest of that party'.² Goodwin, for instance, could say, 'in 1650, they shall begin; but it shall be
45 years before it comes to full head, and blessed is he that comes to
this day'.³

Stoughton sensibly distinguishes between mere millenarians,
theoretical theocrats and practical theocrats.⁴ It was quite possible
to be 'a fervent, injudicious, honest Fifth-Monarchy-man',⁵ and yet
to take 'no part in the struggles of practical politics'.⁶ That 'the
resort to violence, the effort to establish and exercise the rule of the
Saints by force, is not . . . an essential of the Millenarian creed, but
rather a character impressed upon it by a revolutionary era'⁷ is
indicated by the fact that many millenarians did not support Venner's
rising in 1655.⁸ Indeed, Rogers told Cromwell that 'that Fifth-
Monarchy principle, as you call it, is of such a latitude as takes in all
Saints, all such as are sanctified in Christ Jesus, without respect of
what form or judgment he is'.⁹ This 'latitude', as we shall see shortly,
was another expression of 'the liberty of the Spirit', and was the

---

¹ M. Llwyd, *Gweithiau*, II. 250 f.
² T. Richards, *Religious Developments in Wales, 1654–1662*, p. 206; for Chapman, cf. *ib.*,
p. 237, and Sir J. Berry and S. G. Lee, *A Cromwellian Major-General*, p. 262, n. 3.
³ T. Goodwin, *Works*, XII. 79, following the *Explication of Daniel* by T. Brightman, for
whom cf. *D.N.B.*, *s.v.* The sermon 'By T.G.', from which this passage is quoted, is attributed
to H. Knollys by A. Gordon, in *D.N.B.*, *s.v.*, and by A. S. P. Woodhouse, *op. cit.*, p. 233; to
W. Kiffin by W. T. Whitley, *A Baptist Bibliography*, no. 22–641, p. 11, by J. Smith, *Bibliotheca
Anti-Quakeriana*, *s.v.*, and by A. Gordon, in *D.N.B.*, *s.v.* (the double attribution seemingly
having escaped his notice); and to J. Burroughes by H. M. Dexter. *op. cit.*, bibliographical
appendix, no. 736; but the attribution to Goodwin is supported by R. Baillie, *op. cit.*, p. 80:
'T.G. (whom common report without any contradiction that I have heard declares to be
Thomas Goodwin)'.
⁴ J. Stoughton, *op. cit.*, II. 59 f.
⁵ Baxter, of Robert Brown: *R.B.*, ii. 433; cf. J. Berry, of the millenarian manifesto, *A Word
for God*: 'I think that people will not be wrought up to any comotion: . . . they are an affec-
tionate, tender-spirited people that want judgment: . . .' J. Thurloe, *State Papers*, ed. T. Birch,
IV. 394.
⁶ A. Gordon, of V. Powell, in *D.N.B.*, *s.v.*; cf. *ib.*, *s.v.* N. Holmes: 'Although a millenarian,
he only inculcated a spiritual and purified liberty to be enjoyed by the saints . . .'. J. Browne, *op.
cit.*, p. 165, n. ‡, remarks that 'most of the churches [in Norfolk and Suffolk] were tinctured with
millenarian views': cf. J. Thurloe, *op. cit.*, IV. 698: 'The greatest number of these people are in
Norfolk'. Calamy refers to the millenarian notions of several of the ejected ministers. William
Sedgwick, who was not ejected, was called 'Doomsday Sedgwick' from his eschatological
prophecies (cf. A. Gordon, in *D.N.B.*, *s.v.*).
⁷ A. S. P. Woodhouse, *op. cit.*, pp. [82] f.; the word omitted is 'perhaps'.
⁸ Cf., e.g., *D.N.B.*, *s.vv.* C. Feake, T. Harrison, J. James, J. Rogers.
⁹ J. Rogers, *Faithfull Narrative*, printed in E. Rogers, *Life and Opinions of a Fifth-Monarchy-
Man*, p. 215; cf. p. 66.

natural consequence of believing that the Lord 'is coming forth to make you free to suffer a blessed Freedom, a glorious Liberty'.[1]

As time passed, and the hopes of the Millenarians that Christ would appear and would set up His Kingdom upon earth, whether in political or in catastrophic form, proved illusory, there was a gradual *Verinnerlichung* of such convictions, to which an increase of spiritual insight also contributed. 'By 1656 the Fifth Monarchy movement had for many become *vieux jeu*',[2] and Dr. Sippell justly describes Quakerism from this angle as *ganz wesentlich vergeistigter Chiliasmus.*[3] It was, for instance, the congregations ministered to by Vavasor Powell, the 'most fierce and persistent defender in Wales'[4] of Millenarianism, which 'seem to have been the chief source out of which sprang the groups of Friends in Mid-Wales'.[5] Friendly relations, moreover, between Fifth Monarchists and Friends are not far to seek. Sir Henry Vane the younger, for instance, who was interested in Fifth Monarchist speculations,[6] was 'very loving to Friends'.[7] Fox and Nayler both held meetings at the house[8] of the Fifth Monarchist Overton.[9] Sir John Lawson[10] was another Fifth Monarchist whose wife befriended the Quakers.[11] A Fifth Monarchist who is known to have become a Quaker is John Pennyman,[12] but later, perceiving 'a great part of the Quakers to be Degenerated into meer Form, and setting up G. Fox instead of the Spirit of Christ, to be their Lord and Lawgiver', he dissociated himself from Friends and was disowned by them.[13] Dr. Gooch, indeed, asserts that Quakerism itself 'was im-

---

[1] J. Salmon, *op. cit.*, p. 28.
[2] L. F. Brown, *The Baptists and Fifth Monarchy Men*, p. 101.
[3] T. Sippell, *William Dells Programm einer 'lutherischen' Gemeinschaftsbewegung*, p. 10.
[4] T. Richards, *The Puritan Movement in Wales*, p. 186.
[5] *B.Q.*, p. 208; cf. R. Davies, *Account* (1710 edn.), pp. 2, 45, 99. That 'Merionethshire contributed more to the ranks of Quakerism than any other Welsh county, considering its population' (T. M. Rees, *The Quakers in Wales*, p. 146) owed something to Powell's influence, but probably more to the fact that 'in the early seventeenth century there was probably no other district of Wales where such reverence for literature and education flourished' as in the *cantref* Ardudwy in Merionethshire (T. E. Ellis, introd. to M. Llwyd, *Gweithiau*, II. xi, with references to many notable natives), which thus proved fertile soil for the new seed; for its need, cf. J. Jones, in *Transactions* of Lancs. and Cheshire Hist. Soc., N.S. (1861), I. 185: 'What becomes of poore Merionethshire, is that countrey denied the tender of gospel mercies? Is there no prophet, noe messenger of Xt yt will make Duffryn Ardidwey in his way?' (1651). Fox's sounding the day of the Lord on Cadair Idris, ' & since there has a great people risse in those places' (*Journal*, ed. N. Penney, I. 281, 448) is an interesting parallel to his behaviour on Pendle Hill, in another district where the ground had been specially prepared (cf. App. I, *inf.*).
[6] Cf. C. H. Firth, in *D.N.B.*, *s.v.*
[7] J. Nayler, in *Letters of Early Friends*, ed. A. R. Barclay, p. 39; quoted on p. 16, n. 10, *sup.*
[8] G. Fox, *Journal*, ed. N. Penney, I. 32, 402.
[9] Cf. C. H. Firth, in *D.N.B.*, *s.v.*   [10] Cf. *D.N.B.*, *s.v.*
[11] Cf. N. Penney, in his edn. of G. Fox, *Itinerary Journal*, pp. 328 f.
[12] Cf. *D.N.B.*, *s.v.*
[13] Cf. N. Penney, in his edn. of G. Fox, *Journal*, II. 431 f.

pregnated with Millenarian ideas'.[1] This seems an exaggeration. There is a startling passage in John Perrot's *A Wren in the Burning-Bush*, to the effect that 'you the Quakers & Tremblers . . . are *his chosen Generation*, his Royal Priesthood, & most peculiar and ever-lasting inheritance . . . Abraham . . . Lot . . . Noah . . . And Moses . . . saw not such a glory as is now revealed among you';[2] but this was written only a year before Perrot 'runne out'.[3] In Fox's mouth, at least, 'the day of the Lord', which he frequently 'sounds' or 'declares', appears to be void of any particularizing chronological content, and to be little more than a synonym for the divine judgement, which is always imminent, upon sin.[4]

An interesting example of those whose Millenarianism became thus spiritualized without their becoming Quakers is presented by Llwyd. Llwyd's expectations were so keen that they influenced even the naming of his children: in 1650 he writes,

> In soule, in family, & Wales and England peace shall bee
> therefore my litle daughter now is called Peace by mee.[5]

These expectations were confessedly chiliastic,[6] and this influenced Llwyd's attitude to the ordinances; for the apostolic injunction is to observe the Lord's Supper only 'till he come', and if the Lord's coming be at hand, then there is about to be spiritual freedom for the disuse of the ordinance. Llwyd, we saw earlier, was no despiser of the ordinances; but the following context suggests that he expected them soon to be superseded.

> We know that ordinances pure, are in themselves but dry
> yet walke together in known paths loves knot will better tye.

> Two woes are past, the third begins, the judge is now at hand
> the tides do turne, the nation reeles. Stand now (yee faithful) stand.

Indeed, for those who would look, Christ was already come within; and Llwyd bids men look: 'watch ever for Christ at home, on the hearth of your own heart.'[7] The promise was fulfilled, and Christ's Spirit at last was largely present, bringing with it a larger liberty.

---

[1] G. P. Gooch, *English Democratic Ideas in the Seventeenth Century* (1927 edn.), p. 233, n. 2.
[2] J. Perrot, *A Wren in the Burning-Bush*, p. 5; for Perrot, cf. *D.N.B.*, *s.v.*
[3] G. Fox, *Journal*, ed. N. Penney, II. 314; cf. Penney's note, II. 375 f.
[4] Cf. *ib.*, I. 40, 281, 297, 304; II. 2 f. (where the day is treated as past), *et al.*
[5] M. Llwyd, *Gweithiau*, I. 36.
[6] Cf. *ib.*, I. 27:

> Call mee a chiliast if you please
> or giddy headed foole
> when those dayes come whereof I speake
> your wisdomes will bee coole.

R. Farmer, *Satan Inthron'd*, p. 48, does call Llwyd 'hare-brain'd'.
[7] M. Llwyd, *Gweithiau*, I. 16, 145.

This new-found spiritual liberty expressed itself both in a broad tolerance of difference within the fellowship of the Church, and in a demand for toleration as an established policy. The tolerance, which was the source of the demand for toleration, was itself the immediate issue of the contemporary religious enthusiasm, conditioned as we have seen this to be by a new historical sense and by eschatological convictions. In some periods tolerance is the fruit of indifference, but any suggestion that this is true of the seventeenth century betrays complete misunderstanding. Even the Master of Balliol's dictum, that 'toleration of others was in part a price they had to pay for their own passionately held liberty'[1] is misleading. Toleration in the State, like tolerance in the Church, was a natural outcome of faith in 'the liberty of the Spirit'. In the remainder of this chapter it is largely with the underlying tolerance with which we shall be concerned.

A most telling expression of this fundamental conviction is to be found in the farewell speech, from which we quoted earlier, attributed to John Robinson. After stating his persuasion of 'more light and truth yet', we are told,

> he took occasion also miserably to bewail the state and condition of the reformed churches, who were come to a period in religion, and would go no further than the instruments of their reformation. As, for example, the Lutherans, they could not be drawn to go beyond what Luther saw;[2] . . . and so also, saith he, you see the Calvinists, they stick where he [Calvin] left them; a misery much to be lamented; for though they were precious shining lights in their times, yet God had not revealed his whole will to them; and were they now living, saith he, they would be as ready and willing to embrace further light, as that they had received . . . it is not possible that the christian world should come so lately out of such thick antichristian darkness, and that perfection of knowledge should break forth at once.[3]

On this T. H. Green comments justly: 'It is as giving a freer scope than any other form of church to this conviction, that God's spirit is not bound, that independency has its historical interest'.[4]

The Presbyterians, as we have seen repeatedly, did not share the Congregationalists' primary interest in the Holy Spirit. Consequently neither did they share the Congregationalists' spirit of tolerance.

---

[1] A. D. Lindsay, *Toleration and Democracy*, p. 6.
[2] Cf. the titles, *Looke Beyond Luther* (1623) by R. Bernard, and *Luther's Forerunners*, by J. P. Perrin, translated by S. Lennard (1624); for Bernard and Lennard, cf. *D.N.B.*, *s.vv.*
[3] J. Robinson, *Works*, I. xliv. f.
[4] T. H. Green, *Works*, III. 289 f., quoting the passage from Neal's inaccurate version.

H

Baillie complains that 'Independency here is become a uniting Principle'.[1] Milton rejoices that this is so:

> while we still affect by all means a rigid external formality, we may as soon fall again into a gross conforming stupidity, a stark and dead congealment of wood and hay and stubble, forced and frozen together, which is more to the sudden degenerating of a Church than many sub-dichotomies of petty schisms . . . all cannot be of one mind—as who looks they should be? . . . those neighbouring differences, or rather indifferences, are what I speak of, whether in some point of doctrine or of discipline, which, though they may be many, yet need not interrupt the unity of Spirit, if we could but find among us the bond of peace![2]

John Cook also readily accepts Baillie's taunt. The Independent's tolerance of believers' baptism, on the ground that 'if it be an errour, it is a very harmlesse one', we noticed earlier.[3] Cook continues:

> If an Antinomian doctrinall doe not prove an Antinomian practicall, hee thinks some of those opinions are very comfortable . . . He hopes Seekers finde the way to heaven, yet counts it sad that any should wait new Apostles (they may as well seek a new Gospel,) and that those Ordinances which Christ hath purchased with his pretious bloud, should be counted shadows, much derogatory to his love and wisdome; yet he suspects his owne heart, and thinks that possibly some men live at a very high rate in spirituall enjoyments, being wholy at rest in God, and have the lesse need of Ordinances, and for those that thinke the Saints are here in full perfection of grace and glory, his sinfull heart tells him it is an errour; yet hee will not judge any tree to be evill but by its fruits. He knows no hurt in a million of millenary-like errours; who would not be glad to see Jesus Christ?

Such was the Independents' ideal attitude to those Puritans who were more radical than themselves. To the Presbyterians they would be equally tolerant. 'Heads need not breed difference in hearts;' says Cook, 'He counts every godly Presbyterian to be his deare brother, but not to be preferred before the truth', and says of the name Independents, 'and the word Presbyters, as it is used, I wish they were extinct and buryed:'.[4] Cradock similarly remarks that 'Presbytery, and Independency are not two religions: but one religion to a godly, honest heart; it is only a little rufling of the fringe; . . .'.[5]

The tolerance of many Congregationalists towards the Baptists which we observed earlier we can see now to have been in no way

---

[1] R. Baillie, *op. cit.*, p. 93; Baxter says 'the Antinomians were commonly Independants': R.B., i. 162; quoted on p. 60, n. 2, *sup.*
[2] J. Milton, *Areopagitica* (Everyman edn.), pp. 37 f.   [3] Cf. p. 96, *sup.*
[4] J. Cook, *What the Independents would have*, pp. 8, 11 f., 2.
[5] W. Cradock, *Gospel-Libertie*, p. 135.

exceptional but a natural expression of 'the liberty of the Spirit'. As Llwyd says,

> Mens faces, voices, differ much,
> saincts are not all one size
> flowers in one garden vary too
> lett none monopolize.

Again, 'The truth is between you all . . . all your Sects have some pieces of the Truth on their sides;'.[1] Therefore, to turn to Francis Rous' way of putting it,

> When Christ speaks to thee to follow him one way, thou maist not with Peter make quarrels and questions concerning John's other way; for so maist thou receive Peters answer from the Master: what is that to thee? follow thou me. It is the Masters part to allot the way and work of his Disciples, and therefore let both Peter and John walk that different way, to which their Master hath differently directed them.[2]

This extract excellently illustrates the tender spirit of these men. The word 'tender', which is a characteristic word of Fox's,[3] is no less characteristic of other radical Puritans, and pre-eminently of Cromwell, in this, not least, 'our cheif of men';[4] it implies openness to the workings of God's Spirit within,[5] and consequent sensitiveness to the Spirit's workings in others also, according to their measure.

One outstanding quality of John Buchan's study of Cromwell is his insistence 'that he was in essence a mystic, and that the core of his religion was a mystical experience continually renewed. . . . His religion, being based not on fear but on love, for fear had little place in his heart, made him infinitely compassionate towards others'.[6] A classic exposition of the workings of Cromwell's heart is in the letter in which he says of his daughter, Lady Claypole,[7]

> she seeks after (as I hope also) what will satisfy. And thus to be a seeker[8] is to be of the best sect next to a finder; and such an one shall every faithful humble seeker be at the end. Happy seeker, happy finder! Who ever tasted that the Lord is gracious, without some sense

---

[1] M. Llwyd, *Gweithiau*, I. 24; II. 238.   [2] F. Rous, *Works*, p. 645.

[3] Fox, who calls himself 'a tender youth' and Elizabeth Hooton 'a very tender woman', allows of the Baptists in his youth that 'they were tender then': *Journal* (1901 edn.), I. 4 f., 9.

[4] J. Milton, *To the Lord General Cromwell*.

[5] Cf. G. Fox, *Journal*, ed. N. Penney, II. 147, of meetings for worship: 'oh the tendernesse, & brokennesse, & life, & power, . . .'.

[6] J. Buchan, *O. Cromwell*, pp. 67 f.; cf. p. 529: 'Oliver is what Novalis called Spinoza, a *Gottbetrunkener Mann*'. J. M. Murry, *Heaven—and Earth*, p. 126, applies the same epithet to the Ironsides.

[7] Cf. C. H. Firth, in *D.N.B.*, *s.v.*, as Claypoole; G. Fox, *Journal*, ed. N. Penney, I. 327 f.

[8] For the untechnical use of the term 'seeker', cf. M. Llwyd, *Gweithiau*, II. 236 (quoted on p. 107, *sup.*); 262, to Erbury, 'I desire you to let me be a private seeker . . .'; 271, to Baxter: 'I hope you are yet kept by the Lord's spirit a seeker . . .'.

of self, vanity, and badness? Who ever tasted that graciousness of His, and could go less in desire,—less than pressing after full enjoyment?

This inner spiritual dynamic was combined in Cromwell with a clear perception that 'uprightness, if it be not purely of God, may be, nay commonly is, deceived'[1] and that 'we are very apt, all of us, to call that faith, that perhaps may be but carnal imagination, and carnal reasonings'; and the combination made him, more than any other prominent radical Puritan, understanding, compassionate and tolerant. 'They that are the most yielding have the greatest wisdom', he said once; 'I am confident on't, we should not be so hot one with another'.[2]

In the speech with which in 1653 he opened the Nominated Parliament, and of which Morley says, 'so far as the speech can be said to have any single practical note, it is that of Tolerance',[3] Cromwell says:

> we should be pitiful. Truly, this calls us to be very much touched with the infirmities of the Saints; that we may have a respect unto all, and be pitiful and tender towards all, though of different judgments.

This tolerance, with which Cromwell would yield 'the liberty of the Spirit' to all peaceable Christians, without regard to denominational distinction, had been fostered in him by his experience in the Army. In 1645 he wrote:

> Presbyterians, Independents, all have here the same spirit of faith and prayer; the same presence and answer; they agree here, have no names of difference; pity it is it should be otherwise anywhere! All that believe, have the real unity, which is most glorious; because inward, and spiritual, in the Body, and to the Head.

Cromwell was no Anabaptist,[4] but equally he had no antipathy to Anabaptism. In 1644 he wrote to a major-general, who had cashiered a lieutenant-colonel for Anabaptism,

> Take heed of being sharp, or too easily sharpened by others, against those to whom you can object little but that they square not with you in every opinion concerning matters of religion.[5]

The Quakers Cromwell feared politically, with what justification we shall consider later, and consequently he found himself unable to grant to them the degree of toleration which he granted to others;

---

[1] O. Cromwell, *Letters and Speeches*, ed. T. Carlyle, Letters XLI and CXLVI.
[2] O. Cromwell, in *Puritanism and Liberty*, ed. A. S. P. Woodhouse, pp. 8, 59.
[3] J. Morley, *O. Cromwell*, p. 363.
[4] Except in the sense in which he may be called 'the last and greatest of the Anabaptists': G. M. Young, *Charles I and Cromwell*, p. 13.
[5] O. Cromwell, *Letters and Speeches*, ed. T. Carlyle, Speech I and Letters XXXI and XX.

but, whenever he could, he showed them tolerance. 'They would have mee to disown these people,' he said once, 'shall I disown y^m because they will not put of there hatts . . .'.[1] He was always easy of access to Quaker leaders,[2] and Fox gives a touching account of one of the occasions when he and Cromwell met:

> severall times hee saide Itt was very good & truth . . . as I was turneinge hee catcht mee by ye hande & saide these words with teares in his eyes:
> Come againe to my house: for if thou & I were butt an houre in a day togeather wee should bee neerer one to ye other: & y^t hee wisht mee noe more ill then hee did to his owne soule.[3]

'There can be little doubt that Cromwell's moderate carriage towards Friends endeared him to them, and that he and they felt mutual esteem for one another.'[4]

Cromwell's religious establishment Firth calls 'a confederation of Christian sects working together for righteousness',[5] but, in intention at least, it was less even of 'a confederation of sects' than a channel for 'ye power of god before sects was'. [6] By all the normal standards of creed, liturgy or organization, as Stoughton says, 'it was not a Church at all. . . . it had no Church courts, no Church assemblies, no Church laws, no Church ordinances. . . . Not even the two great sacraments of Christianity were mentioned'.[7] These negative statements are true, but their significance is likely to be missed unless it be realized that Cromwell's religious establishment was the result of tolerance, and that its purpose was to allow as large a measure as possible of 'the liberty of the Spirit'. How large a measure in fact was possible we may examine, as in the next chapter we pass from 'the liberty of the Spirit' in ideal to 'the government of the Spirit' in practice.

---

[1] W. Dewsbury, quoted by N. Penney in his edn. of G. Fox, *Journal*, I. 400.

[2] 'Few rulers were more accessible to petitioners': C. H. Firth, in *D.N.B., s.v.*

[3] G. Fox, *Journal*, ed. N. Penney, I. 167 f.   [4] *B.Q.*, p. 440.

[5] C. H. Firth, *O. Cromwell* (1935 edn.), p. 368.

[6] G. Fox, *Journal*, ed. N. Penney, I. 379; Cromwell would have been at one with Fox over this.

[7] J. Stoughton, *op. cit.*, II. 89.

CHAPTER VIII

THE GOVERNMENT OF THE SPIRIT

SYNOPSIS OF ARGUMENT

   i. Tolerance naturally expressed in toleration.
'The government of the Spirit' the obverse of 'the liberty of the Spirit.'
  ii. Church polity the link between 'the government of the Spirit'
in personal and in political life.
Puritan politics the application of a spiritual principle.
 iii. The duty of 'the saints' to 'judge the world'.
Conditions favouring the rise of Fifth Monarchism.
The Nominated Parliament: its constitution;
hopes;
policy;
failure.
Fifth Monarchists become plotters;
or Quakers.
 iv. Cromwell's faith in 'the government of Spirit';
reliance on providential 'dispensations';
concern for liberty to worship in freedom of conscience.
  v. Anglicans and Roman Catholics in theory excluded from toleration.
Reasons for this.
Extent of connivance at use of Prayer Book;
episcopal ordinations.
 vi. Reasons for Cromwell's suspicion of Quakers.
Nature and extent of persecution of Quakers during the Commonwealth.

'he that is spiritual judgeth all things' (1 *Cor.* ii. 15).
'the saints of the most High shall take the kingdom, and possess the
kingdom for ever, even for ever and ever' (*Dan.* vii. 18).

A T the close of the last chapter, we observed the tolerance towards
others which arose in Puritanism from the consciousness of a new
'liberty of the Spirit' within; but we were driven constantly to the
very bounds of any description of this attitude as purely personal, or
as confined to the fellowship within the Church, and were made to
look beyond, towards a consideration of the demand for toleration
in the State. The distinction between tolerance and toleration is a

genuine one; but the two things are as closely related as the similarity of the words suggests, and the last chapter would be inadequate, if not followed by a wider study. In Puritanism there is no longer the old separation between religious and secular, between the Church and the State: Calvin's attempt to identify the holy community with the Genevan community at large is always before men's eyes as an ideal. In England, religion and politics have never been more inseparably intertwined than during the Civil War and the Commonwealth; and especially in those circles imbued with millenarian enthusiasms, which in the years 1650–55 were intensely fashionable, there is a perpetual overflow of spiritual convictions into political channels. If freedom be a keynote in Puritanism, so is theocracy; freedom is demanded, but in order to facilitate obedience to God; those in whom the Spirit of God is must bear their responsibility in judging the world and in ruling others; the obverse of 'the liberty of the Spirit' is 'the government of the Spirit'. We see this most clearly in the Fifth Monarchy movement, the influence of which reaches its climax in what Gardiner calls 'the high-water mark of Puritanism in Church and State',[1] the Nominated Parliament. We see it also in the peculiarly political quality attaching to the spiritual experience of Cromwell, the representative *par excellence* of the inarticulate common man:[2] the convictions of 'the government of the Spirit' and the methods of discerning it, recorded in many a Puritan diary, are apparent in Cromwell's faith in 'waitings', 'dispensations' and 'providences', and by him are interwoven with the government of the State.

The intervening stage between 'the government of the Spirit' in personal experience and in the State is 'the government of the Spirit' in the polity of the fellowship within the Church. Here those lessons were learned, which, later, men sought to apply on a larger scale. As their name suggests, the Congregationalists, with their Separatist forebears, were the pioneers. The distinctive feature of the Congregational polity was the church-meeting, in which not only chosen officers but every member had an equal share in the church's government. In this development from Presbyterianism may be seen the expression in religion of the general tendency of the period towards individualism and democracy. Indeed, the word *democracy* is not absent from

[1] S. R. Gardiner, *History of the Commonwealth and Protectorate*, II. 340; *id., Cromwell's Place in History*, p. 84.
[2] 'in the world of action what Shakespeare was in the world of thought, the greatest because the most typical Englishman of all time': *ib.*, pp. 115 f. Professor Ernest Barker uses the same comparison in *British Statesmen*, p. 40; cf. also J. M. Murry, *Heaven—and Earth*, p. 178, for a similar comparison of Cromwell's 'creative experience' with Shakespeare's.

contemporary discussions of the subject. Erbury, for instance, with
his eye for sequence, remarks

> the Prelatick Church was Monarchical . . .: The Presbyterian Church
> is an Aristocracy . . .: The Independent or baptized Churches (both is
> one) are a pure Democracy. . . .[1]

Baxter says, 'I like not the democratick formes', and consequently
objects to the Congregationalists' 'principles of Popularity'.[2] Such a
correlation is of value, so long as two things are remembered: first,
that it is formal rather than material, the democratic form of the
church-meeting being not an end in itself but a means of discovering
'the government of the Spirit'; and secondly, that it was the church-
meeting which gave birth, in England, to political democracy, not
vice versa.[3]

For the future of civilization it may be that what proved, in the
event, to be most fruitful was this application in the political sphere of
the democratic form of the church-meeting, when, partly through
the influence of that 'principle of segregation' which Professor
Woodhouse so skilfully delineates but (it may be argued) ante-dates,[4]
its original spiritual purpose had been allowed to fade from memory.
That spiritual purpose, however, was still strongly present in those
who first effected the political application, and who themselves are
described more fitly as theocrats than as democrats. What Troeltsch
says of the Pauline ethic is true here. Christian equality is essentially
an equality before God, not before man, is 'a negative equality over
against the infinite holiness of God',[5] and consequently an equality
only within the Christian fellowship. Without, 'he that is spiritual
judgeth all things', and 'the saints' form a spiritual aristocracy, who
are to 'judge the world', if that is possible, but who in any case are
other, and better, than 'the world' and those who are 'without God
in the world'. Apart from such a conclusion, the reality of the work
of the Holy Spirit within the hearts of the elect would be under-
mined, and its value rendered worthless.

For a period men believed that for the saints to judge the world
and to possess the kingdom *was* possible. The eschatological expectations mentioned in the preceding chapter undoubtedly contributed

---

[1] W. Erbury, *Testimony*, p. 63.

[2] R. Baxter, *A Holy Commonwealth*, Preface; *R.B.*, iii. 141.

[3] The earliest instance of *democratical* (1589) in the *Oxford English Dictionary*, and the second instance of *democracy* (1574; the first refers to Athens) are both from religious, not political, controversy.

[4] Cf. A. S. P. Woodhouse, *Puritanism and Liberty*, pp. [57] ff.

[5] E. Troeltsch, *op. cit.*, i. 72.

to this belief. Mixed with them was a rising nationalism of the kind which reaches its peak in Milton's *Areopagitica* (1644):

> Lords and Commons of England, consider what Nation it is whereof ye are, and whereof ye are the governors: . . . the favour and the love of Heaven, we have great argument to think in a peculiar manner propitious and propending towards us. . . . Now once again by all concurrence of signs, and by the general instinct of holy and devout men, . . . God is decreeing to begin some new and great period in His Church, even to the reforming of Reformation itself: what does He then but reveal Himself to His servants, and as His manner is, first to His Englishmen?[1]

A little earlier, Sibbes had pointed the moral:

> Is there any outward thing that advanceth our kingdom before Turkey, or Spain, &c.? Nothing. Their government, and riches, and outward things are as much as ours, if not more. The glory of places and times are from the revelation of Christ, that hath the Spirit accompanying of it.[2]

A little later, Sterry addresses the members of the Long Parliament thus:

> You are Substitutes and Vice-gerents to the Lord Jesus. Look then to Jesus the Beginning and End of your Authority. God hath laid the Government on his Shoulder. What is his sufficiency for it? The Spirit of the Lord resteth on him. . . . Can You be able to rule over any spot of this earth; when Jesus Christ was not fit for the government of the whole; without the Spirit?[3]

When as early as 1645 the Commons could thus suffer themselves to be regarded as having no title but as instruments of 'the government of the Spirit', the experiment of the Nominated Parliament becomes less surprising.

Furthermore, the execution of Charles I acted as an explosion in a powder-magazine. When one recalls the 'one loud burst of horror and indignation over Europe'[4] at the execution of Mary Stuart, one may imagine something of what the reaction to regicide still was. For England to be kingless surely heralded the end of all things. Moreover, as with the Elizabethan religious settlement men transferred their allegiance from the Virgin Mary to their Virgin Queen,[5] so now, conversely, many transferred their allegiance from King

[1] J. Milton, *Areopagitica* (Everyman edn.), pp. 31 f.; for a study of Milton as 'inevitably driven towards arguing for a state ruled by Christ' (p. 62), cf. G. Wilson Knight, *Chariot of Wrath* (1942).
[2] R. Sibbes, *Works*, IV. 303.
[3] P. Sterry, *The Spirits Conviction of Sinne*, Epistle Dedicatory.
[4] A. Jessopp, in *D.N.B.*, *s.v.* Elizabeth.
[5] Cf. E. C. Wilson, *England's Eliza*, pp. 57, 195, 220.

Charles to King Jesus, whose reign on earth seemed brought appreciably nearer by the abolition of human kingship. 'Fifth Monarchism arose, in a great measure, out of the ruins of English monarchism'.[1] A telling instance of this intertwining of religious and political conviction is provided in the charge brought by his parishioners against Dell in 1660, that he said Charles I 'was no king to him, Christ was his king, Venice and Holland without kings, why not England?'[2].

The men who held these convictions had an opportunity for putting them into practice, greater than they well could have expected, in what is known as the Nominated, Little or Barebones Parliament. By any constitutional criterion, its title of Parliament was but *soi-disant*,[3] for it was an assembly of 'the saints', a hundred and thirty-nine in number, nominated by Congregational and Baptist churches throughout the country, and selected, with some replacements, by army officers, with representatives from Scotland, Wales and Ireland, and with six co-opted members; but an assembly which had Rous as Speaker and counted 'for the most part men of worth, substance, and standing'[4] among its members, scarcely deserved to receive for sobriquet the name of a member who 'does not seem to have spoken at all'.[5] The scheme came from Harrison, the Fifth Monarchists' political leader, and not from Cromwell, who accepted it only with hesitation; but, if one may judge from the speech with which he opened Parliament, a speech which has been called 'the companion-piece to the *Areopagitica*',[6] Cromwell had the keenest hopes of what the assembly might accomplish. 'Indeed', he said, 'I do think somewhat is at the door: we are at the threshold.'[7] 'Harrison himself could not have addressed them in ecstasy more rapt.'[8]

Whatever hopes he cherished were soon dashed, chiefly by the impatience and fissiparous tendencies inherent in radical Puritanism

---

[1] J. Stoughton, *Religion in England*, II. 61.

[2] *C.R.*, *s.v.*; the Venetian constitution was an ideal in seventeenth-century England before Charles' death was so much as contemplated: cf. G. M. Young, *Charles I & Cromwell*, p. 57.

[3] Cf. S. R. Gardiner, *Cromwell's Place in History*, p. 82.

[4] J. Morley, *O. Cromwell*, p. 361. S. R. Gardiner, *History of the Commonwealth and Protectorate*, II. 308, n. 1, prints a complete list of the members. For notes on them, cf. H. A. Glass, *The Barbone Parliament*, pp. 69–86, who points out that among them, besides Cromwell and his son Henry, Harrison, Ireton and Lambert, were one peer, three future peers, ten baronets or knights, four future Lord Mayors, the Court physician and Admiral Blake. Of the 145 members 42 are the subjects of articles in *D.N.B.*

[5] *D.N.B.*, *s.v.*, as Barbon.

[6] J. M. Murry, *op. cit.*, pp. 171 f.; Mr. Murry adds, 'Cromwell's speech is imbued with the one quality that the *Areopagitica* has not—tenderness' (p. 174).

[7] O. Cromwell, *Letters and Speeches*, ed. T. Carlyle, Speech I.

[8] S. R. Gardiner, *op. cit.*, II. 287.

and manifest earlier in the 'Troubles of Frankfort' and in the Separatist divisions in Holland.[1] In Baxter's words:

> in the Little Sectarian Parliament, it was put to the Vote, whether all the Parish Ministers of England should at once be put down or no? And it was but accidentally carried in the negative by two Voices: And it was taken for granted, that the Tythes and Universities would at the next Opportunity be voted down;[2]

This, which was the policy of the extremist minority, caused alarm to the moderate majority and consequent disruption. Within five months of its opening, the Nominated Parliament abdicated, and Cromwell, in whom the 'quality of knowing when to pull up was a distinguishing feature',[3] accepted the abdication and immediately assumed the title of Lord Protector. 'By that act he destroyed the most cherished hopes of the fifth-monarchy men, when they seemed almost to have reached fruition.'[4]

Henceforth the Fifth Monarchists had no chance of any legal establishment in fulfilment of their convictions; some became plotters, others became Quakers. At Blackfriars, which 'claimed to be independent of the municipal authorities of London', with 'the privileges of sanctuary',[5] Fifth Monarchist preachers fulminated against Cromwell's new title, in face of Christ's kingly rule,[6] claiming that 'they could not refuse to utter words with which they were inspired by the Holy Spirit'.[7] John Rogers, 'though there is no proof that he was actually concerned in any plot',[8] openly told Cromwell, 'I am ready, for one amongst the Lord's Remnant, to side with just principles in the strength of the Anointing, whether it be *praedicando*, *precando* or *praeliando*'; and when questioned, 'Said you not *praeliando*?', he replied, 'Yes, in the Spirit of the Lord'.[9] Christopher

---

[1] The 'Wisbech Stirs' (cf. T. G. Law, *The Conflicts between Jesuits and Seculars in the reign of Queen Elizabeth*) are a sufficient reminder that these tendencies were not endemic to Puritanism.

[2] *R.B.*, i. 113; cf. M. Llwyd, *Gweithiau*, I. 92:
> The hott yong Parliament
> would pull all mountaines downe
> Christ being the heire by right discent
> yet they gott small renowne.

[3] S. R. Gardiner, *Cromwell's Place in History*, p. 28.

[4] *D.N.B.*, *s.v.* J. Rogers.

[5] J. Stoughton, *op. cit.*, II. 64.

[6] The Broadmead Baptist Church, Bristol, was equally disapproving: cf. E. Terrill, *Broadmead Records*, ed. N. Haycroft (1865 edn.), p. 37: 'Oliver Cromwell, called Lord Protector when as God alone was yᵉ Protector of his people; (*but we sinned*.)'.

[7] S. R. Gardiner, *History of the Commonwealth and Protectorate*, II. 321; Cromwell brought Sterry and others 'to oppose spirit to spirit'.

[8] *D.N.B.*, *s.v.*

[9] J. Rogers, in E. Rogers, *Life and Opinions of a Fifth-Monarchy-Man*, pp. 211 f.

Feake, who 'occupies a middle position between the quiet dreamers and the armed fanatics',[1] asked, more moderately,

> Whether between an immoderate and unruly Spirit on the one hand, despising and trampling upon Authority, which is a beam of God, and a spirit of baseness and flattery on the other hand, dawbing over unrighteousness, and having the persons of men in authority in admiration, is there not between both a middle way, wherein the Spirit of God upon a man may lead him forth to bear his witness against the unrighteousness or backslidings of the Rulers, and yet in the same Act hold an holy reverence to the Authority itself . . . ?[2]

The party's leader, Harrison, who, it was said, had claimed a revelation 'that the Spirit told him that it was impossible to settle this government but in a monarchical way, and it was revealed unto him that there would speedily be a king again, but . . . a king anointed with the Spirit',[3] went into retirement; but he held fast to his convictions even at his execution for regicide in 1660, after which he was expected by some 'to rise again, judge his judges, and restore the kingdom of the saints'.[4] Five of the members of the Nominated Parliament are noted by Braithwaite as having become Quakers, and three others as having been 'at one time or another well-wishers'.[5] Thus evaporated the Fifth Monarchists' attempt to judge the world by 'the government of the Spirit'.

Cromwell remained; and Cromwell believed in 'the government of the Spirit' no less keenly than did the Fifth Monarchists, and put it into practice far more effectually. To perceive the dealings of God with the soul in the day's events was a Puritan commonplace; Cromwell's significance is that, being 'interested first in religion, and then in politics',[6] he carried the perception out of the individual sphere and applied it in the realm of politics. Moreover, Cromwell's

---

[1] A. Gordon, in *D.N.B.*, *s.v.*

[2] C. Feake, *Sighs for Righteousness*, as quoted by L. F. Brown, *op. cit.*, pp. 52 f.

[3] S. R. Gardiner, *op. cit.*, II. 276.   [4] C. H. Firth, in *D.N.B.*, *s.v.*

[5] *B.Q.*, p. 119, n. 3; Thomas French, one of the members for Cambridge, may be added (cf. N. Penney, in his edn. of G. Fox, *Journal*, II. 373). Five other members are among those called 'moderate men' in lists from Quakers in several counties in 1659, suggesting suitable Justices of the Peace (cf. *Extracts from State Papers relating to Friends*, ed. N. Penney, pp. 106–112), and a sixth is called 'A Moderate man' in a Quaker document dated 1707 (cf. *First Publishers of Truth*, ed. N. Penney, p. 125). Five other members in 1656 were among those who urged moderate measures against Nayler (cf. *B.Q.*, pp. 258 f.); one of these, Lambert, when in 1673 visited by a Quaker, Miles Halhead, said: 'Friend, I would have you know, that some of us never made Laws, nor consented to Laws to persecute you, nor none of your Friends; for Persecution we were ever against' (M. Halhead, *Sufferings and Passages*, p. 24). John Bradshaw, the judge presiding at Charles I's trial, who did not sit in the Nominated Parliament, but was continued by it in the chancellorship of the duchy of Lancaster, is another who was sympathetic towards Quakerism (cf. *D.N.B.*, *s.v.*, and N. Penney's edn. of G. Fox, *Journal*, I. 409).

[6] S. R. Gardiner, *Cromwell's Place in History*, p. 23.

faith in the Spirit was a faith less doctrinaire than the Fifth Monarchists' faith: it was far more expectant, more dynamic. His remark to the French Ambassador in 1647, that a man never rose so high as when he did not know where he was going,[1] had a spiritual foundation. In the following year he wrote to Robert Hammond:

> We in this Northern Army were in a waiting posture; desiring to see what the Lord would lead us to . . .
>
> Thinkest thou, in thy heart, that the glorious dispensations of God point out to this? or to teach His people to trust in Him, and to wait for better things . . .?[2]

In Cromwell's experience there is a constant dependence of 'the government of the Spirit' upon 'the liberty of the Spirit', a principle to which, with its resultant tenderness and tolerance, we have seen him to be acutely sensitive. How this affected him will become apparent from some passages in his letters and speeches.

'I am one of those', he said in 1647, 'whose heart God hath drawn out to wait for some extraordinary dispensations, according to those promises that he hath held forth of things to be accomplished in the later times, and I cannot but think that God is beginning of them.'[3] That he was aware of a tendency in his enthusiasm to exaggerate is clear from a remark which he made about Sir Henry Vane the younger in the following year: 'I pray he make not too little, nor I too much, of outward dispensations'. How much, in fact, Cromwell did make of 'outward dispensations' appears in the letter to Hammond already quoted:

> As to outward dispensations, if we may so call them: we have not been without our share of beholding some remarkable providences, and appearances of the Lord. His presence hath been amongst us, and by the light of His countenance we have prevailed. . . .
>
> seek to know the mind of God in all that chain of Providence. . . . I say again, seek that spirit to teach thee; which is the spirit of knowledge and understanding, the spirit of counsel and might, of wisdom and of the fear of the Lord . . . so that . . . thou shalt judge for the meek of the Earth . . .
>
> My dear Friend, let us look into providences; surely they mean somewhat. They hang so together; have been so constant, so clear, unclouded. . . .
>
> Dear Robin, beware of men: look up to the Lord. . . . and thou shalt

---

[1] Cf. C. H. Firth, *Oliver Cromwell*, p. 479.

[2] O. Cromwell, *Letters and Speeches*, ed. T. Carlyle, Letter LXXXV.

[3] O. Cromwell, in *Puritanism and Liberty*, ed. A. S. P. Woodhouse, pp. 103 f.

be able through Him, without consulting flesh and blood, to do valiantly for Him and His people.[1]

Acting on this principle, Cromwell found that it always surpassed his expectations. As he said of his men, 'such men as had the fear of God before them, as made some conscience of what they did', 'they were never beaten'. Sometimes, he admitted, he had to go blindfold. But that, he claimed, 'is not to be objected to a man. For who can love to walk in the dark? But Providence doth often so dispose. . . . The case may be that it is the Providence of God that doth lead men in darkness'. Moreover, this going blindfold he turned to advantage. In his exhortation to the Nominated Parliament, he says:

> I say, own your call; for it is of God. Indeed, it is marvellous, and it hath been unprojected. . . . And indeed this hath been the way God dealt with us all along, To keep things from our eyes all along, so that we have seen nothing, in all His dispensations, long beforehand; which is also a witness, in some measure, to our integrity.

So again, in dissolving the First Protectorate Parliament, he said:

> I would be loath to call it a Fate; that were too paganish a word. But there has been Something in it that we had not in our expectations. . . . These issues and events have not been forecast; but sudden Providences in things: . . .

In this speech, the date of which is eight years later than the earliest passage quoted above, Cromwell shows 'the government of the Spirit', thus manifest in providential dispensations, to have been, amidst all the apparent inconsistencies of his policy, the one unbroken guiding thread in his public life. Many a man, he says,

> submits not to the Appearances of God in the World; and therefore lifts up his heel against God, and mocketh at all His providences; laughing at the observations, made up not without reason and the Scriptures, and by the quickening and teaching Spirit which gives life to these other; calling such observations enthusiasms: such men, I say, no wonder if they 'stumble and fall backwards . . .'. The Scriptures say, 'The Rod has a voice . . .' By this voice has God spoken very loud on behalf of His people, by judging their enemies in the late war, and restoring them a liberty to worship, with the freedom of their consciences, and freedom in estates and persons when they do so.[2]

With this last passage we come to the subject of freedom of conscience, or toleration. If 'the liberty of the Spirit' involves tolerance, 'the government of the Spirit' involves toleration. This Cromwell

---

[1] O. Cromwell, *Letters and Speeches*, ed. T. Carlyle, Letters LXVII and LXXXV.
[2] *Ib.*, Speeches XI, I and IV.

realized from the first, and the attainment of toleration, in a measure then without parallel, he counted his chief claim to reputation. As early as 1644 he said, 'to seek to maintain our opinions in religion by force . . . we detest and abhor'. In the following year he proclaimed it to be fundamental that 'for brethren, in things of the mind we look for no compulsion, but that of light and reason'. In his speech opening the Nominated Parliament he said, 'if the poorest Christian, the most mistaken Christian, shall desire to live peaceably and quietly under you,—I say, if any shall desire but to lead a life of godliness and honesty, let him be protected'. To the Second Protectorate Parliament, once more, he said:

> If men will profess,—be they those under Baptism, be they those of the Independent judgement simply, or of the Presbyterian judgement—in the name of God, encourage them, countenance them; so long as they do plainly continue to be thankful to God, and to make use of the liberty given them to enjoy their own consciences. For, as it was said today, this is the peculiar Interest all this while contended for.[1]

'In adhesion to the general doctrine of liberty of conscience,' says John Morley, 'he had never wavered. Perhaps it was the noblest element in his whole mental equipment.'[2]

The most striking expression by Cromwell of his belief in toleration occurs in a remark made by him when considering the scheme for religious settlement proposed by Owen in 1652. He said then that 'he had rather that Mahometanism were permitted amongst us than that one of God's children should be persecuted'.[3] In this is perceptible not only his 'tenderness' but his sturdy faith in the power of the Holy Spirit to lead into all truth. 'Your pretended fear lest Error should step in', he wrote to the Scottish Presbyterians, 'is like the man who would keep all the wine out of the country lest men should be drunk.'[4] One is reminded of the words of his Latin Secretary of State:

> though all the winds of doctrine were let loose to play upon the earth, so Truth be in the field, we do injuriously, by licensing and prohibiting, to misdoubt her strength. Let her and Falsehood grapple; who ever knew Truth put to the worse, in a free and open encounter?[5]

---

[1] *Ib.*, Letters xxIII and xxxI; Speeches I and v.
[2] J. Morley, *op. cit.*, p. 382.
[3] R. W., *The Fourth Paper*, Preface, as quoted by D. Masson, *Milton*, IV. 394; Masson's identification of the author with Roger Williams (*ib.*, p. 396, n. 1) is accepted by H. M. Dexter, *op. cit.*, bibliographical appendix, no. 1610, and by W. T. Whitley, *op. cit.*, no. 11–652, p. 46.
[4] O. Cromwell, *Letters and Speeches*, ed. T. Carlyle, Letter cxLvIII.
[5] J. Milton, *Areopagitica* (Everyman edn.), p. 36.

The same spirit breathes in John Cook's *What the Independents would have*:

> did God for the safety of a sheep dispence with his own law, and are men so wolvish to prefer an inferiour Law of uniformity to the royall law of love, which is the life of a Kingdome? but men may ruine themselves, they can never ruine the truth.[1]

The toleration granted in Cromwell's 'government of the Spirit' combines with tolerance for the Spirit's workings in others an undoubted faith in the Spirit's convincing might.

Such was Cromwell's ideal; and, after the work performed so thoroughly by Gardiner and Firth, there can be no excuse either for accusing him of hypocrisy in proclaiming it or for complaining that it was never wholly fulfilled. Firth thus succinctly dismisses both suggestions: 'A study of Cromwell's letters and speeches leads irresistibly to the conclusion that he was honest and conscientious throughout';[2] 'Cromwell's was the most tolerant government which had existed in England since the Reformation'.[3]

The toleration attained was not, it is true, complete. In theory, the Roman Catholics and Anglicans were explicitly excluded; so also, to a large extent, were the Quakers. The reason for this was the inextricable confusion of religion with politics. Precisely as, for political reasons, the Established Church under Elizabeth had, in theory, granted no quarter to Roman Catholics, allowing innocent, saintly men such as Campion to be put to death because of plotters such as Persons, so now, for political reasons, Cromwell was unable to grant toleration to those whose Common Prayer Book 'remained the very badge of Royalism'.[4] His work had been 'In obtaining that liberty from the tyranny of the Bishops to all species of Protestants to worship God according to their own light and consciences', in obtaining it from those who had sought 'to eat out the core and power and heart and life of all Religion by bringing on us a company of poisonous Popish Ceremonies, and imposing them upon those that were accounted the Puritans of the Nation...'.[5] One can hardly be surprised if to Cromwell our modern question, 'Shall Toleration be given to Intolerance?',[6] did not present itself.

In point of fact, there was a considerable degree of connivance at, if not of toleration of, Anglican worship. The freedom given to

---

[1] *Op. cit.*, p. 14.   [2] C. H. Firth, in *D.N.B.*, *s.v.*   [3] *Id.*, *O. Cromwell*, p. 367.
[4] S. R. Gardiner, *Cromwell's Place in History*, p. 112; horse-racing was prohibited for six months for the same extrinsic, political reason (cf. C. H. Firth, *op. cit.*, p. 350).
[5] O. Cromwell, *Letters and Speeches*, ed. T. Carlyle, Speeches IV and XVI.
[6] J. M. Murry, *op. cit.*, p. 179.

James Ussher, Archbishop of Armagh, who did not resign his Preachership at Lincoln's Inn until rendered incompetent by the loss of his teeth,[1] and who later was ordered a State funeral by Cromwell, might be thought exceptional, on account of his combination of moderate views with renowned learning; but it was not so. In the City of London, always a stronghold of Puritanism and under the eye of the Government, there were Thomas Fuller, the ecclesiastical historian, preaching at St. Bride's, St. Andrew's and elsewhere; George Hall, afterwards Bishop of Chester, at St. Botolph's, Aldersgate; John Pearson, also afterwards Bishop of Chester, at St. Clement's, East Cheap; Peter Gunning, afterwards Bishop of Ely, at Exeter House chapel, in the Strand, which was 'a frequent resort for churchmen'; Anthony Farindon at St. Mary Magdalene's, Milk Street, 'the scholars' church'; Robert Mossom at St. Peter's, Paul's Wharf, where came a 'great concourse of nobility and gentry'; Nathaniel Hardy at St. Dionys' Backchurch, Fenchurch Street, who maintained a monthly 'Loyal Lecture' and usually preached on the 'Royal Martyrdom'; and, until his execution for implication in Stapley's plot, John Hewit at St. Gregory's, by St. Paul's, who married Cromwell's daughter to Lord Fauconberg. Attending Hewit on the scaffold was John Barwick, who used the Prayer Book service daily in his brother Peter's house in St. Paul's Churchyard, and George Wild, afterwards Bishop of Derry, who used the liturgy regularly in a house in Fleet Street. Jeremy Taylor, afterwards Bishop of Down and Connor, also for a time officiated to a private congregation in London, till he was given Cromwell's personal pass for proceeding to a living in Northern Ireland.

This will be allowed to represent considerable connivance; and what is known of London was probably true to some, if not to the same, extent of other cities. At Oxford, for instance, Owen, as Vice-Chancellor, connived at the holding of the Prayer Book service in Thomas Willis' house in Merton Street by John Fell, afterwards Bishop of Oxford, John Dolben, afterwards Archbishop of York, and Richard Allestree, afterwards Regius Professor of Divinity in the University. At Lincoln there was a private congregation ministered to by Robert Mapletoft, afterwards Dean of Ely. At Bristol George Bull,[2] afterwards Bishop of St. David's, and at Boothby Pagnell, Lincolnshire, Robert Sanderson, afterwards Bishop of Lincoln, were permitted in their churches to use the Anglican liturgy

---

[1] Cf. A. Gordon, in *D.N.B.*, *s.v.*
[2] For his marriage in 1658 by Prayer Book rites, cf. *D.N.B.*, *s.v.* W. Master.

I

memoriter or in a modified form. In these cases the facts are known because the men concerned later rose to eminence; it may be presumed that they obtained in many unknown cases, where the clergyman's name now is forgotten. Clergymen admitted to country livings despite their political views are exemplified in Nehemiah Rogers, 'as uncompromising a royalist as a friend of Laud's was likely to be', and Richard Owen, familiar as a visitor to John Evelyn's home at Sayes Court, Kent.

The protection of the sequestered clergy by royalist gentry was made illegal after the Penruddock plot, which exacerbated the Government, much as Spanish designs on the Elizabethan Government had resulted in a stiffening of the penal laws against Roman Catholics. Here again, however, 'the Declaration . . . was seldom, if ever, put in practice against the clergy. Not a single one of the reports of the Major-Generals—so far as they have reached us—even alludes to the ejection of clergy from private houses'.[1] At Richings Lodge, Buckinghamshire, the home of Mrs. Salter, the sister of Brian Duppa, Bishop of Salisbury, the Anglican service continued to be read by John Hales, 'the ever-memorable', and Henry King, Bishop of Chichester. William Juxon, afterwards Archbishop of Canterbury, read it regularly at Chastleton House, Oxfordshire, where is still preserved the Bible which he had used on the scaffold at the execution of Charles I.[2] The most notable shelter for sequestered clergy was Westwood, Worcestershire: here Lady Pakington welcomed Allestree, Pearson, Gunning, John Fell, Henry Hammond, Charles I's chaplain, Humphrey Henchman, afterwards Bishop of Salisbury, and George Morley, afterwards Bishop of Winchester.

Nor are examples lacking of permission by the Government to its pronounced opponents to retain their livings. John Hacket, for instance, afterwards Bishop of Lichfield and Coventry, remained at Cheam, Surrey; Edward Pococke, the first Laudian Professor of Arabic at Oxford, at Childrey, Berkshire; Robert Skinner, Bishop of Oxford, at Launton, Oxfordshire. Skinner was the most active of those bishops who ensured the Anglican succession by continuing privately to consecrate priests. He was assisted in this work by Ralph Bathurst, Fellow of Trinity College, Oxford, who acted as Archdeacon, and by Thomas Lamplugh, afterwards Archbishop of York, who 'is said to have made not less than three hundred journeys for that purpose from Oxford to Launton'. Other bishops who are known to have conse-

---

[1] S. R. Gardiner, *History of the Commonwealth and Protectorate*, III. 336.
[2] Cf. M. Dickins, *Chastleton House*, p. 18.

crated priests during the Commonwealth include Duppa, King, Joseph Hall, Bishop of Norwich, Ralph Brownrig, Bishop of Exeter, Thomas Morton, Bishop of Durham, Thomas Sydserff, Bishop of Galloway, and Thomas Fuller, Bishop of Ardfert.[1]

Even the Roman Catholics, according to the French Ambassador, 'received better treatment under the Protector than had been accorded to them by any former Government, whether Royal or Parliamentary',[2] and this although they were Royalist in sympathies, almost to a man. It is noticeable that, whereas between 1641 and 1646 twenty-one Roman Catholic priests were hanged, between 1649 and 1660 only two thus suffered,[3] and one of these Cromwell would have spared.[4]

The same reasoning which excluded the Anglicans and Roman Catholics from toleration in effect also excluded the Quakers. That in 1656 Henry Cromwell should say, 'Our most considerable enemy now in our view are the Quakers',[5] may seem strange; the reason for his remark was, as his father said a year later, that 'they were against both magistracy and ministry'.[6] Fox himself might assure Cromwell, 'with the carnall weapon I doe not fight', but he could also write, 'And yᵉ Nations will I Rock being on them atopp'.[7] There is no evidence that he ever advised the soldiers, who came in numbers to his meetings, to throw away their arms. On the contrary, in 1657 he wrote *To the Councill of Officers of the Armie . . . And for the Inferior Officers and Souldiers to Read*, allowing the turning of the sword against violent doers, and saying,

> to them that do well, the sword is a praise . . . And if ever you Souldiers and true Officers come again into the power of God which hath been lost, never set up your Standart until you come to Rome, and it be a top of Rome, then there let your Standart stand.[8]

[1] For the statements in the last four paragraphs, cf. *D.N.B.*, *s.vv.*; other names, with some of those mentioned above, may be found in J. Stoughton, *op. cit.*, II. ch. ix. Other Irish bishops who *probably* consecrated priests during the Commonwealth are John Leslie, Bishop of Clogher, and Henry Leslie, Bishop of Down and Connor (cf. *D.N.B.*, *s.vv.*, where Bagwell assumes Henry Leslie to be the Bishop of Meath referred to by Evelyn, *s.d.* May 7, 1656, since he was already 'provided' to Meath, though he was not translated thither until 1661).

[2] S. R. Gardiner, *op. cit.*, IV. 19.

[3] Cf. C. A. Newdigate, *Our Martyrs: a chronological list*, pp. 28 ff.

[4] Cf. C. H. Firth, *O. Cromwell*, p. 362.

[5] H. Cromwell, in J. Thurloe, *State Papers*, ed. T. Birch, IV. 508.

[6] Cf. *Letters of Early Friends*, ed. A. R. Barclay, p. 50; H. Cromwell continues: 'I thinke their principles and practises are not verry consistent with civil government, much less with the discipline of an army': J. Thurloe, *loc. cit.* F. A. Inderwick, *The Interregnum*, p. 286, writing from the legal point of view, describes the Quakers as 'the chief source of trouble to the Commonwealth'.

[7] G. Fox, *Journal*, ed. N. Penney, I. 161, 343.

[8] *Op. cit.*, p. 8; I provide the year-date from the mention of Monck's cashiering of Quakers (cf. p. 132, *inf.*) and of the proposals for a House of Lords. Miss M. E. Hirst, in *The*

Two years later Edward Burrough wrote similarly 'To the English Army, to Officers and Souldiers',

> hew down the Tops, strike at the Branches, make way, that the Ax may be laid to the Root of the Tree, that your Sword, and the Sword of the Lord, may neither leave Root nor Branch of Idolatry, Oppressions and Tyranny . . .[1]

'It is clear that the uncompromising condemnation of war', which soon became a fundamental testimony of the Quakers, 'was not at first deliberately adopted, but was thrust upon them, like their very name, by the hostility of outsiders',[2] the departure of Quakers from the armed forces being not always voluntary but sometimes a cashiering for insubordination, as in 1657 by General Monck.[3] Weingarten's judgement, that *nur für seine Person hat Fox die Theilnahme an den Kriegen der Republik abgelehnt, nicht aber grundsätzlich*, and that for the Quakers as a whole *stand das Recht der Waffen zweifellos fest*[4], may be extreme in point of fact, but very well represents the Protector's view. Even after his death, Quakerism was popular among Lambert's forces in Cheshire.[5] Nor would such links as we have observed between the Fifth Monarchists and the Quakers be hidden from an intelligence service then unparalleled for its efficiency.[6]

Even so, 'apart from the proceedings against James Nayler, there was no special legislation directed against Friends'. 'So far as the central authorities were concerned, it was as persons causing disturbance that the Quakers suffered and not because of their religion.'[7] 'Oliver and his Council ordered the liberation of Friends on several occasions after searching enquiry had been made into the causes of their commitment.'[8] Twice Cromwell sought to release Fox from prison,[9] and the persecution of Nayler was against his will.[10] 'In

Quakers in Peace and War, p. 122, and in *New Appreciations of G. Fox*, p. 116, n. 2, doubts the ascription of this tract to Fox, on the ground of its being signed 'F.G.'; but the ascription was accepted in 1680 by J. Pennyman, *Works* (1703), p. 112, and the signature is found in others of Fox's tracts, e.g. *Concerning Sons and Daughters, and Prophetesses speaking and Prophecying*, and in his high-flown letter to Cromwell which is endorsed by Fox, 'gff to olefer croumull', but is signed 'ff. G. who is of the world called George ffox who A new name hath which the world knowes not' (*Journal*, ed. N. Penney, I. 162). The omission of the tract from Fox's *Works* is significant. The form 'F.G.' is found also in the Swarthmore MSS., as is 'N.J.' for J. Nayler. Cf. Howe's signing a letter 'H.I.' in H. Rogers, *Life of J. Howe*, p. 296.

[1] E. Burrough, *Works*, p. 538.
[2] M. R. Brailsford, *A Quaker from Cromwell's Army: James Nayler*, p. 25.
[3] *Ib.*, p. 19; cf. *Extracts from State Papers relating to Friends*, ed. N. Penney, pp. 14, 27.
[4] H. Weingarten, *Die Revolutionskirchen Englands*, pp. 245, 248.
[5] Cf. P. Henry, *Diaries and Letters*, ed. M. H. Lee, p. 69.
[6] Cf. C. H. Firth, in *D.N.B.*, *s.v.* J. Thurloe. Additional suspicion was caused by the frequent association of the Quakers in the popular mind with the Jesuits (cf. p. 163, *inf.*).
[7] W. C. Braithwaite, in *First Publishers of Truth*, ed. N. Penney, pp. 345, 350.
[8] N. Penney, in his edn. of G. Fox, *Journal*, I. 456.
[9] *Ib.*, I. 168, 237 f.   [10] Cf. *B.Q.*, p. 264.

practice, he was more lenient than the laws.' 'To the great majority of the nation', however, 'even the more limited amount of religious freedom which the laws guaranteed seemed too much.'[1] Consequently, 'much of the suffering during this period was caused by those in local authority, and was not prompted by the central Government'.[2] Even then, the actual amount of imprisonment was relatively small. In 1657 Fox says, 'above twenty hundred have been persecuted and imprisoned within these few years for conscience sake towards the Lord:'.[3] At the close of the Commonwealth, he says, 'there was about 700 freinds in prison' throughout the country.[4] Within a year of the Conventicle Act of 1664, 'there had been over 2100 imprisonments on account of attendance at . . . five meetings'[5] in London alone. The Quakers may then have appreciated more fully than they did at the time Cromwell's efforts towards realizing his ideal of 'the government of the Spirit'. Considering the novelty of the ideal and the shortness of his Protectorate, we are bound to recognize also the remarkable degree to which he succeeded.[6]

---

[1] C. H. Firth, *O. Cromwell*, pp. 367 f.   [2] N. Penney, *loc. cit.*
[3] G. Fox, *To the Councill of Officers* (cf. p. 131, n. 8, *sup.*).
[4] *Id., Journal*, ed. N. Penney, I. 385.   [5] *S.P.Q.*, p. 42.
[6] Cf. also G. F. Nuttall, 'Cromwell's Toleration', in *Transactions* of Congregational Historical Society, XI. 6, pp. 280 foll.

CHAPTER IX

THE LIFE AND FELLOWSHIP OF THE SPIRIT

SYNOPSIS OF ARGUMENT

i. Puritan contrast between 'historical' and justifying faith:
> Baxter, Petto;
> 'God beyond the stars' and Holy Spirit near at
> hand: Dewsbury, Howgill, G. Winstan-
> ley, R. Coppin.

ii. Personal assurance of Holy Spirit's nearness:
> Cromwell, Cradock, Baxter, Petto.
> Ineffability of the experience: Brereley, T. Goodwin.
> Analogy from sense-perception: Sterry, Rous.

iii. Gentleness of 'the voice of the Spirit': Petto, J. Goodwin, Llwyd.
> Duty of not grieving the Spirit: Sibbes, T. Goodwin.

iv. Presence of Holy Spirit the test of 'the fellowship of the Spirit':
> Cradock.
> in others recognized by Holy Spirit in ourselves:
> Cradock, Baxter.
> Analogy from animal instinct: Rous, Llwyd, Cradock.

v. Puritan Christology: Sibbes, Sterry, T. Goodwin.

vi. Puritan mysticism: Cradock, Sterry, Rous, Llwyd.

'If we live in the Spirit, let us also walk in the Spirit' (*Gal.* v. 25).
'grieve not the holy Spirit of God' (*Eph.* iv. 30).

THE excursion into politics, which has been made in the last
chapter, from a modern point of view may seem an irrelevance.
To the Puritan it would not seem so. Indeed, the extent to which
imaginatively we have entered into the Puritans' conviction may be
measured by our ability to see their political life, or at least their
political ideals, in the way they saw these, as springing directly from
the spiritual principle which was central to their faith and experience.
It may assist in our recovery of their conviction, if we turn in again
towards that centre, and observe the way in which, both personally
and socially, the doctrine of the Holy Spirit controlled their devotional
life.

Throughout this study the Puritan movement, in its various phases,
has evinced itself to be a movement towards immediacy in relation
to God. The same fact appears in the contemporary discussion

concerning what was called a merely historical, as opposed to a justifying, faith.[1] Men felt keenly that it was insufficient to believe in the gospel simply as a true story of what happened once long ago. If the gospel were to be powerful and saving, it must be realized as affecting the believer now and particularly: the word must be very nigh, in the mouth and in the heart. In Baxter's words:

> An historical belief, which is true in its kind, . . . you may come to by rational persuasions, without special grace: but not that deep and firm belief, which shall carry over the will effectually to God in Christ, and captivate the whole man into the obedience of his will.[2]

The distinction appears clearly in Petto's exegesis of *Psalm* xxxv. 3, in which he stresses the possessive pronouns thus:

> say *to my soule*, they were internall speakings he prayed for: . . . say *I am thy salvation, i.e.* not onely that he which beleeveth shall be saved, but let me be particularized, *thy* salvation: . . .[3]

Equally, it was insufficient to contemplate and adore God as the Creator, eternal but distant in the heavens. God must be found in direct personal experience, present now by His Holy Spirit in the heart, making men able to say with Job, 'I have heard of thee by the hearing of the ear; but now mine eye seeth thee'.

It is striking to note how frequently the confessions of the spiritual pilgrims who abounded at this time are in these terms of finding God to be no longer far away but close at hand. William Dewsbury, for instance, tells how he used to 'pray to a God I knew not where he was, but expected him without, looking up towards the Firmament . . . but I felt the hand of the Lord within me'.[4] Francis Howgill says similarly, 'I knew not where God was, but in my Imagination imagined a God at a Distance'.[5] Anthony Pearson, again, says, 'All my religion was but the hearing of the ear, the believing and talking of a God and Christ in heaven or a place at a distance, I knew not where,' until he found 'that Lord discovered to be near me that I ignorantly worshipped'.[6]

These three men all became Quakers, and Cotton Mather records that 'the Quakers scoffed at our imagined God beyond the stars';[7]

---

[1] Cf., e.g., J. White, *A Way to the Tree of Life* (1647), vii. (3): 'Of Faith, and the two sorts of faith, Historicall, and Iustifying'.

[2] R. Baxter, *Works*, xx. xxix; cf. G. Fox, *Journal* (1901 edn.) II. 291: 'no man . . . by reading history . . . could declare or know the generation of Christ'.

[3] S. Petto, *The Voyce of the Spirit*, p. 33.   [4] W. Dewsbury, *Testimony*, p. 45.

[5] F. Howgill, *Works*, p. 40.

[6] A. Pearson, in Swarthmore MSS. (Friends House), I. 87 (spelling modernized); quoted inaccurately in *Letters of Early Friends*, ed. A. R. Barclay, p. 10, n.*; for Pearson, cf. *D.N.B.*, *s.v.*

[7] C. Mather, *History of New England*, VII. iv; for Mather, cf. *D.N.B.*, *s.v.*

but this must not be taken to indicate that the perception of this contrast was characteristic of Quakerism only, and not of Puritanism generally. At the time of which they write in the passages quoted, neither Dewsbury nor Howgill were yet radical Puritans: Dewsbury had Presbyterianism, Congregationalism and Anabaptism still to pass through, and Howgill the last two of these states. Moreover, precisely the same perception is to be found in some who did not become Quakers. The Leveller, Gerrard Winstanley, for instance, tells men, 'you do not look for a God now, as formerly you did, to be ⟨in⟩ a place of glory, beyond the sun, moon and stars, nor imagine a divine being you know not where, but you see him ruling within you . . .'[1] The Universalist, Richard Coppin, is another who says of his earliest days, 'I heard of a God afar off, one that lived above the skies'.[2] Coppin, it is true, asserts that even when, later, he was among the Presbyterians, Congregationalists and Baptists, he knew no more than 'that there was a God afar off, and not within me, which I still knew but by hear-say'.[3] There is always a time-lag in all reforms, and doubtless many among the Puritans, especially among the Presbyterians, remained content with the profession of a largely 'notional' religion. We have seen before, however, that the Puritan movement as a whole was a movement away from such complacency; and, though the overwhelming consciousness of the Holy Spirit's nearness was felt by the Quakers to be their own special possession,[4] it is a consciousness which appears at once in any examination of radical Puritan devotion.

Something was said earlier of the mystical core of Cromwell's religion.[5] Certainly Cromwell cannot be understood without an appreciation of his devotional life, with its full assurance of the Holy Spirit's nearness.

> the true knowledge is not literal or speculative, but inward, trans-forming the mind to it. It's uniting to, and participating of, the Divine Nature.
>
> I dare not say, He hideth His face from me. He giveth me to see light in His light.
>
> And in this poor condition I obtain mercy, and sweet consolation through the Spirit . . . His presence hath been amongst us, and by the

---

[1] G. Winstanley, *Works*, ed. G. H. Sabine, p. 44; for Winstanley cf. Professor Sabine's introduction to the volume; the article in *D.N.B.* is inaccurate.

[2] R. Coppin, *Truths Testimony*, p. 10; for Coppin, cf. A. Gordon, in *D.N.B.*, *s.v.*

[3] *Ib.*, p. 12.

[4] Cf. R. Williams, *George Fox Digg'd out of his Burrowes*, ed. J. L. Diman (Narragansett Club Pubs., v), p. 264: 'The Spirit say the Quakers, why thats our Weapon !'.

[5] Cf. p. 115, *sup.*

light of His countenance we have prevailed. . . . we can humbly say, We know in whom we have believed; . . . [1]

'Run aside sometimes from your companie,' wrote Thomas Harrison to Cromwell in 1650, 'and gett a word with the Lord. Why should not you have three or four pretious soules allwaies standing at your ellbow, with whom you might now and then turne into a corner? I have found refreshment and mercie in such a waie.'[2]

One of such 'pretious soules' was Walter Cradock, who eighteen months later wrote to Cromwell of the 'prayer and praises, which sometimes I make my business in a ditch, wood, or under a hey-mow, in your behalfe'.[3] That this was no idle phrase, used in order to curry favour, is indicated by passages in Cradock's sermons, in which he exhorts his hearers to strive after being able to say,

> God hath appeared two hundred times, two thousand times to my soule. I have seene him one while in the Sacrament, I have seen him among the Saints, I have seene him in such a country, in such a condition, in such a place, in such a medow, in such a wood, when I read his word, and called upon his name.

> God may be out of sight, and out of ken, and yet you may be Saints: but there is a more glorious life, when a man always walks in Gods sight, God seeing him, and he seeing God . . . there be Saints that live gloriously, that are fond of God, that are always with him, sleeping and waking, at bed, and board, they are never out of his sight.[4]

This assurance of the Holy Spirit's nearness, in personal communion with the believer, is such a notable feature of Puritan devotion that it may be well to observe it more closely. It is not confined to the radical Puritans, though among them it is more evident. Of Baxter, whose cautiousness with regard to all enthusiasms we have observed, Matthew Sylvester says in his funeral sermon,

> He wondred to hear others speak of their so sensibly Passionately strong Desires to Die, and of their transports of Spirit when sensible of their approaching Death: when as he himself thought he knew as much as they; and had as rational satisfaction as they could have, that his Soul was safe; and yet could never feel their Sensible Consolations.[5]

The honest wonder is typical of Baxter, as is his answer to Sylvester's question, 'Whether much of this was not to be resolved into Bodily Constitution?', that 'He thought it might be so'; but no less typical

---

[1] O. Cromwell, *Letters and Speeches*, ed. T. Carlyle, Letters CXXXII, II, LXXXV.
[2] T. Harrison, in *Original Letters*, ed. J. Nickolls, p. 10.
[3] W. Cradock, *ib.*, p. 85.
[4] *Id.*, *Gospel-Holinesse*, p. 23; *Divine Drops Distilled*, p. 56.
[5] M. Sylvester, *Elisha's Cry after Elijah's God* (printed in *R.B.*, *ad fin.*), p. 15.

is his cry at the end of his long work on *The Reasons of the Christian Religion*:

> Thy presence makes a crowd a church; thy converse maketh a closet, or solitary wood or field, to be kin to the angelical choir.[1]

One further illustration may be provided from the 'Experiences of A. M.', printed by Petto in his *Roses from Sharon*:

> I found immediately an invincible power bearing up my heart, to cast helpe upon one that is mighty, Jesus Christ, and so evidently and certainly, that one should sooner perswade me, that a man which I see and have conference with, is not a man, then that I did not see Christ by faith.[2]

Petto himself elsewhere thus sums up the soul's assurance of its enjoyment of the Holy Spirit's witness:

> The Spirit by a secret touch irresistibly striketh the soule into such cleare, firme, and strong apprehensions and perswasions of its adoption, that . . . it cannot but say, as *Job* 19. 25 I *know*—or as *Romans* 8. 38, *I am perswaded* . . .[3]

As is so often the case with an experience of this type, the inner certitude of the reality of the Holy Spirit's presence was accompanied by a sense of the difficulty of adequately describing the experience, in such a way that others might be convinced of its genuineness and might be helped to enter into the experience for themselves. Roger Brereley, for instance, admits

> Which as I take it on me to expresse it:
> So 'tis most true; I cannot; I confesse it;
> Nor do hereby boast my self to know it,
> But sure I am some of God's Children do it:[4]

Thomas Goodwin uses an historical illustration by way of intimating the difficulty:

> I remember one once said of the late Queen Elizabeth, I have seen her picture, saith he, but I have one picture of her that I will not sell for all the pictures of her in the world. And what was that? I saw her but once, saith he, and the image of her remains still in me; which image he could convey to no man living. . . . Therefore, now, if you ask me what it is the saints know, which another man knows not? I answer you fully, he himself cannot tell you, for it is certain, as to that impression which the Holy Ghost leaves upon the heart of a man, that man can never make

---

[1] R. Baxter, *Works*, xxi. 391.   [2] *Op. cit.*, p. 12.
[3] S. Petto, *The Voyce of the Spirit*, p. 71.   [4] R. Brereley, *Of True Christian Liberty*, p. 15.

the like impression on another; he may describe it to you, but he cannot convey the same image and impression upon the heart of any man else.[1]

It is natural that those who seek to explain their inability adequately to describe the experience should thus fall back on the analogy of sense-perception, the frequency of which in their argument we noted earlier.[2] Peter Sterry makes the following comparison:

> I can no more convey a sense of this difference (between Reason and Spirit) into any soule, that hath not seen these two Lights shining in it self: than I can convey the difference between Salt and Sugar; to him, who hath never tasted sweet or sharp. These things are discerned only by exercise of senses, *Heb.* 5. 14.[3]

In view of Locke's use of 'the relish of that celebrated delicious fruit', the pineapple, in support of his philosophical argument,[4] it is of interest to find Rous using the same illustration:

> after we have tasted those heavenly things whereof we were possessed, from this taste there ariseth a new, but a true, lively, and experimental knowledge of the things so tasted. And indeed this is a knowledge which no art, eloquence or expression of man can teach us. For even in natural fruits there are certain relishes, and, as I may call them, Idaea's and characters of tastes, which nothing but the tast it self can truly represent and shew unto us. The West-Indian Piney cannot be so expressed in words, even by him that hath tasted it, that he can deliver over the true shape and character of that taste to another that hath not tasted it.[5]

Sometimes, as in the passages quoted from Cradock and Thomas Goodwin, the experience is described in visual terms; sometimes, as in those from Sterry and Rous, it is in terms of taste; most frequently, perhaps because of the Hebraic influence upon their minds through Scripture, the Puritans preferred auditory terms. The title of Petto's book, *The Voyce of the Spirit*, is characteristic. In this work Petto says wisely,

> Christians thinke to have assurance all at once, upon a sudden, and are apt to be very much troubled if it commeth not in by the lumpe: whereas the will of God is, to let it in sometimes by little and little; and the soule may be a long time in attaining it.[6]

This recognition that the assurance of God's presence is not bound to be 'by the lumpe' but may be 'by little and little' is not common.

---

[1] T. Goodwin, *Works*, iv. 297.   [2] Cf. pp. 38 ff., *sup.*
[3] P. Sterry, *The Spirits Conviction of Sinne*, p. 24.
[4] Cf. J. Locke, *An Essay Concerning Human Understanding*, ed. A. S. Pringle-Pattison, ii. i. 6; iii. iv. 11.
[5] F. Rous, *Works*, pp. 622 f.   [6] S. Petto, *op. cit.*, p. 20.

Baxter has the judicious remark that 'Education is Gods ordinary way
for the Conveyance of his Grace, and ought no more to be set in
opposition to the Spirit, than the preaching of the Word; . . . the Soul
of a Believer groweth up by degrees'.[1] The more radical Puritans,
however, as we have seen,[2] distrusted education in connexion with
religious experience, preferring to conceive such experience in terms
of the hearing of a voice, which in the nature of the case was more
sudden and momentary.[3]

Petto, nevertheless, is not the only writer who allows that 'the voice
of the Spirit' may not always be 'by such invincible operations as doe
not leave the soule to freedome whether it will owne them or not',
but may sometimes act 'in a more milde, gentle, and secret indiscern-
able way'.[4] John Goodwin, also, says that 'the voice of the Spirit of
God in men, by which he guideth them, is but very soft and low, at
least ordinarily'.[5] Morgan Llwyd, like Whittier after him, refers
to Elijah's experience in 1 *Kings* xix:

> God is not in the earthquake, fire or whirl-winde, nor in wars, blood-
> shed, and carnal animosities, but in the still, small, private voice.[6]

Perhaps the finest expression by any of the Puritans of that experience
which lay at the heart of their religion, the experience of what elsewhere he calls 'the inexpressible voice in the spirit',[7] is the following
sentence from Llwyd: here each phrase is in itself simple and biblical,
but the cumulative effect created is remarkable.

> When the true shepherd speaks, and a man hears him, the heart burns
> within, and the flesh quakes, and the mind lights up like a candle, and
> the conscience ferments like wine in a vessel, and the will bends to the
> truth: and that thin, heavenly, mighty voice raises the dead to life, from
> the grave of himself, to wear the crown, and wondrously renews the
> whole life to live like a lamb of God.[8]

Llwyd's devotion was more mystical than was that of most of his
contemporaries; and to this we shall return. The tenderness, however,
which breathes warmly in such a passage as that just quoted, and
which informs all Llwyd's writing, is a widespread characteristic of
Puritan piety, appearing, for example, in the frequency with which
Puritan authors dwell upon the duty of not grieving the Holy Spirit.
Especially in the writings of Richard Sibbes, the source of so much in

[1] R.B., i. 6 (3).   [2] Cf. pp. 83 ff., *sup.*
[3] The Quaker experience of 'hearing a voice' (cf. e.g., G. Fox, *Journal* (1901 edn.), I. 11;
J. Nayler, *Works*, p. 12; M. Halhead, *Sufferings and Passages* (1690), p. 3; M. Stephenson, in
G. Bishope, *New-England Judged* (1703), p. 132) may be seen thus to be entirely in the tradition.
[4] S. Petto, *op. cit.*, p. 21.   [5] J. Goodwin, Πλήρωμα τὸ πνευματικόν, p. 401.
[6] M. Llwyd, *Gweithiau*, II. 236.   [7] *Ib.*, I. 225.   [8] *Ib.*, I. 219.

Puritan devotion, nor only in his sermons explicitly from *Ephesians* iv. 30, entitled *A Fountain Sealed: . . . Wherein Many things are handled about the Holy Spirit, and grieving of it*,[1] but throughout his works, occur constant exhortations not to grieve God's Spirit.

> There will be a wonderful care not to grieve the Spirit.
> There is nothing in the world so great and sweet a friend that will do us so much good as the Spirit, if we give him entertainment.
> What greater unkindness, yea, treachery, to leave directions of a friend to follow the counsel of an enemy?
> We must take especial heed of slighting any motion, as being the Spirit's messenger.
> let us give him way to come into our souls when he knocks by his motions. . . . Grieve not the Spirit by any means.[2]

Thomas Goodwin is another who repeatedly returns to this text, and who in his exegesis of it uses terms most tender and personal:

> we grieve him when we sin against such a working of his, as wherein, like a father, and as a friend, he gives counsel and direction to the contrary.
> To grieve him is more than to anger him. . . . here, as when a man's wife that lies in his bosom, or his child, shall wrong him; . . . As when a father that is a magistrate, or as one that maintains a student in a college, if either punisheth a child or pupil in his purse, he punisheth himself; so must God afflict himself to afflict you.[3]

One might suppose that a devotion in which the Holy Spirit is thus central, an experience so inexpressible, a concern above all else not to grieve the Spirit within, might lead to a quietistic self-centredness in religion; but this is not so. 'A strong, fond saint takes less care for his owne salvation, but he cares much for the service of Jesus Christ,'[4] says Cradock, a representative of many at this point. There is, in fact, a 'fellowship of the Spirit', the warmth and personal quality of which is a reflection of the spiritual experience shared by, and uniting, its members. Who precisely these members are, may not be always clear; and Cradock wisely warns against spiritual pride and exclusiveness in judging others. With reference to the departure of the rich young man, he comments:

> but many that are first shall be last, and the last shall be first. As if he should say, I would not have you to be proud, and to crow over that poor man that is run from me, because you are old Disciples; it may be

---

[1] Sibbes refers to the Holy Spirit as both 'it' and 'him'; Baxter appears usually to call the Spirit 'it'; Owen always 'him'.
[2] R. Sibbes, *Works*, v. 370, 431, 416, 426; iv. 236.
[3] T. Goodwin, *Works*, vii. 321; iii. 416.   [4] W. Cradock, *Divine Drops Distilled*, p. 59.

that man may come back again to me, and be my best servant when you may run away: for many that are first shall be last, and the last shall be first.

it may be because of my fleshliness I think him to be an heretick or a Schismatick, and it may be he is a Saint, and childe of God, and one of his hidden ones.

And indeed Beloved, I doubt not but that there is many a poore sinner that now follows the ale-house, and drinking, and swearing, and whoreing, that yet may be in Heaven before thee and mee.[1]

At the same time, Cradock never has any doubt that the presence of the Holy Spirit is the only genuine basis and test of 'the fellowship of the Spirit':

O such a one doth great things, he prayes, and hears, and reads, and disputes much: I [ay] but hath he the spirit, or no?

The greatest difference (that I know) in all the Book of God, between Saints and Sinners is, that the one hath the Spirit, and the other hath not.[2]

Then how, it may be asked, is one to know whether a man 'hath the Spirit, or no'? Here also, for all his tenderness towards sinners, Cradock is in no doubt. He turns to the world of nature, where he finds an analogy in animal instinct. In the same way that 'a Saint follows the Holy Ghost with a kinde of sagacity (if I may compare it with reverence) just as we see the Dog follow the Hare: there is something in Nature that the Dog knows which way the Hare went, when a wiser creature knows not', so

a man that hath the spirit may know the spirit in another by the spirit. . . . a man that hath the spirit of God, he can see as clearly as a natural man can with his eyes. How can a poor lamb know the dam among a thousand?[3]

Saltmarsh similarly extends the analogy of sense-perception from the sphere of the soul's perception of God's Spirit in his own heart to its perception of the Spirit in other men:

This Manifestation of Spirit is that in which Spiritual men are known and revealed to each other, and have as full assurance of each other in Spirit and in Truth as men know men by the voice, features, complexions, statures of the outward man.[4]

Nor is this assurance of 'the fellowship of the Spirit' confined to the more enthusiastic type of Puritan. In 1658 Barbara Lambe wrote to Baxter on behalf of her husband,[5] who, on account of his conversion

---

[1] *Ib.*, pp. 138, 91; *Gospel-Holinesse*, p. 175.   [2] *Id.*, *Divine Drops Distilled*, pp. 209, 208.
[3] *Ib.*, pp. 168, 210.   [4] J. Saltmarsh, *Sparkles of Glory*, p. 92.
[5] Cf. A. Gordon, in *D.N.B.*, *s.v.*, T. Lambe.

by Samuel Fisher[1] to the duty of believers' baptism, had separated from the congregation to which John Goodwin ministered, and who now, through Fisher's defection to Quakerism, was in the distress of uncertainty whether or no to return to Goodwin's congregation. The first paragraph of Baxter's reply conveys something of his deeply pastoral nature and explains much of the devotion felt for him; it also expresses admirably this 'fellowship of the Spirit'.

> Dear Mrs. Lambe,
> How true did I feel it in the reading of your Husband's Lines and yours . . ., that unacquaintedness with the Face is no hindrance to the Communion of the Saints: So much of Christ and his Spirit appeared to me in both your Writings, that my Soul in the reading of them was drawn out into as strong a Stream of Love, and closing Unity of Spirit, as almost ever I felt it in my Life. There is a Connaturality of Spirit in the Saints that will work by Sympathy, and by closing uniting Inclinations, through greater Differences and Impediments than the external Act of Baptism: As a Load-Stone will exercise its attractive Force through a Stone Wall. I have an inward Sense in my Soul, that told me so feelingly in the reading of your Lines, that your Husband, and you, and I are one in our dear Lord, that if all the self-conceited Dividers in the World should contradict it on the account of Baptism, I could not believe them.[2]

By such intimate, detailed concern as this with the particular distresses of 'the fellowship of the Spirit' on earth it was that Baxter's passionate faith in 'the communion of saints' in heaven as on earth received its nourishment.

> Still we are centred all in thee,
>   Members, tho' distant, of one Head;
> In the same Family we be,
>   By the same Faith and Spirit led.

> Before Thy Throne we daily meet
>   As joynt-Petitioners to thee;
> In spirit we each other greet,
>   And shall again each other see.[3]

Baxter's illustration of the 'Connaturality of Spirit in the Saints' from a 'Load-stone', still more Cradock's pointing to animal instinct as an analogue for spiritual experience—'How can a poor lamb know the dam among a thousand?'—is characteristic of the Puritans, who

---

[1] Cf. *D.N.B.*, *s.v.*   [2] *R.B.*, App. III, p. 54.
[3] R. Baxter, *Poetical Fragments* (1699 edn.), p. 41.

allowed a considerable place in their thought to natural theology in this sense. Rous, for instance, argues:

> We see in natural things, how joyfully the young ones run to their Dams, yea, children with earnestness apply themselves to the brests of their mothers. Surely, Man hath but one true and very Father, but one true Cause and Creator; and how joyfully should Man run to this his Original, how earnestly should he suck from God by prayer, the nourishment and increase of that spiritual life, which himself hath begotten in us?
>
> The young Lamb knows her Dam by that instinct, and notion, which neither it, nor we, can understand or express. How much more should those that are begotten by God, own God for their Father, by a secret acknowledgment and ⟨y⟩earning?[1]

Llwyd has the same illustration in a passage in which, once more, he refers to 'the voice of the Spirit':

> How do you discern the voice of the Holy Spirit from the others? Do you not know that a little lamb can discern its own mother's voice from a hundred others?[2]

Cradock himself, perhaps, refers more frequently than any other Puritan writer to 'something in Nature': 'for the creatures are Gods Characters'.[3] In his *Divine Drops Distilled* there is a long passage[4] in which he says that 'grace is like the springing of the sea; or the springing of the year . . . (for we should learn something from the creatures)':

> So it is in experience, in the beginning the Lord makes a Saint glad of a Primrose, of a little turning of the water, that the flood, that the stream, is turned; if he begin to hear the word, that hated it, and to rejoyce in the company of good neighbours, that hated it, two or three little Primroses . . .
>
> Didst thou ever see a Dog (let me instance in that vile creature) (for God would have us learn from the creatures, and God hath cast them so that they should not be onely for our use, but every thing in reference to his Gospel, that we may not only occasionally draw such things that hap hazard fall out, but to observe their nature and qualities, and learn somewhat from them) . . .[5]

It may be asked whether the readiness in Puritan piety thus to see the workings of God's Spirit in natural as well as supernatural spheres

---

[1] F. Rous, *Works*, pp. 61 f., 597.   [2] M. Llwyd, *Gweithiau*, I. 218 f.
[3] W. Cradock, *op. cit.*, p. 36.
[4] This passage, the simple, sustained rhythms of which are not unworthy of comparison with the swayings and swellings of Donne's prose, is quoted *in extenso* in *Transactions* of Congregational Historical Society, XXII. 1, pp. 20 f.
[5] *Op. cit.*, pp. 45 f. (45 is numbered 39 in error).

affected Puritan Christology, in weakening the sense of uniqueness in the revelation of God through Christ. Through going 'as far as mortals could go in removing intermediaries between God and man: the church, the priest, the magical sacraments, the saints and the Virgin', the Puritans, Professor Perry Miller has said, 'even minimized the rôle of the Savior in their glorification of the sovereignty of the Father'.[1] The last phrase sufficiently indicates that Professor Miller is thinking here primarily of the more conservative Puritans, upon whom Calvin's influence was strong. In more radical circles, also, a result somewhat similar followed from the emphasis on the doctrine of the Holy Spirit. There is truth in Troeltsch's words, despite their exaggerated expression, that 'spiritual religion' in general 'feels no need of the doctrine of the Atonement', that 'forgiveness of sins recedes into the background, and it is replaced by a direct experience of God and actual victory over sin . . .'.[2] The fact that the centre of reference in Puritan piety was the Holy Spirit was thus bound to have effect upon Puritan Christology.

Puritan writers refer frequently to the fact that Jesus' earthly life was in closest dependence upon God's Spirit. Sibbes, for instance, quotes 'I will put my Spirit upon him' as 'the qualification of Christ for his calling', and says 'Whatsoever Christ did as man, he did by the Spirit'. 'When he entered upon his calling, he had more of the Spirit'; for 'without God and the work of the Spirit, not man, not an angel, not Christ himself, can work upon an obstinate stubborn soul'.[3] Sterry, similarly, asks the Long Parliament, 'Can You be able to rule over any spot of this earth; when Jesus Christ was not fit for the government of the whole: without the Spirit?'.[4] The Holy Spirit, Sibbes points out further, 'is the bond of union between Christ and us'.[5] Thomas Goodwin also asserts, 'Now for the manner of the indwelling of the Holy Ghost's person; it is no error to affirm that it is the same in us and the man Christ Jesus'.[6] 'The difference betwixt his being in Christ and us', says Sibbes, 'is, that the Spirit dwells in Christ in a fuller measure . . .';[7] therefore,

> The more the free grace and love of God in Christ alone is made known to the church, the more Spirit there is; and again back again,

---

[1] P. Miller, *The New England Mind: the seventeenth century*, p. 45.
[2] E. Troeltsch, *op. cit.*, II. 747 f.
[3] R. Sibbes, *Works*, I. 15, 17; v. 239; IV. 384. Cf. L. Muggleton, *Spiritual Epistles*, p. 488: 'this is to be minded, that Christ never did any miracle till after the descending of the Holy Ghost upon him, then it was he received his commission from Heaven . . .'.
[4] P. Sterry, *The Spirits Conviction of Sinne*, Epistle Dedicatory; quoted on p. 121, *sup*.
[5] R. Sibbes, *Works*, I. 17.   [6] T. Goodwin, *Works*, VI. 66.
[7] R. Sibbes, *Works*, v. 413.

K

the more Spirit the more knowledge of Christ; for there is a reciprocal going of these two, the knowledge of Christ and the Spirit.[1]

It will be seen that those who held an adoptionist Christology of this type would be likely to conceive salvation in terms of communion rather than of atonement, if these words may be used in their secondary, not their etymological, sense. Sibbes says,

> The Holy Ghost is the substantial vigour of all creatures whatsoever.
> Every creature hath a beam of God's glory in it. The whole world is a theatre of the glory of God.[2]

At the same time, there is no inclination to weaken insistence upon the unique quality of the workings of God's Spirit in Christ, and through Christ in men's hearts. 'Something in Nature' may have 'reference to his Gospel' but can never go beyond it. 'Those things which are written in the book of nature do not cross anything written in the Scripture'.[3] Puritan piety admits no attempt to seek communion with God's Spirit except as within the bounds of the revelation through Christ.

Sibbes' words, 'the whole world is a theatre of the glory of God', might be a paraphrase from the *Itinerarium Mentis ad Deum* of St. Bonaventure; and there is not a little in Puritan writers with the unmistakable marks of mysticism. Mysticism is a word used loosely and therefore abused. Here, there is meant by it a sense of being carried out beyond the things of time and space into unity with the infinite and eternal, in which the soul is filled with a deep consciousness of love and peace, a unity so intimate as to make erotic terms the most natural on which to draw. Puritan mysticism is a field still almost entirely unexplored. Many might doubt or deny its existence, even its possibility, and not without a degree of justification. Within Christianity at least, the mystic worships normally in an atmosphere of rich symbolism; the Puritans preferred plainness in worship and a stern independence of creaturely aids. Again, the mystic commonly has a highly developed imagination, which he uses as a ladder wherewith to ascend to God; the Puritans checked 'the imaginations of their hearts'[4] on the same ground that they repudiated images,

---

[1] *Ib.*, iv. 214 f.   [2] *Ib.*, iv. 213, 241.

[3] J. Goodwin, Πλήρωμα τὸ πνευματικόν, p. 478.

[4] In the seventeenth century *imagination* meant what we now call *fancy*, generally fancy of an evil kind. This appears from an analysis of the word's associations in Shakespeare and the Authorized Version, and from reference to Burton's *Anatomy of Melancholy* (cf. index, *s.v.* 'Imagination, what'); cf. the use of the word in passages quoted on p. 135, *sup.* Professor H. J. C. Grierson, *Two Dutch Poets*, p. 5, remarks 'the comparative absence . . . of the transfiguring, idealizing work of the imagination' in seventeenth-century Dutch art. The word owes its redemption largely to Coleridge.

namely, that they were a dishonour to God, Who was beyond imagining, and that they too easily became a barrier between God and the soul. Thirdly, although many of the greatest mystics were men and women of action, the mystical experience *per se* is one of yielding to that which takes possession; the Puritans kept an active and firm control of their personalities, allowing small place for relaxation or passivity. For each of these reasons, Puritan mysticism might seem almost a contradiction in terms. Yet, in a piety which was essentially a movement towards immediacy in communion with God, it would be strange if mysticism were to find no place. In point of fact, it is evident that the type of experience defined was keenly desired and gladly welcomed by at least the more radical among the Puritans.

Thus Cradock says,

> I remember, in such a Countrey, in such a Chamber, in such a place, where God shew'd himself to me, & I was satisfied; I saw every thing vanish before me, and I desired nothing but that . . .[1]

Nor does he suggest that this was an experience in any way private or unusual:

> when a man's ways please God, the stones of the street shall be at peace with him. . . . that is, he shall be at peace with every thing. Why so? because there is an infinite, unspeakable quiet in his own soul.

For

> a Saint . . . can say, I cannot tell what shall become of England, or Scotland, or Ireland, but I am sure I know a back door that leads me into a Kingdom that cannot be shaken, to go into the middle Region, where no storms of the Air shall trouble me; and there I can rest my spirit.[2]

Similarly, Rous says of the soul,

> Let her often go out of the body, yea out of the world by heavenly contemplations; and treading on the top of the earth with the bottom of her feet, stretch herself up, to look over the world, into that upper world, where her treasure, her joy, her beloved dwelleth.[3]

This passage, as also that quoted earlier from Rous about the 'endless circle of tasting, loving, and knowing, which grows still greater, the more we round it',[4] comes from a work actually entitled *The Mystical Marriage, or Experimental Discoveries of the heavenly Marriage between a Soul and her Saviour.* Rous was Provost of Eton,

---

[1] W. Cradock, *Gospel-Holinesse*, pp. 36 f.   [2] *Id., Divine Drops Distilled*, pp. 197, 19.
[3] F. Rous, *Works*, p. 726; for George Fox's frequent use of 'the top' and 'looking over', cf. Q.S.M., pp. 40 ff.
[4] *Ib.*, p. 624; quoted on p. 40, *sup.*

and his references to Pseudo-Dionysius, St. Bernard of Clairvaux and Gerson suggest a consciousness of mystical tradition greater than that of other Puritan writers; but, from the constant output of Puritan sermons and commentaries on the *Song of Songs*[1], the idea of such a 'marriage' was before men's minds, and the use of erotic terms in description of the soul's state when enjoying 'the life of the Spirit' is not infrequent. Sterry, for instance, expresses himself thus:

> You have seen how a Sugar-loafe dissolves, and weeps it selfe away, when it is dipt in wine. So hearts dissolve, so they melt, dip't in the sweet sense of Divine Love.[2]

Cradock, once more, says:

> As they say of love, one that is in love, sees nothing with her eyes, nor hears nothing with her ears but love; so a Saint that is fond of God, bring him meat, he sees the love of God in Christ in it; bring him cloathes, or any thing, his eyes is fastened more upon the love of God in Christ, then upon the thing.[3]

Of all the radical Puritans, the writer who is most consciously and consistently mystical in his language is Morgan Llwyd. Llwyd is in a somewhat different category from other writers, both because he was strongly under the influence of Boehme, two of whose works he translated into Welsh,[4] and because of his devotion to Wales and the Welsh. The Celtic element present in radical Puritanism is very noticeable, Cradock and Erbury being born in Wales and Rous being a Cornishman, while Owen was 'of an old Welsh family',[5] Roger Williams has a suggestively Celtic surname, Cromwell had distant Welsh ancestry, and Baxter came from the Welsh Marches; but no other leading Puritan save Vavasor Powell spent practically his whole life[6] in Wales as did Llwyd, whose Welsh writings are considered to-day a fountain-head of the modern language at its purest. Whatever weight may be attributed either to Boehme's influence or to Welsh tradition and feeling,[7] Llwyd expressed his conviction that the doctrine of the Holy Spirit was primary in language deeply mystical, in which metaphor follows metaphor in profusion. The

[1] E.g., *An Exposition on the whole Book of Solomon's Songs* (1652), by J. Robotham, for whom cf. p. 36, *sup.*

[2] P. Sterry, *op. cit.*, p. 19.   [3] W. Cradock, *op. cit.*, p. 60 (numbered 52 in error).

[4] Cf. p. 16, n. 5, *sup.*   [5] *D.N.B., s.v.*

[6] Llwyd was in England with the parliamentary forces for a short period, during part of which he lodged (cf. T. Edwards, *Gangraena*, iii. 62) with Giles Calvert the chief publisher of radical Puritan and Quaker works and the publisher of some of Boehme's works, who himself at least once attended a Quaker meeting (cf. 'Giles Calvert's Publishing Career', in *Journal of Friends' Historical Society*, xxxv. 45).

[7] Cf. 'Anthropos' in his edn. of Llwyd's *Llyfr y tri Aderyn*, p. 13: 'his mysticism is a part of himself. His thoughts have a Welsh mould, not a German'.

following passage, like many earlier quotations, is from his *Llyfr y tri Aderyn*, a discussion between three birds, of which the dove represents that 'life of the Spirit' which Llwyd owned himself:

> Dove: But if a man will deny himself and follow the Lamb, the New Birth, and endure to the end, and be saved, let him not extinguish the light which is in his conscience, but blow it till it shine, and let him follow the light of God, and the morning star within, and the sun will rise brightly upon him.
>
> Eagle: What is that morning star?
>
> Dove: The certainty of knowledge, the pledge of the Spirit, the sure eye of faith, the earnest of perfection, Jehovah's seal, and the witness of the three in one, the anchor of the soul, and all this happens when a man in the light knows the love of God towards him, in him, and through him, in might and a wondrous peace.[1]

In another discussion by Llwyd, written in English, between Goodman Past, Goodman Present and Goodman Future, Goodman Past says:

> Rulers, look no more too much out at your windows upon Time, and the flowers and motions of time, but look in upon Eternity in your own chamber, that ye may come to the ground of all things, and of your selves.[2]

Mystical language such as this is to be found throughout Llwyd's writing, always within the bounds of an emphasis upon the Holy Spirit. Indeed, if no Puritan is more mystical, it may be said also that no Puritan is more imbued with this emphasis. In the *Llyfr y tri Aderyn* the dove says:

> no church but the spiritual, no spirit but the second Adam, no temple of God but the pure thought of man, no enduring temple for man but the Almighty, and the Lamb, no unity but the unity of the Everlasting Spirit, no singing, no communion, no union, no praying, no membership in any Church, but when the Spirit of the Head rules in might.[3]

Mr. E. Lewis Evans justly comments: 'The Quakers did not teach more plainly, or ever go further, than this.[4]' Why, then, did Llwyd not eventually became a Quaker? and what was it which, despite the frequent similarities which we have observed between other radical Puritans and the Quakers, made the Quakers a people apart? In our final chapter we turn to a consideration of the contra-distinguishing character of Quakerism.

---

[1] M. Llwyd, *Gweithiau*, I. 221.   [2] *Ib.*, II. 239.   [3] *Ib.*, I. 207.
[4] E. Lewis Evans, *M. Llwyd*, p. 82; for a brief analysis of Llwyd's mysticism, cf. ch. v (*Cyfriniaeth*).

CHAPTER X

THE SPIRIT IN EVERY MAN

SYNOPSIS OF ARGUMENT

i. Much in Quakerism a carrying forward of developments in radical
   Puritanism.
   The case of Morgan Llwyd.
ii. Four important points of disagreement between Puritanism and
    Quakerism:
    (a) the relation between the Spirit and reason;
    (b) the relation between the Spirit and the Word of God in Scripture;
    (c) whether spiritual revelations and inspirations were extraordinary
        and had ceased, or ordinary and continued;
    (d) whether the Spirit gave intellectual infallibility and moral per-
        fectibility.
iii. Fundamental Quaker conviction that the Spirit is in every man.
     Fox's use of *seed*.
     Genesis iii. 15 primary in Fox's thought: identification of 'the seed of
     the woman' with Christ.
     Effect of this on Quaker theology.
iv. Puritan objection to Quaker teaching that the Spirit of Christ
    (a) was in Old Testament characters;
    (b) is in the heathen;
    (c) is in sinners.
v. Quaker conviction condemned by Puritans as unsound in reference
   to Christ: universalist.
   Discussion of *John* i. 9.
   Puritan association of Quakers with Papists.
vi. Quaker concern to 'answer that of God in every man' issued in Quaker
    testimonies against war, personal retaliation, capital punishment,
    oaths, flattering speech, 'hat-honour'.
    Quaker meeting for worship;
                         business.

'The spirit of man is the candle of the Lord' (*Proverbs* xx. 27).
'the true Light, which lighteth every man that cometh into the world'
(*John* i. 9).

THROUGHOUT this study it has appeared constantly that
Quakerism grew, as all movements of men's spirits must grow,
out of the soil and climate of the time. We have seen how much in

Quaker conviction was in line with the current interest in the doctrine of the Holy Spirit; was but the carrying forward of a development already well advanced within radical Puritanism; was an emphasis, a fusing and a systematization of beliefs which had appeared earlier but which had then been more hesitant, sporadic and unrelated. Yet throughout the second half of the seventeenth century, more particularly during the decade 1650–60, the Quakers and the Puritans counted each other their bitterest opponents; and, although in a time of fierce controversy disputes over minor matters often rage with a fury out of proportion to their importance, it is clear that there was something in Quakerism which was genuinely contrary to the Puritans', even to the radical Puritans', beliefs and which excited their keenest antipathy. In this final chapter we attempt an analysis of this specific, contradistinguishing character of Quakerism. By way of recapitulating first the marks of Quakerism which were not without precedent in radical Puritanism, we may attend more closely to the case of the Puritan whose position most nearly approximated to that of the Quakers: Morgan Llwyd.

The first certain expression by Llwyd of interest in Quakerism can be placed as early as 1652, for in that year Fox wrote to him a letter[1] which implies that Llwyd had written to him already. The correspondence preceded the venture which Fox records thus:

> And there was a preist att Rexam in Wales one ffloyde: hee sent two of his preachers Into ye north to try us & see what a manner of people wee was . . . & one of y^m stands a fine minister for Christ to this day: one John appe John: . . .[2]

This expedition is mentioned by Fox during his account for the year 1653. The year-date is confirmed, as Mr. E. Lewis Evans has observed, in an account by John ap John, in which he says:

> the 21 day of the 5 month 1673. this tim 20 years Agooe was ye tim that J John ap John was At Swart Moore with Gorge ffoox in Lankashire, it was ye ffurst tim y^t I soa Go ffox.[3]

Later in the same year Fox wrote 'To the people of Hexam [i.e. Wrexham] in Wales',[4] and a return visit was paid by 'Richard Hubberthorne and John Lawson, both of Lancashire, . . . haueing a testimony to beare for ye Lord', who 'were not received'.[5] There is

[1] Cf. H. J. Cadbury, *Annual Catalogue of G. Fox's Papers*, p. 37, no. 6, 95 A.
[2] G. Fox, *Journal*, ed. N. Penney, I. 141; partly quoted on p. 99, *sup.*
[3] J. ap. John, memorandum, printed in W. G. Norris, *John ap John*, p. 6, with facsimile.
[4] Cf. H. J. Cadbury, *op. cit.*, p. 45, no. 22, 13 A. The importance of Wrexham at this time is shown by its choice for the centre of the whole area (Wales, Shropshire and Herefordshire) controlled by James Berry as Major-General.
[5] *First Publishers of Truth*, ed. N. Penney, p. 17. For Hubberthorne and Lawson, cf. *D.N.B.*, *s.v.* Hubberthorn; E. Brockbank, *R. Hubberthorne*.

a detailed account of their visit in a letter by Lawson among the Swarthmore MSS., in which he relates that 'Richard had something given him to speak to the priest who was much strucken . . . the priest was silent . . . the priest sat sobin'.[1] Whatever emotional effect Hubberthorne's testimony may have had upon Llwyd, it did not 'convince' him. In 1657 Fox himself 'came Into Rexam att night: where many of Floydes people came to us: but very rude & wilde & ayry they were & litle sense of truth they had yett there was some convinct in ye tounde';[2] but, again, Llwyd was not among these last-mentioned.

Phrases in Llwyd's *Llyfr y tri Aderyn*, which appeared in the former year, 1653, have been supposed to bear antagonistic reference to the Quakers, but without justification. The sarcastic question, concerning the Pope, 'Is he among the quakers? Why is he quaking?',[3] is admittedly startling; but it may be noted that in the original edition, as reprinted in Llwyd's *Gweithiau*, the word is 'quakers' (*crynwyr*), not 'Quakers' (*Crynwyr*)[4], and that the verb 'quake' (*crynnu*) is used in a passage quoted earlier,[5] in which the effect of the presence of the Holy Spirit is described, without suspicion of reference to the Quakers. Other phrases, such as 'new lights', 'doctrine deep, strange and abstruse', and 'the deaf and dumb, foaming, bewitching and astonishing the simple',[6] have been assumed to refer to Quakerism,[7] but probably wrongly.[8] *Llygadtynnu* here may with greater propriety refer to 'John Robins' Witchcraft spirit';[9] and *goleuni newydd* we have seen to be a catchword of the time, the phrase actually being used of Llwyd's own congregation at Wrexham.[10]

The very fact that these phrases are antagonistic makes it unlikely that Llwyd had Quakerism in mind, for the passages in his letters which without doubt refer to Quakerism are by no means hostile. In 1656 he wrote to Baxter, 'You condemne the generation of the Quakers. If I were intimate with you I might better aske why?' Later in the same year he wrote, again to Baxter, 'Neither shall men

---

[1] J. Lawson in Swarthmore MSS. IV. 66; it is quoted, not quite correctly, by E. L. Evans, *M. Llwyd*, p. 72.

[2] G. Fox, *Journal*, ed. N. Penney, I. 284 f.   [3] M. Llwyd, *Gweithiau*, I. 176.

[4] 'Anthropos', in his edn. of Llwyd's *Llyfr y tri Aderyn*, p. 32, erroneously prints *Crynwyr*; L. J. Parry, in his translation of this work in *Transactions of National Eisteddfod of Wales for 1896* (1898), p. 207, and J. E. Southall, 'Morgan Llwyd and his Times', in *Friends' Quarterly Examiner*, LIII. 31, also erroneously print *Quakers*.

[5] Cf. p. 140, *sup.*   [6] M. Llwyd, *Gweithiau*, I. 250 (*bis*), 263.

[7] Cf. T. Richards, *Religious Developments in Wales, 1654–1662*, p. 243.

[8] Cf. E. L. Evans, *op. cit.*, p. 81.

[9] Cf. L. Muggleton, *Spiritual Epistles*, p. 57; quoted on p. 44, n. 6, *sup.*

[10] Cf. p. 51, *sup.*

agree in God, till the fleshly mind (that perks up in man's heart to judge of God's mind) bee mortifyed. (And in that the Quakers say well as I thinke.)' In 1658 to his mother, who had inquired his opinion of the Quakers, he wrote the wise but tantalizing words, 'They say the truth, but not the whole truth'.[1] These three explicit references in Llwyd's letters provide evidence of his genuine interest in Quakerism, and the evidence is borne out by the general tone of his writings.

There is no need to pause over superficial similarities, such as his use of numbers in place of the pagan names of the days and months. This was a commonplace in radical Puritanism, from Barrow onwards. Passages such as 'but we do not read that he ever took a text from the Bible, except once from Isaiah . . .', 'They write their sermons, but only for reward from men . . .' and 'We know that ordinaunces pure, are in themselves but dry'[2] are more remarkable. They might certainly be expected from a Quaker, in whose armoury they found a regular place,[3] rather than from a 'hireling' minister, who continued to preach from texts and to observe the ordinances. The *rapprochement*, however, was on a deeper level than this. The two following passages from his *Llyfr y tri Aderyn* indicate how completely Llwyd shared the most radical convictions.

> Eagle: When does a man's prayer reach God's bosom?
> Dove: When God's Spirit groans (without adulteration) in a man.
> . . .
> Dove: . . . Immanuel, God with us in our flesh.
> Eagle: What is that? Is he in *our* flesh?
> Dove: He is, if we are in *his* Spirit.[4]

The parenthesis 'without adulteration' (*yn ddigymmysg*) in the first

[1] *Ib.*, II. 271, 274, 269, partly quoted on p. 41, n. 6, *sup.*; for the last phrase in another context, cf. II. 218.
[2] *Ib.*, I. 186, 190, 16 (quoted on p. 112, *sup.*).
[3] Objection to preaching for hire and from texts, and to the observation of the ordinances, is expressed in the queries presented by the Quakers in different parts of the country: cf. e.g., R. Baxter, *The Quakers Catechism* (1655), pp. 21, 23; J. Parnell, *Goliah's Head Cut off with his own Sword* (1655), pp. 30, 46 (the first of two so numbered), 44 (the second of two so numbered); *An Answer to a Book which Samuel Eaton Put up to the Parliament . . . And he cals the Title of his Book Quakers Confuted* (1654), pp. 21, 26; *Some Quaeries to be answered in Writing or in Print, by the Masters, Heads, Fellows, and Tutors of the Collegde they are setting up at Durham* (⟨1657⟩), pp. 8 f., 14; R. Sherlock, *The Quakers Wilde Questions* (1656), pp. 2 f.; T. M⟨orford⟩, *XX. Queries Propounded to George Long, High Priest of Bathe, and Priest Sangers of London*, printed in his *The Deceit and Enmity of the Priests, Manifested* (1659; but note postscript: 'This Book should have been printed long ago'), pp. 34 f. A collation and analysis of these and other queries, which thus appeared at much the same time in Durham, Lancashire, Cheshire, Worcestershire, Huntingdonshire and Somerset and elsewhere (cf. *Certain Quaeries and Antiquaeries concerning the Quakers (so called) in and about Yorkshire* (1653)), is much to be desired.
[4] M. Llwyd, *Gweithiau*, I. 222, 202.

passage, and the emphatic final 'our' (*ni*) in the Eagle's reply in the second, are noteworthy here. Even more significant is Llwyd's constant exhortation to look within:

> . . . look in upon Eternity in your own chamber, that ye may come to the ground of all things, and of your selves.
>
> whilst some expect fountains of waters to spring from afar upon them, I desire to find (not notionally, and after the flesh), a spring in us the hope of glory, (the flowers in our own gardens, the hope of Summer,) . . .
>
> And there is a book within every man . . .
>
> And there are some others (miserable creatures) who seek a God afar off, and also cry for him outside, not seeing that there is a spring and a root within, seeking to burst forth and grow through them. For he is with every man, however evil he be, lighting every man that comes into the world . . .[1]

This last sentence is the most remarkable of all. In the words 'however evil he be' (*er cynddrwg yw*) it may be said to include the primary differentia of Quakerism.

In the analysis of the differences between Quakerism and Puritanism the greatest care is imperative. Out of the mass of anti-Quaker literature which was produced,[2] we may pay attention to works by two writers whom continually we have found to be judicious and with some understanding of enthusiasms which they could not altogether share: Baxter and Owen. Baxter wrote *The Quakers Catechism* in 1655 and *One Sheet against the Quakers* in 1657; Owen wrote *Pro Sacris Scripturis Adversus hujus temporis Fanaticos* in 1658. Even here it is necessary to disregard things in Quakerism to which these writers took objection, but which from our more detached position we can see to have been in no way genuine characteristics of the new movement. Baxter complains, for instance, of the use by the Quakers of coarse and intemperate language:

> they have called me Dog and Devil, and abundance of such names . . .
> Nay I have had more railing language from one of them in one letter, then I ever heard from all the scolds in the Countrey to my remembrance this twenty years.[3]

Such *argumenta ad hominem* must be counted out of court; and, although according to their own principles they should have refrained

---

[1] *Ib.*, II. 239, 261; I. 186, 227, partly quoted on pp. 86, n. 4, *sup*. For other references by Llwyd to flowers and gardens, cf. *ib.*, I. 24; II. 239, 274.

[2] As early as 1659 Fox replies in *The Great Mistery of the Great Whore* to 110 anti-Quaker works.

[3] R. Baxter, *One Sheet against the Quakers*, pp. 5, 4; cf. *eund.*, *The Quakers Catechism*, pp. 1 f., 29; cf. p. 27, n. 3, *sup*.

from abuse, the Quakers had no monopoly of it. All enthusiastic movements tend towards violent and unbridled language in their beginnings, and Quaker examples of this, however regrettable, were not specifically Quaker.

Nor is it desirable to lay emphasis on the obvious external differences in worship which existed, or even on the Quaker disuse of the ordinances. These were real differences and aroused keen and vocal opposition; but, apart from the fact that much in radical Puritanism was in sympathy with Quaker practice, these differences are clearly but the expression of something deeper and more theological. Four points which are frequently under dispute, all relating to the doctrine of the Holy Spirit, come nearer to the fundamental difference, although none of them is identical with it. These four points concern:

(*a*) The relation between the Holy Spirit and reason.

(*b*) The relation between the Holy Spirit and the Word of God in Scripture. These two points may be associated in the one larger problem of 'the discerning of spirits' and of the criterion by which to judge.

(*c*) The question whether spiritual revelations and inspirations had been an extraordinary dispensation and had ceased, or had been an ordinary dispensation and still continued. A possible position was that they had recurred, because the present age was an extraordinary, and perhaps the last, age.

(*d*) The question whether or no the presence and guidance of the Holy Spirit involved intellectual infallibility and moral perfectibility.

Each of these points has received considerable attention already in its own place in the development of the argument.[1] The first point troubled a divine so eminently rational as Baxter, who was confident that it was 'our duty to study and meditate continually day and night', and who entirely repudiated any suggestion that 'the Spirit excluded Reason';[2] but we have seen a deep suspicion of 'fleshly reason' in many Puritans more radical than Baxter who yet never became Quakers: 'a thief within is the reasoning of man,' says Llwyd, 'which locks the door of every mind against the waft of the Holy Spirit'.[3]

The second point, concerning the relation between the Spirit and the Word, went deeper. Here there was a real difference, evident, for

---

[1] For the first point, cf. ch. II; for the second, cf. ch. I; for the third, cf. ch. VII; for the fourth, cf. ch. III; for Quaker worship and disuse of the ordinances, cf. chh. IV–VI.
[2] R. Baxter, *The Quakers Catechism*, pp. 20, 22.   [3] M. Llwyd, *Gweithiau*, I. 190.

example, in Fox's remark when summing up the argument for women ministers:

> And if there was no Scripture for our Men and Womens meetings, Christ is sufficient.[1]

Over this point, however, there was considerable misunderstanding. The Puritans accused the Quakers of setting up the Spirit *against* the Word. The Quakers replied that they were not guilty of such a charge, because they possessed the *same* Spirit as inspired those who gave forth the Word. Consequently, the attempts made to treat this point in isolation could meet with no success. Conviction with regard to it depended upon the position taken over the third point, whether the New Testament dispensation of the Spirit was ordinary or extraordinary, and could, or could not, be repeated for contemporaries.

On the conservative Puritan assumption that the New Testament dispensation was extraordinary, Quaker teaching about the relation of the Spirit and the Word was clearly erroneous; but, since the Quakers held that dispensation to be ordinary, it was necessary for the Puritans to attack this conviction, if their teaching about the Spirit and the Word was to be shown to be false. Owen says plainly,

> *Argumentum ideo nostrum primum ita se habet: si Revelatio voluntatis divinae in Scripturis facta, ita sit perfecta, integra atque omnibus numeris absoluta . . .*[2]

Consequently, he ridicules the Quaker claim to be θεοπνεύστοι. To this the Quaker Samuel Fisher retorts, ironically picking up Owen's argument:

> the Canon is compleated, the Standard sealed, no immediate motion now, no such mission as the Prophets had now, no speaking by divine inspiration now, no extraordinary infallible guidance of men by the infallible Spirit of God now . . .
>
> As if there were none at all now, nor ever to be any more while the world stands (because your selves are not so) any such, as were heretofore ἀναμαρτήτοι, θεοπνεύστοι φερόμενοι ὑπὸ πνεύματος ἁγίου ἅγιοι Θεοῦ ἄνθρωποι . . .
>
> Let not J.O. in any wise say so, for there are yet (though himselfe is none of them) 7000 of the people of Christ in England . . . many of

---

[1] G. Fox, *Epistles*, p. 388; quoted on p. 89, *sup.*

[2] J. Owen, *op. cit.*, p. 78; for the Quaker claim to the continuation of 'revelation', cf. R. Baxter, *The Quakers Catechism*, p. 12; J. Parnell, *Goliahs Head Cut off*, p. 15; *Some Quaeries to be answered*, p. 9.

whom . . . have . . . the promises thereof made good unto them concerning the gift of the holy Spirit of the Lord . . .[1]

This matter was scarcely patient of logical resolution: to state position and counterposition was all that was possible.

The Quaker argument here involved the fourth point, for the claim was made, as by Fisher, to possess 'infallible guidance' and to be ἀναμαρτήτοι.[2] This claim was especially obnoxious to Baxter, whose natural modesty led him to regard it as no more than spiritual pride.[3] 'I have no such Infallibility,' he says, and

> Can that man that hath one spark of grace believe that he hath no sin? Can he have so little knowledge of himself? For my part, I am one that is sick and have need of the Physician.[4]

To this the Quaker reply may be given in Fox's words:

> then did ye Preistes Roare up for Sinne in their pullpitts, & preach up sin y^t people said never was ye like hearde. Itt was all their workes to plead for itt . . .
> And soe when professors came to mee to dispute & discourse I shold feele y^m before they came to plead for sin & imperfection, & I asked them whether they beleived? & they said yes, y^n I asked y^m: In whome? & they said, In Christ, & I said to y^m: if you beleive you are past from Death to Life, & soe from ye sinne y^t bringeth Death & they saide they beleived noe such thinge y^t any could bee free from sin while upon ye earth.[5]

'Pleading for sin' seems a strange phrase to apply to Christian ministers of any persuasion, but it was almost a technical term in the controversial vocabulary of Fox,[6] who believed that he had come into a newness of life in which he had dominion over sin.

This dispute over sin brings us to what was the fundamental difference between the Quakers and the Puritans, the difference which arose over Quaker conviction that the Holy Spirit was in every man. 'That every man was enlightened by the divine light of Christ'[7] was regarded by Fox, as we have seen, as a primary 'opening'. Sometimes, as here, Fox uses the term *light*. This we have seen to be a commonplace in radical Puritanism.[8] Sometimes he uses the term *seed*. This

---

[1] S. Fisher, *Rusticus ad Academicos*, iv. 2, 11, 3.

[2] For this claim, cf. R. Baxter, *op. cit.*, pp. 10, 24; J. Parnell, *op. cit.*, pp. 8, 51; R. Sherlock, *The Quakers Wilde Questions*, p. 2; T. M⟨orford⟩, *XX Queries*, p. 36; *An Answer to a Book*, pp. 12, 18; *Some Quaeries to be answered*, p. 9.

[3] Cf. F. J. Powicke, 'Richard Baxter and the Quakers', in *Friends' Quarterly Examiner*, LIII. 193.

[4] R. Baxter, *op. cit.*, pp. 10, 29.   [5] G. Fox, *Journal*, ed. N. Penney, I. 2 f.

[6] Cf. G. Fox, *Journal*, ed. N. Penney, I. 188, and index, *s.v.*, to *Journal* (1901 edn.) and to *Gospel-Truth Demonstrated*.

[7] *Ibid.*, (1901 edn.), I. 34; quoted on p. 52, *sup.*   [8] Cf. p. 40, *sup.*

image likewise is not confined to Quaker apologetic. It is used continually by Rous, for instance; by Saltmarsh, who says, 'that by which the people of God, or all true Christians, are born, is the seed of God, or Word of God, or the divine nature of Jesus Christ, or the Spirit of God . . .';[1] and by Muggleton, for whom 'Reason is the seed or nature of the Devil; Faith the seed or nature of God'.[2] To say that 'Fox is very fond of what might be called a garden symbolism of regeneration',[3] still more to connect his terminology with his country background, is beside the point. The parable of the Sower was much in men's thoughts in the seventeenth century,[4] and *seed* is a natural metaphor for those interested in spiritual birth or new creation. So far, there is force in the suggestion that 'The metaphor seems to show how Fox wished to express his consciousness that, whether in the individual soul or in the community, the Divine immanence involves a process of living and organic growth'.[5] As the same writer, however, has urged, 'Fox was no theologian trained to analyse, to explain in scientific terms these great realities of which he was conscious'.[6] What lies behind his references to the seed, in fact, is not primarily the parable of the Sower or 'organic growth' at all; it is the passage in *Genesis* iii. 15, where it is said that enmity will be put between the seed of the serpent and the seed of the woman, and that the seed of the woman will bruise the head of the serpent. This passage was primary in Fox's thought, and to it he constantly returns. In 1654 he addresses Friends, 'All freinds every where know ye seed of god which bruseth ye seed of ye serpent . . .'. In 1657 he tells Rice Jones, the 'proud Quaker',[7] 'it was the serpent in him, that had . . . done hurt' and bids him wait 'in the fear of God, for the Seed of the woman, Christ Jesus, to bruise the serpent's head in him'. In 1673 the subject forms the staple of his first vocal ministry in worship on his return from America. In 1678 he still exhorts Friends, 'O, keep all in this Seed . . . for . . . In this Seed all nations, and ye, are blessed, which bruiseth the head of the seed that brought the curse . . .'.[8]

---

[1] J. Saltmarsh, *Sparkles of Glory*, p. 55.
[2] Cf. A. Gordon, *The Origin of the Muggletonians*, (cf. *sup.*), p. 275.
[3] R. H. King, *George Fox and the Light Within*, p. 76.
[4] *The Parable of the Sower and of the Seed*, by Thomas Taylor the Puritan (cf. *D.N.B.*, *s.v.*; he is to be distinguished from Thomas Taylor the Quaker, for whom cf. p. 178, n. 10, *inf.*), first published in 1621, appeared in a third edition in 1634 and was translated into Dutch.
[5] T. E. Harvey, *The Rise of the Quakers*, p. 139.
[6] *Id.*, introd. to G. Fox, *Journal*, ed. N. Penney, i. xxv.   [7] Cf. p. 17, *sup.*
[8] G. Fox, *Journal*, ed. N. Penney, i. 142; 1901 edn., i. 416; ed. N. Penney, ii. 259 foll.; 1901 edn., ii. 335; cf. *eund.*, *Gospel-Truth Demonstrated*, pp. 904 f., and the titles of two tracts, W. Dewsbury, *The Discovery of the great enmity of the Serpent against the seed of the Woman*

The fact that this passage which was primary in Fox's thought was not from the New Testament but from *Genesis*, had an effect on early Quaker theology. Fox is careful always to give the passage a Christian reference, by identifying 'the seed of the woman' with Christ. In this very identification, however, he so 'telescopes' the divine processes of creation and redemption as inevitably to reduce the significance for redemption of the coming of Christ and His Holy Spirit in history. Since 'the seed of the serpent' is the evil principle which has been in man from the beginning, Christ and His Holy Spirit, as identified with 'the seed of the woman', has been in man equally from the beginning, and is now in every man. It was this conclusion, which the Quakers did not hesitate to draw, which to the Puritans was abhorrent. Without possessing the much more recent interest in the historical details of Jesus' life, the Puritans allowed full value to His life, death and resurrection, and to the coming of His Holy Spirit at Pentecost, as dividing history into two parts through the provision of a possibility of redemption which previously had not existed. This sense of a Christian watershed in history was lacking in Quaker conviction. As Professor H. G. Wood has said with reference to Penn's *Christian Quaker* rather later, it 'lacked . . . an adequate conception of the *history* of salvation'.[1]

That the seed, light or spirit was in every man was, then, the contra-distinguishing Quaker principle; and in 'every man' were included both those who lived in Old Testament days before Christ came, and those who have lived since He came and who live now, both heathen and sinners. About each of these three groups Fox is quite clear. In his work entitled *The Heathens Divinity, Set upon the Heads of all called Christians, That say they had not known that there had been a God or a Christ, unless the Scriptures had declared it unto them*, Fox enumerates persons in the Bible in whom the Spirit of God was at work 'without Scripture'. Apart from a developed Logos Christology such as was held by Penn and Barclay rather than by Fox, it is not easy to see how the Old Testament characters mentioned can be said to illustrate the knowledge 'without Scripture' of *Christ*, which the title leads the reader to expect, and which is the point at issue. It would appear that Fox relied on such a strained, but at that time universal, interpretation as is implied in his question, 'Was it not a

(1655) and J. Whitehead, *The Enmity between the Two Seeds* (1655). 'What is the Serpents head that must be bruised?' was part of the seventeenth query addressed to Baxter: cf. R. Baxter, *op. cit.*, p. 13; cf. also *Some Quaeries to be answered*, p. 8.

[1] H. G. Wood, 'William Penn's *Christian Quaker*', in *Children of Light*, ed. H. H. Brinton, p. 23; Professor Wood adds, 'I think we Friends still lack it'.

Divine Principle in Nebuchadnezzar that caused him to utter these words . . . "One was like the Son of God" ?'.[1] In the New Testament Fox mentions Cornelius;[2] but he seems not to have paid adequate attention to the cardinal word in Baxter's fifteenth counter-query, 'had Co⟨r⟩nelius sufficient light within him before Peter preached to him?',[3] which is *sufficient*.[4]

With regard to the contemporary heathen, Baxter's fourteenth counter-query runs similarly:

> Is not he a Pagan and no Christian that thinks that the light which is in all the Indians, Americans, and other Pagans on earth, is sufficient without Scripture?[5]

In his reply to Baxter in *The Great Mistery of the Great Whore*, Fox passes this query by. In reply to other opponents who asked a similar question, Fox says,

> 'the light which doth enlighten every man that cometh into the world', by whom the world was made, was before natural conscience was, or natural light either, or the blurr'd light as thou cals it; And many of the Indians do shew forth more in their conversations of the light then you do;[6]

The genuineness of his conviction here is shown in letters which he wrote to Quakers in captivity among the heathen, exhorting the Quakers to

> get the Turks and Moors Language, that you might be the more inabled to direct them to the Grace and Spirit of God in them, which they have from God, in their Hearts.[7]

Moreover, that the Quakers found nothing in this conviction incompatible with work among the heathen is indicated by the extraordinary fervour and extent of their missionary activity abroad in the first generation.[8] By 1660 they had already visited 'Germany, America, and many other islands and places, as Florence, Mantua, Palatine, Tuscany, Italy, Rome, Turkey, Jerusalem, France, Geneva,

---

[1] G. Fox, *Gospel-Truth Demonstrated*, p. 332; Fox can hardly be blamed for an interpretation of *bar ᵉlahîn* in *Dan.* iii. 25 which the translators of the Authorized Version presumably shared and intended to convey. For another mention by Fox of Nebuchadnezzar, cf. *ib.*, p. 532.
[2] Cf. *ib.*, p. 335.   [3] R. Baxter, *op. cit.*, p. 30.
[4] Cf. H. G. Wood, in *op. cit.*, p. 18: 'We are faced with a strange paradox. The light within is at once sufficient and insufficient'.
[5] R. Baxter, *loc. cit.*   [6] *Op. cit.*, p. 185; cf. p. 262.
[7] G. Fox, *Epistles*, p. 493; cf. pp. 455, 477, 503.
[8] Cf. *B.Q.*, ch. xvi, 'Work beyond seas'. The missionary fervour Baxter shared; cf. *R.B.*, i. 213 (23): 'No part of my Prayers are so deeply serious, as that for the Conversion of the Infidel and Ungodly World. . . . '

Norway, Barbadoes, Bermuda, Antigua, Jamaica, Surinam, New-foundland'.[1]

That the Spirit of Christ was also in the third group mentioned, that 'wicked men had ye spiritt of God'[2] was to the Puritans the worst of Quaker blasphemies. Neave Brayshaw justly describes Fox's conviction that it was a duty to 'answer that of God in every man' as 'one of the dominating thoughts of . . . his life'.[3] He did not apply the principle universally. In those who were supposed, by himself as well as by others, to be witches,[4] he seems to have made no attempt to appeal to 'that of God'. To many others besides witches he did not always practise what he preached—'Love gives noe names'.[5] At the same time, even his use on occasion of virulent language and aggressive behaviour can be seen to imply no abandonment of the root-principle. On one occasion he begins a letter, 'To ye light in thy conscience I speake y^u child of ye devill', and continues, 'to ye light in conscience I doe speake which will . . . let y^{ee} see y^t y^u art as a beast'.[6] On another occasion, while on his trial, after perceiving that the judge was contemplating sharp practice against him, Fox says, in revealing phrase, 'I looked him in ye fface, & ye Witnes started up in him, & Made him blush . . .'.[7] These two illustrations, which could easily be multiplied, are more convincing evidence of his fundamental belief that 'wicked men had ye spiritt' than any arguments *ad hoc* could be.[8] To the Puritan way of thinking, however, the belief was so foreign that Puritan controvertists appear to stop short at the Quaker teaching that the Spirit of Christ was in Old Testament characters and in the heathen. Perhaps they regarded the further Quaker teaching that the Spirit was in sinners as but the natural concomitant of the Quaker claim to freedom from sin in themselves through the Spirit, a claim which the Puritans considered sufficiently blasphemous and dealt with in its own place. The connexion between the two positions on either side may be expressed thus. The Puritans held that the Holy Spirit indwells only the converted, and them incompletely (some would add, metaphorically), and does not

---

[1] *Letters of Early Friends*, ed. A. R. Barclay, p. 286, n.* (the passage quoted is printed on p. 292).
[2] G. Fox, *Journal*, ed. N. Penney, II. 63.
[3] Q.S.M., p. 54; references to 80 instances of Fox's use of this phrase are printed, *ibid.*, n. 3.
[4] Cf. G. Fox, *Journal*, ed. N. Penney, index, *s.v.* Witchcraft: A. M. Gummere, *Witchcraft and Quakerism.*
[5] G. Fox, *Journal*, ed. N. Penney, II. 59.
[6] *Ib.*, I. 90; 'yee' and 'yu' are abbreviations for 'thee' and 'thou'.   [7] *Ib.*, II. 77.
[8] From this belief sprang very soon the Quaker testimony against war, that Christians must behave towards all men redemptively, in the way '*the most likely* to reach to the inward witness' which is in every man, however sinful, 'and so change the evil mind into the right mind': Q.S.M., p. 131; cf. p. 164, *inf.*

L

indwell the unconverted at all.[1] The Quakers held that the Holy Spirit indwells all men, the converted completely and the unconverted incompletely.

To the Puritans the Quaker position was thus faulty, as allowing sufficient importance neither to the reality of sin nor to the redemption from sin achieved through Christ at a certain point in history: ἠγοράσθητε γὰρ τιμῆς. Hence Thomas Goodwin's remark that 'the very notion of the Quakers' was 'that which in those days the Pelagians held'.[2] Hence Owen's assurance that one need only 'Convince any of them of the Doctrine of the Trinity, and all the rest of their Imaginations vanish into Smoak'.[3] Hence the phrase which Ralph Farmer prints after his name on the title-page of his anti-Quaker tract, *The Great Mysteries of Godlinesse and Ungodlinesse*: 'a Servant of that Jesus Christ that was crucified at Jerusalem above sixteen hundred years ago'. Fox attributed 'the slaunder raised upon us yᵗ ye Quakers shoulde deny Christ yᵗ dyed & suffered att Jerusalem: which was all utterly false: & never ye least thought of it in our heartes'[4] to the malice of Rice Jones: but, although we have recognized Fox's Christocentric and ethical criterion, it must be allowed that the 'slaunder' had deeper causes than personal antipathies. Even to Baxter it seemed that the Quakers 'deny that there is any such Person as Jesus Christ who suffered at Jerusalem . . . and only call somewhat within themselves by the Name of Christ',[5] speaking 'allegorically and equivocally when they mention his name and nature'.[6]

In addition to this general objection, there was the further inevitable abhorrence of the Quaker position felt by those whose theology was Calvinist. To the Quaker assertion *Lumen illud omnibus aeque inesse mortalibus*, Owen, for instance, replies that *Christus nulla sub consideratione lumen salutare omnibus & singulis hominibus indulsit.*[7] In this connexion the number of converts to early Quakerism from among the *General* Baptists may be observed.[8]

In an argument quoted earlier, Fox referred in defence to *John* i. 9, and Owen remarks, *Nihil crebrius in ore habent, quam verba illa de*

---

[1] J. Goodwin, Πλήρωμα τὸ πνευματικόν, pp. 24 f., is exceptional; cf. further pp. 174 f., *inf*.

[2] T. Goodwin, *Works*, IV. 344; partly quoted on p. 38, *sup*.

[3] J. Owen, Πνευματολογία, I. iii. 4; cf. J. W. Graham, *The Divinity in Man*, p. 256: 'You could not make a Trinity nor even a Duality out of his [i.e. Fox's] teaching. Friends have always followed him in this, and have never accepted the Trinitarian formula'.

[4] G. Fox, *Journal*, ed. N. Penney, I. 11.

[5] R. Baxter, *op. cit.*, p. 30.

[6] *Id.*, *One Sheet against the Quakers*, p. 3; cf. J. W. Graham, *op. cit.*, p. 251: 'George Fox never offers any explanation of the relation between the historic Jesus and the Inward Christ'.

[7] J. Owen, *Pro Sacris Scripturis*, pp. 5, 104.   [8] Cf. p. 13, n. 7, *sup*.

Christo, Ioh. 1. 9.[1] Owen himself points out that *Christus dicitur lux hominum, non lux illa quae est in hominibus,* and that *Non dicitur Christum illuminare omnem hominem venientem in mundum, sed quod ipse veniens in mundum omnem hominem illuminat.* He then asserts the true interpretation of the verse to be:

> *filius Dei, aeternus λόγος, φῶς aeternum,in mundum veniens . . . vitam &*
> *immortalitatem . . . in lucem produxit, perque Evangelium innotescere fecit; atque*
> *insuper Spiritum sanctum . . . emisit, ad quosvis homines ex iis qui natura*
> *tenebrae erant illuminandos . . .*[2]

Baxter, who had no Calvinist axe to grind, answers the Quaker query, 'Whether Christ enlighteneth every one that cometh into the world?', not by reducing *omnes* to *quosvis . . . illuminandos,* but by interpreting *mundum* in a double sense:

> Yea, he doth so; All that come into the world of nature, he enlighteneth with the light of Nature . . .; And all that come into the world of grace he enlighteneth with the light of supernatural Revelation.[3]

With such a distinction as this Fox had no patience and to it he makes no further reply than to denounce Baxter as 'ignorant of Johns doctrine, and the Scriptures; a man not fit to teach . . .'.[4]

In the passage quoted above, Baxter continues, 'we cannot be ignorant who are your Teachers', and refers to the Jesuits. This aspersion was made frequently. To-day it seems strange; but, although in point of fact there was no connexion whatever between the Quakers and the Jesuits, it was less beside the point than might be thought. What Baxter had in mind appears in the three following passages:

> We know how earnestly the Jesuites would perswade us . . . that by the good use of natural light men may certainly get supernatural; and that it is in mens own power, what light soever they have to improve it to salvation.
>
> we hear the croakings of your Papist guides in that word [*Infallible;*] that's the pillar of their Kingdom, and the master-point of their New Religion, That their Church is infallible.
>
> The Papists make the Scripture a dead letter, no sufficient Rule of faith, or Judge of Controversies; and so do they [i.e. the Quakers].[5]

---

[1] J. Owen, *op. cit.,* p. 112; for the Quaker query, 'Whether Christ enlighteneth every one that cometh into the world?', cf. R. Baxter, *The Quakers Catechism,* p. 7; J. Parnell, *op. cit.,* p. 51; T. M⟨orford⟩, *op. cit.,* p. 34; *Some Quaeries to be answered,* p. 9.
[2] *Ib.,* pp. 113 f., following St. Augustine: cf. *Patrologia Latina,* ed. J.-P. Migne, t. 40, c. 280.
[3] R. Baxter, *op. cit.,* p. 7.
[4] G. Fox, *The Great Mistery of the Great Whore,* p. 28.
[5] R. Baxter, *op. cit.,* pp. 8 f.

We may also recall Mucklow's charge:
    What difference is there in these things between George Fox and the
Papists? the one saith, No Liberty out of the Church; the other saith,
No Liberty out of the Power . . .[1]

In the popular mind Quakerism was associated with Roman Catholi-
cism, less for theological or ecclesiastical reasons than because of the
Quakers' refusal to take the oath abjuring papal authority and the
doctrine of transubstantiation.[2] It is curious that in these ways the
Quakers, who, in giving more emphasis to the doctrine of the Holy
Spirit than it had ever received before, represented 'the fag-end of
Reformation',[3] should have been thought to return, in effect, to the
Roman Catholic position, against which the whole impetus of the
Reformation had been in revolt.

The Quaker principle of 'the Spirit in every man' issued in various
'testimonies' which, though their negative expression entailed misunderstanding and persecution, rested upon the positive duty of
'answering that of God in every man'. As early as 1650, Fox says,

    they woulde have had mee to bee Captaine off y^m to goe foorth to
    Worcester fight & ye souldyers cryed they woulde have none butt mee:
    . . . Butt I tolde y^m I lived in ye virtue of y^t life & power y^t tooke away
    ye occasion off all warrs . . .[4]

We have seen that the testimony against war was not immediately
adopted by all Quakers;[5] but in 1660, when explicitly asked whether
Friends might join a new regiment of militia-foot, Fox 'forbad,
and said it was contrary to our principles, for our weapons are
spiritual and not carnal'.[6]

Fox's refusal to retaliate (except with his tongue) is evident throughout his life. Two striking examples may be given, each instinct with
his conviction that the Holy Spirit was even in those who maltreated
him. In 1652

    I stoode uppe againe in ye eternall power of God & stretched out my
    armes amongst y^m all & saide againe with a loude voice strike againe[7]
    heere is my armes my head & my cheekes: . . . & I was in ye love of
    God to y^m all y^t had persecuted mee.

[1] ⟨W. Mucklow,⟩ *The Spirit of the Hat*, p. 12; quoted on p. 46, *sup.*
[2] Cf. W. C. Braithwaite, in *First Publishers of Truth*, ed. N. Penney, p. 346.
[3] R. H., *The Character of a Quaker*, p. 1; quoted on p. 13, *sup.*
[4] G. Fox, *Journal*, ed. N. Penney, I. 11 f.
[5] Cf. p. 131, *sup.*   [6] Cf. *B.Q.*, p. 462.
[7] Cf. J. Rogers, *Jegar Sahadvtha*, printed in E. Rogers, *Life & Opinions of a Fifth-Monarchy-Man*, pp. 235, 265; 'strike on'.

In 1660 he said to another persecutor

> heere is Gospell for thee heere is my haire & heere is my cheeke & heere is my shouldors & turned it to him . . . & ye truth came soe over him y^t hee grew loveinge: . . .[1]

The fully conscious testimony against capital punishment arose only later, but Fox himself says that 'puttinge men to death for Catle & for money . . . for such small thinges . . . was . . . contrary to ye law of God'.[2] His concern for the life of every man, because for the Spirit in every man, appears also in his testimony in Cornwall against the custom of plundering shipwrecks, 'not regarding to save the men's lives': 'endeavour to preserve their lives, and their goods for them; for that shows a spirit of compassion, and the spirit of a Christian'.[3]

The same concern to 'answer that of God in every man' issued in the testimonies against oaths, flattering speech and 'hat-honour', as opposed to the prevailing perjury, deceit and insincerity. These testimonies, as also those mentioned earlier, the Quakers defended with Scriptural references, especially to the Sermon on the Mount.[4] They were also in intentional neglect of 'those differences in rank and position which amount to nothing in the sight of God'.[5] The use of 'thou' and 'thee' Fox further sought to defend on grammatical grounds in 'quite the most curious book sent out by the early Quakers',[6] *A Battle-Door for Teachers & Professors to learn Singular & Plural*. The primary purpose, however, was to appeal to 'the Spirit in every man'. Seeing that men 'profess Love and Friendship to one another, and with the same Mouth wish ill one to another, and one destroy another', Fox urged that, on the contrary, 'Plainness and Truth, and Uprightness, and Honesty may come to rule in People . . . that the Witness of God in all may arise . . .'.[7] Merchants and traders Fox exhorted in similar language; and though at first

> the people were shy of them, and would not trade with them; so that for a time some Friends could hardly get money enough to buy bread . . . afterwards, when people came to have experience of Friends' honesty and faithfulness and found that their yea was yea and their nay was nay, . . .

---

[1] G. Fox, *Journal*, ed. N. Penney, I. 58; II. 4. The use in the second passage of 'Gospell' in this context is indicative of its ethical connotation for Fox.
[2] *Ib.*, I. 13.   [3] *Id., Journal* (1901 edn.), I. 459.
[4] For this as in the tradition of the sect-type, cf. E. Troeltsch, *op. cit.*, I. 332.
[5] *B.Q.*, p. 495; on the especial relevance of 'hat-honour', cf. *ib.*, pp. 493 ff.; *P.G.F.*, pp. 117 ff.
[6] N. Penney, in his edn. of G. Fox, *Journal*, II. 379; cf. *B.Q.*, pp. 496 ff.
[7] G. Fox, *Gospel-Truth Demonstrated*, p. 107.

the lives and conversations of Friends did preach, and reached to the witness of God in the people.[1]

The same concern is to be seen, once more, in the procedure followed in Quaker meetings for business. Here, the practice of obtaining a majority by counting votes was considered spiritually injurious and was not observed. It was replaced by an attempt to discover 'the sense of the meeting' as a whole, in tender 'willingness to *wait* and *persuade* until a large measure of spiritual unity is reached'.[2] Edward Burrough thus finely expresses the ideal:

> to hear and consider, and if possible to determine the same in justice and truth, not in the way of the world, as a worldly assembly of men, by hot contests, by seeking to outspeak and over-reach one another in discourse as if it were controversy between party and party . . .; not deciding affairs by the greater vote, or the number of men, as the world, who have not the wisdom and power of God; . . . But in the wisdom, love and fellowship of God, in gravity, patience, meekness, in unity and concord, submitting one to another in lowliness of heart, and in the holy Spirit of truth and righteousness, . . . by hearing and determining every matter coming before you, in love, coolness, gentleness, and dear unity; I say, as one only party, all for the Truth of Christ, and for the carrying on the work of the Lord, and assisting one another in whatsoever ability God hath given; and to determine of things by a general mutual concord, in assenting together as one man in the spirit of truth and equity, and by the authority thereof.[3]

We may recall Dr. Sippell's judgement that *das Quäkertum ist in erster Linie Zeugnis; es ist der in Permanenz erklärte Gewissensappell an alle Menschen.*[4] It is so, because its contradistinguishing character is this fundamental and far-reaching faith in 'the Spirit in every man'.

---

[1] *Id., Journal* (1901 edn.), I. 186.
[2] *Q.S.M.*, p. 168; cf. L. Richards, *Planning for Freedom*, pp. 46f., on this procedure, in which, with 'a deeply religious impulse as its operative motive', 'personal initiative is . . . combined with group authority in a living and creative fellowship'. The *procedure* was one observed in Dutch politics: cf. G. J. Renier, *The Dutch Nation*, p. 21; for the *motive* cf. also p. 6, n. 8, *sup.*
[3] E. Burrough, in *Letters of Early Friends*, ed. A. R. Barclay, p. 305.
[4] T. Sippell, *Werdendes Quäkertum*, p. 109; quoted on p. 42, *sup.*

CRITICAL CONCLUSION[1]

IN a historical study it is imperative to allow the characters so far as possible to speak for themselves, within the ambit of their own age, interests and experience, and not to introduce extraneous comments,

[1] Cf. G. F. Nuttall, 'Towards a Theology of the Holy Spirit', in *Congregational Quarterly*, Oct. 1944.

similarities or contrasts from the detachment of another century. 'A vision or an idea is not to be judged by its value for us, but by its value to the man who had it.'[1] In any case, the writer's personal interpretation will be expressed sufficiently in his selection and arrangement of the material on which he works. Accordingly, in the foregoing pages an attempt has been made to present 'The Holy Spirit in Puritan Faith and Experience' fairly and objectively, as a study in historical theology, with sympathetic understanding but without independent criticism. The question has not been asked where the Puritans were right, and where they were wrong, in the implications for their lives which they believed the doctrine of the Holy Spirit to possess; nor has judgement been pronounced upon the issue between the Puritans and the Quakers. At the same time, it would seem not altogether adequate to leave those implications and that issue 'in the air', as if entirely without relevance to present concerns. Provided that the historical presentation is kept distinct from the succeeding judgement, nothing is lost by attempting in conclusion to pronounce such judgement. Even then, it remains desirable not to confuse two separate judgements. There is the judgement on past conviction still as within its own period, in which certain perceptions now attained had not yet risen above time's horizon. There is also the judgement on that conviction in the light of any such additional later insights.

Of these later insights it is clearly impossible entirely to divest oneself; nor is it to be desired. It is, in fact, these insights which make it possible to write history of value, such history as reveals much of men's minds which was hidden from themselves, such history as yields a sense of the whole towards which, unwittingly, the partial and (for the present) conflicting convictions of men are often travelling. In the fifteenth century, for instance, the rationalism of Bishop Pecock and the biblicism of the Lollards are opposed.[2] In the sixteenth century the same tendencies on a larger scale combine in Renaissance and Reformation and together break the unity of the Middle Ages, substituting a different unity therefor. In the same way, it may prove possible for the conflicting convictions of Puritans and Quakers eventually to be embraced in a new unity; and it is historical judgement which perceives this as a possibility, even though the way to the realization of such a unity be not yet clear.

In the last chapter, for example, in the dispute over sin, it is imposs-

---

[1] F. M. Powicke, *S. Langton*, p. 161.
[2] Cf. G. F. Nuttall, 'Bishop Pecock and the Lollard Movement', in *Transactions* of Congregational Historical Society, XIII. 2, pp. 82 foll.

ible not to feel now how much truth was present on both sides. Baxter, with his 'need of the Physician', has more insight into men's hearts and, personally, more humility and saintliness as well as more reasonableness. Yet Fox's enthusiastic assurance of triumph over sin through the Holy Spirit equally represents something without which Christian experience would be shorn of a major glory. To combine such a consciousness of triumph over sin with a consciousness of continuing sinfulness, although logically it may seem impossible, is not impossible psychologically, if one may judge by St. Paul's experience; but it is rare. One of the insights which we have gained is that our minds, being individual and finite, cannot at the same time see all the varying aspects of 'the truth as it is in Jesus'. We perceive also that our experience must be allowed to be influenced considerably by differences of temperament and education. In already perceiving this Baxter was exceptional:

> I must say that our different Educations, I doubt not, is a great cause of our different sentiments. Had I never been a Pastor, nor lived out of a Colledg . . . I might have thought as you do. And had you converst with as many Country people as I have done, and such, I think you would have thought as I do.[1]

It is such an admission as this which inspires confidence in Baxter's judgement; and it is consonant with it that, although multitudes sought his advice on all manner of subjects, he formed no party but kept a position of his own which was so central as at the time to seem eccentric.

The skill in pastoral psychology for which Baxter was famed appears also in his perception of the nature of the apprehension of the Holy Spirit in its more ordinary forms. The line which his argument follows is this:

> Doth the Spirit work on a man as on a beast or a stone? and cause you to speak as a clock that striketh it knoweth not what; or play on man's soul, as on an instrument of music that hath neither knowledge of the melody, nor any pleasure in it? No, the Spirit of God supposeth nature, and worketh on man as man; by exciting your own understanding and will to do their parts.[2]

Baxter is right in this insistence that God's Spirit 'worketh on man as man', on the whole man, and primarily by the normal activities of man's reason and conscience. One danger of an emphasis upon the doctrine of the Holy Spirit is that the abnormal in man may be

---

[1] R. Baxter, *An Answer to Mr Dodwell and Dr Sherlocke*, p. 93.
[2] *Id., Works*, IV. 226.

exaggerated at the expense of the normal. For this there is, unfortunately, abundant precedent in the Old Testament, in which the Spirit 'strikes', 'beats', 'falls suddenly on' or 'breaks in upon'[1] a man, in a way violent and at first non-moral, quite of a piece with the manner in which in early Quakerism 'the power' comes on men in Meeting and makes them quake. Even in the New Testament the Pentecostal experiences are still notably abnormal. It is to St. Paul that we owe it, not only that the Holy Spirit is equated with Christ and so personalized, ethicized and (from our point of view[2]) spiritualized, but that the Spirit's activity through the understanding and conscience is placed on a higher level than is such an abnormal activity as 'speaking with tongues'.[3]

At the same time, we accept to-day the distinction between intuition and discursive reason, and allow the necessity of intuition in the mental activities of a complete personality. Consequently, we understand the radical Puritan and Quaker suspicion of 'notions' and 'fleshly reason', and their preference for 'openings' and 'experiences', in which *ogni dimostrazion mi pare ottusa*.[4] Baxter erred in rejecting such modes of apprehension of the Holy Spirit.

> The Holy Spirit assisteth us in our hearing, reading, and studying the Scriptures, that we may come, by diligence, to the true understanding of it; but doth not give us that understanding, without hearing, reading, or study.
>
> the Spirit worketh not on the will but by the reason: he moveth not a man as a beast or stone, to do a thing he knoweth not why, but by illumination giveth him the soundest reason for the doing of it.[5]

This was to go too far. This may be indeed 'that way of ordinary illumination'; but the extraordinary way remains, the way which St. Paul took when he went 'bound in the Spirit unto Jerusalem, not knowing the things that shall befall me there'. Without such reliance upon the leadings of the Spirit, going far out beyond the findings or confirmations of discursive reason, Christianity might never have reached Europe; and in reviving the practice of such reliance the

---

[1] In representing all these activities by the mild expression 'come upon', the Authorized Version is inadequate, and appears to have misled Dr. Edwyn Bevan, *Symbolism amd Belief*, pp. 174 f.

[2] In the Old Testament *rûaḥ* is always *stofflich vorgestellt* (cf. H. Gunkel, *Die Wirkungen des heiligen Geistes*, p. 45). It is so still in Islam, a fact which creates one of the major difficulties in the attainment of understanding between Christianity and Islam (cf. L. Levonian, *Studies in the Relationship between Islam and Christianity*, pp. 19 f.).

[3] The almost complete absence of 'speaking with tongues' in Quakerism, as also of remarks upon its absence by opponents of Quakerism, is worthy of note.

[4] Dante, *Paradiso*, XXIV. 96; quoted on p. 37, n. 6, *sup.*

[5] R. Baxter, *Works*, II. 104; IV. 295; quoted on p. 47, *sup.*

Quakers, whose own missionary activity we noticed, did a real service to the Church. The more intuitive way may remain the extraordinary way. We may also hold that it was more open to 'persons of the acutely responsive type' such as those with whom 'the Commonwealth period abounded'[1] than it is to Christians at the present day. That is no reason for excluding it, or even for failing to recognize that, just because it is extraordinary, it is often the way in any age for those whose spirits are the most delicately attuned to God's Spirit and whose influence upon other Christians is consequently most filled with blessing.

Our recognition of the place of intuition in mental activity also assists us in appreciating the movement towards immediacy in communion with God, which expresses itself throughout Puritanism. At the same time, we should no longer use the Puritans' illustrations. We have abandoned the '*naïve* realism' which prevailed in the epistemology of Locke's century. The analogy of the immediacy of sense-perception no longer carries conviction; we have become more aware of the extent to which all sense-perception is saturated with, and conditioned by, interpretative activity. We should turn for analogy less to perception of objects and more to aesthetic apprehension. The Puritans, through the exaggeration in Roman Catholicism of the sensuous aspect of worship, tended largely to neglect the aesthetic element in man's mental constitution. We are free to accept its importance, and to study its relation to intellectual intuition. There is an unreflective, undifferentiating immediacy in the apprehension of beauty which is not present in ratiocination, and there is something of the same immediacy in the apprehension of the Holy Spirit. The latter may be said to bear to the former much the same relation as reverence bears to wonder. This may be taken as an indication that it is more distinctively personal.

The concept of personality is a late-comer into theology. It could not be elaborated explicitly in Scripture, because it is partly dependent upon Hellenic influences which then were not yet felt; but the doctrine of the Holy Spirit is a doctrine of a personal God, revealed in a Person and present in personal relationship with persons. The mediaeval tendency, following Aristotle, to treat God as an *ens* rather than as a Person inevitably resulted in neglect of the doctrine of the Holy Spirit; and the Puritan emphasis on the doctrine was, equally, in part on account of the rediscovery of God as a Person. In philosophy, more especially in ethics, few recent concepts have proved more

---

[1] R. M. Jones, introd. to *B.Q.*, p. xxvii.

fruitful than the concept of personality. It is the more curious that theology should be loth to give primary place in its own discipline to what has thus unobtrusively fertilized much outside. A theology based on the doctrine of the Holy Spirit would start from faith in God as at least not less than personal, as not abstract, ideal or a principle of coherence or perfection, as not 'it' but 'he' (if not always 'thou'). In all its elaborations it would keep firmly to the personal level, allowing no impersonal or subpersonal relations, whether between God and Christ or between God and man.

Our general acceptance of the concept of personality implies our recognition of the conditioning of all experience by the personal element. This applies to apostolic experience no less than to contemporary experience. We may believe that the holy men of old, who ὑπὸ Πνεύματος ʽΑγίου φερόμενοι ἐλάλησαν ἀπὸ Θεοῦ, were usually men whose intuitive powers were well developed, babes and sucklings in discursive reason to whom were revealed things hidden from the wise and prudent. We should not hold that therefore they were infallible. We believe that the Holy Spirit worked upon the writers of Scripture, as upon others, 'as men'; and infallibility is not a human quality. The divine inspiration uses, but does not over-ride or even *completely* sanctify, the personalities of men, however great their spiritual influence. The Puritans were right in rejecting Quaker claims to ʽfallibility; but in arguing that the Quakers could not possess the same Spirit as inspired the Apostles, for then they would be infallible, *quod erat absurdum*, they were wrong.

To-day we accept also the discipline of history with greater seriousness. In the seventeenth century the sense of history, as we understand it, was yet in its infancy, as we have seen. Even in reference to recent centuries men were but beginning to possess it. To Scripture they had no thought of applying it. We, on the contrary, perceive how greatly all experience is influenced, not only by the personal element, but by the *Zeitgeist*; and we are conscious of this influence in Scripture, as also in Christian doctrine since the Canon was closed. We see Scripture in terms of development, process, *Werden*, γένεσις. In the interests of history we differentiate between one book and another, and between passages in the same book, in a way which for the Puritans was not possible. We acknowledge the inspiration of Scripture, but we do not conceive it as over-riding contemporary thought-forms. Our conception of inspiration is less mechanical and static, is more personal and dynamic.

Because of this broader conception, the difficulties raised for the

Puritans by the relation of the Holy Spirit to Scripture are largely surmounted. We believe Scripture to be inspired not otherwise than are inspired all productions, whether literary or not, in which God's Spirit is at work, but to be more inspired than other productions, because here, more than elsewhere,

Thy words do find me out.[1]

In order to check our belief in inspiration, whether Scriptural or not, we still use such criteria as the Puritans used—reason, conscience, *sensus communis*; but in the last resort we accept inspiration as self-authenticating. In Coleridge's phrase, 'whatever *finds* me, bears witness for itself that it has proceeded from a Holy Spirit . . .'.[2] In the sphere of theology such a criterion in experience is quickly condemned as thin and subjective; but the condemnation is not found in other mental disciplines.

> Why should religious knowledge be the one field in which the limitation and fallibility of our minds are supposed to vitiate the process of our learning and allowed to sap our trust in the accessibility of truth? . . . despite the margin of uncertainty, we have through our inward, spiritual powers—as through our powers of seeing and hearing—such measure of knowledge, light, and certainty as is sufficient for our daily need; and we have no right or reason to demand more.[3]

In theology 'the margin of uncertainty' is accepted with special reluctance, because the issue is so great. Yet without the acknowledgement there can be no genuine Christianity, at once spiritual and intelligent. Here more, not less, than elsewhere 'we see through a glass, darkly'; 'for we walk by faith, not by sight'.

We are also aware to-day that Scripture includes many types of literature, much of it poetic, symbolic, mythical literature rather than historical or scientific. We still acknowledge the working of God's Spirit in their composition, for His Spirit inspires poetry no less than history; but we cannot build upon the early chapters of *Genesis*, for instance, the kind of theology which was built upon them so long as they were believed to be historical. It is possible for an account to be historical and at the same time to possess great symbolic value, as is the case, for instance, with the account of the crucifixion; but any doubt of the historical nature of the crucifixion would inevitably alter the doctrine of the atonement. Something of the kind has happened with the doctrine of original sin. So long as Christians held

---

[1] G. Herbert, *The Holy Scriptures*, II. iii.
[2] S. T. Coleridge, *Confessions of an Enquiring Spirit* (1840), p. 10.
[3] C. J. Cadoux, *Catholicism and Christianity*, p. 174.

their own version of the pagan belief in an original golden age, the present state of man could be explained only by a theory of degeneration. The doctrine of original sin through Adam's disobedience to God's Spirit was an explanation of that degeneration. To-day we find no evidence for pristine human innocence and believe rather in the evolution of man from animal stock. There is consequently no need for any theory of degeneration or any doctrine of original sin. We believe that in some sense God's Spirit is in all creatures, 'seeing he giveth to all life, and breath': 'the whole world is a theatre of the glory of God'.[1] Through the divine gift of the Spirit to man in a greater degree than to other creatures, a tension arises in man between the animal motions towards self-centredness, which for the animal are natural and right, and the new spiritual motions towards God-centredness. God also gives man free will to set his life in either direction, and such setting involves struggle: 'all spiritual graces are with conflict'.[2]   In this conflict, or temptation, is nothing sinful. Man sins when he yields to the animal motions towards self-centredness, which for him are unnatural and wrong because in disunity with God's Spirit in its fuller degree of bestowal upon him.

In postulating the Spirit of God in every man, including the heathen and sinners, the Quakers, therefore, were right. Where they erred was in identifying this bestowal of 'the Spirit of God as Creator, or of the Father' with the fuller bestowal of 'the Spirit of Christ the Redeemer'[3] granted in and through Christ. Fox's fondness for the contrast between 'the seed of the woman' and 'the seed of the serpent' may be thought dimly to foreshadow our contrast between man and animal; but in identifying 'the seed of the woman' with Christ, he suggests that there is no difference between the Spirit in the unconverted 'man as man' and the Spirit in the converted 'man as Christian'. This last alone can be called justly the Spirit of Christ. Between the Spirit in every man and the Spirit of Christ there is clearly no $\mu\epsilon\tau\acute{a}\beta a\sigma\iota\varsigma$ $\epsilon\acute{\iota}\varsigma$ $\acute{a}\lambda\lambda o$ $\gamma\acute{\epsilon}\nu o\varsigma$; but there is a distinction vital to Christianity, which, if it was exaggerated by the Puritans, was no less underestimated by the Quakers. St. Augustine expresses the difference as being between the initial, creative and general grace, *qua condita est humana natura (haec enim Christianis Paganisque communis est)*, and the second and *major gratia*, which is peculiar to Christians.[4]   Both are *gratia*, but the distinction remains. Baxter makes a triple distinction between (1) 'the gifts of the Spirit common to hypocrites and the unbelievers'; (2)

---

[1] R. Sibbes, *Works*, IV. 241; quoted on p. 146, *sup.*
[2] *Ib.*, IV. 145; quoted on p. 60, *sup.*   [3] Cf. R. Baxter, *Works*, xx. 6.
[4] Cf. *Patrologia Latina*, ed. J.-P. Migne, t. 38, cc. 173 ff.; t. 37, c. 1552.

'that work of the Spirit by which we first repent and believe'; and (3) 'that gift of the Spirit which is promised to believers; which is . . . some notable degree of love to our reconciled Father'.

So that Mr. Tho. Hooker saith more truly than once I understood, that vocation is a special grace of the Spirit, distinct from common grace on one side, and from sanctification on the other side. Whether it be the same degree of the Spirit which the faithful had before Christ's incarnation, which causeth men first to believe, distinct from the higher following degree, I leave to inquiry: . . .[1]

The Quaker abhorrence of such 'notional' distinctions was unfortunate. It led them to reduce, at least in theory, the difference between the creature and the 'new creation', and to neglect the necessity for a genuine repentance and reconciliation. Their opponents' charges that by the light within they meant no more than the natural light of the unconverted man's conscience, and that they denied 'Christ y^t dyed & suffered att Jerusalem', are also made intelligible thereby. The later development of Quakerism suggests, furthermore, that the charges were not without a degree of justification.

It has been said that the Quakers made an 'identification of our Lord Jesus with the living Spirit of the Indwelling God'.[2] It would be more correct to say that implicitly they identified the Logos or eternal Christ with the Holy Spirit. This was an error according to orthodoxy, for which the Logos is identified not with the Spirit but with the Son. Before the Incarnation, the Logos, as the agent by which the world came into being, is in the world, as the world's sustaining life and light, and is at times manifested, as in Isaiah's temple vision; but the Logos is not in men, as the Spirit is in men. The Logos is in Jesus only, and in Him is incarnate; the Spirit is not incarnate in Him, but is in Him as the principle of union between the Logos and His humanity, whereby the Incarnation takes place. The relation of the Spirit to the Logos is not discussed by the writer of *John*; and the Quakers can hardly be blamed for lack of clarity over a passage which puzzles professional theologians. It may be remarked, however, that they laid stress on 'every man' in *John* i. 9 at the expense of 'but as many as received him' in verse 12, and that they paid no attention whatever to the words in *John* vii. 39, 'for the [Holy (A.V.)]Ghost was not yet [given (A.V.)]; because that Jesus was not yet glorified'.

However important it is to divest the manifestation of the God-man on the earth of the appearance of a mutation in God or in His purpose,

[1] R. Baxter, *Works*, v. 351; for another reference to Hooker, cf. xx. 7.
[2] J. W. Graham, *The Divinity in Man*, p. 247.

and of the abrupt in relation to creation and pre-Christian history, the novelty and originality of the manifestation of Christ ought to be just as little removed.[1]

About the very nature of the doctrine of the Holy Spirit there is a certain largeness and elasticity which makes it capable of being used as a permanent foundation for theological superstructures, however these may alter with men's changing thought-forms, mental disciplines, insights, interests and concerns. We saw earlier the radical Puritans' readiness to acknowledge 'fresh light', to 'know their own homes', to learn from 'something in Nature' and to draw upon current philosophical terminology. In this conclusion we have suggested ways in which the doctrine, and a theology in which the doctrine is treated as primary, may be related to more recent and more adequate thought-forms[2] in the spheres of history, psychology, science and philosophy. Such a theology has the further advantage of retaining a genuinely substantial identity with an important New Testament theology. It cannot be called *the* New Testament theology, for the New Testament contains many theologies; but it is *a* New Testament theology and an early theology, in whose formation Jesus Himself took a part. In effect, modern New Testament scholars justify the Puritan conviction that the presence of the Holy Spirit was a primary character of the faith, experience and resultant theology of Christianity in its earliest form.

> The conception of Jesus as inspired by the Holy Spirit is primitive and . . . certainly belongs to the claim which Jesus publicly made for himself.[3]
> The Apostolic age was, above all things, the age of the Spirit: and the New Testament writings must be read in the light of this fact.[4]
> It is not too much to say that the New Testament Church is the community of the Spirit.[5]

In so far as the New Testament remains the ideal for the life, if not for the letter, of Christianity, it is imperative that the doctrine of the Holy Spirit should receive attention in theology, and that the presence of the Holy Spirit should, above all else, be sought in Christian faith and experience. That Christians will all agree upon the liturgical

---

[1] I. A. Dorner, *A System of Christian Doctrine*, tr. A. Cave and J. S. Banks, III. 297.
[2] Our thought-forms can claim no finality; but *we* can use no others: cf. O. Spengler, *The Decline of the West*, tr. C. F. Atkinson, I. 41 foll.
[3] K. Lake and H. J. Cadbury, in *The Beginnings of Christianity*, ed. F. J. Foakes Jackson and K. Lake, IV. 3, on *Acts* i. 2.
[4] J. V. Bartlet, in *A Commentary on the Bible*, ed. A. S. Peake, p. 644.
[5] V. Taylor, in *The Doctrine of the Holy Spirit* (a symposium), p. 49; cf. further G. Johnston, *The Doctrine of the Church in the New Testament* (1943), p. 75 *et passim*.

implications of the doctrine is not to be expected. There is no reason why extempore prayer and read prayer, 'prophesying' and formal preaching, silent meetings and sacramental services should not be recognized, all in their several ways, as capable of divine inspiration and as means whereby men come into personal communion with God through Christ. The sense of inspiration in and through different liturgical practices may well vary with different temperaments. So long as each practice is kept free from the mechanical, impersonal corruptions introduced by sacerdotalism, each may have its place in Christian worship. To combine them may prove difficult, but at least each may claim toleration and the inner tolerance from which toleration proceeds. Such a tolerance we saw exemplified in the most spiritual among the Puritans, such as Cromwell, Bunyan, Cradock, John Jones and John Cook, and in this we may learn from them.

The strict Presbyterian Baillie might complain that Independency was become 'a uniting Principle';[1] the Independents gladly accepted the taunt, believing that they put first things first, and only first things. What was fundamental was not the 'shadowish or figurative ordinances',[2] but the baptism of the Spirit and the feeding upon spiritual bread; was not episcopacy or ministerial ordination or ecclesiastical polity of any kind, for 'the true Succession' was 'through the Spirit'[3], and the Spirit blew where it listed; was not in creeds or catechisms or liturgies or any forms which might quench the Spirit and darken what fresh light might be given. What was fundamental was the personal reception, both individually and communally, of the Spirit; was in the possession of the Spirit's gifts and graces; was in not grieving the Spirit.

An opportunity was provided thereby, and is provided still, for united Christian witness to fundamentals of faith on a New Testament basis. The original demand made of the Christian remains the one binding demand; namely, that by his personality and life he should proclaim 'Jesus is Lord', which 'no man can say . . . but by the Holy Spirit'; and 'if any man have not the Spirit of Christ, he is none of his'. There is no requirement either in life or in theology which is simpler or more primitive. There is also none more testing.

---

[1] R. Baillie, *Dissuasive from the Errours of the Time*, p. 93; quoted on p. 114, *sup.*
[2] J. Bunyan, *Works*, I. 425; quoted on p. 96, *sup.*
[3] O. Cromwell, *Letters and Speeches*, ed. T. Carlyle, Speech I; quoted on p. 85, *sup.*

M

APPENDIX I

THE GRINDLETONIAN MOVEMENT

The influence of Roger Brereley,[1] perpetual curate of Grindleton in the parish of Mitton in Craven, Yorkshire, and of his Antinomianism, in preparing the way for Quakerism is noticed by Professor R. M. Jones in his volume on *Mysticism and Democracy in the English Commonwealth*.[2] Professor Jones also mentions Giles Wigginton,[3] who was suspended from his living at Sedbergh and founded a Separatist congregation there, but makes no reference to Baxter's association of the fanatical group led by William Hacket,[4] of whom Wigginton was one, with the Grindletonians. Of Hacket's group Baxter says that they 'lived a while as wrapped up in the Spirit, and in antinomian fancies'; of the 'Grundletonians' he says, 'I had an old, godly friend that lived near them, and went once among them, and they breathed on him as to give him the Holy Ghost'.[5]

Professor Jones also mentions the spiritual influence of John Webster,[6] Vicar of Mitton, who in his *Academiarum Examen* refers to Brereley, of whom he was evidently a disciple. He does not observe, however, the further link provided by the fact that at Kildwick in Craven, where Webster was curate before moving to Mitton, and where Brereley had preceded Webster in the curacy,[7] there had been another Separatist congregation under another suspended clergyman, John Wilson, who was also an associate of Wigginton.[8] In view of these links, it is significant that it was at Sedbergh that George Fox received the 'people in white raiment' whom he had seen in vision after climbing Pendle Hill, over against Mitton and Grindleton;[9] and that this people's leader, Thomas Taylor,[10] who was now 'convinced',

[1] So A. Gordon, in *D.N.B.*, *s.v.*

[2] pp. 79–84, as Brierly; following T. Sippell, *Zur Vorgeschichte des Quäkertums*, pp. 3–13, as Brerely. Dr. Sippell has since printed extracts from Brereley's published sermons in *Werdendes Quäkertum*, *Beilage* II. One Grindletonian, Thomas Barcroft, is known to have become a Friend (cf. *B.Q.*, p. 24).

[3] Cf. *D.N.B.*, *s.v.*   [4] Cf. *D.N.B.*, *s.v.*   [5] R. Baxter, *Works*, xx. 296.

[6] Cf. *D.N.B.*, *s.v.*; W. Self Weeks, 'John Webster' and 'Further Information about Dr. John Webster', in *Transactions* of Lancashire and Cheshire Antiquarian Society, xxxix and xlviii. In 1657 the Quaker, Robert Widders, disputed with Webster who, he says, 'had been partly convinced and turned back again, Simon Magus like' (R. Widders, *Life and Death*, p. 5; J. Whiting, *Persecution Expos'd*, p. 170, correctly supplies the year-date from internal evidence).

[7] Cf. *Kildwick-in-Craven Parish Register*, ii (Yorkshire Parish Register Society Pubs., lv), pp. 3, 10, 15, 96; this curacy of Brereley's appears to have escaped notice hitherto.

[8] Cf. *The Seconde Parte of a Register*, ed. A. Peel, ii. 225 foll.

[9] Cf. G. Fox, *Journal*, ed. N. Penney, i. 40, 42.

[10] Cf. *D.N.B.*, *s.v.*; Taylor was at this time Lecturer, and minister to a congregation of Seekers (cf. W. C. Braithwaite in *Journal* of Friends' Hist. Soc., v. 3–10), at Richmond, the

had 'naturall frends and former acquaintance' at Carleton in Craven,[1] almost the next village to Kildwick.

There is also considerable evidence of widespread Antinomianism in the parish of Halifax, 'a town early distinguished for its adherence to Puritanism'[2] and its 'prophesyings'. Robert Town, for instance, who was accused of Grindletonianism when at Heywood, later became curate of Elland, where another Antinomian, Thomas Robinson, of Rastrick, was buried. Again, at St. Anne's, *alias* Chapel le Brears, Richard Coore,[3] who was of such pronounced views that in 1672 he applied for a licence as an Antinomian,[4] was succeeded in the curacy[5] by Thomas Taylor's brother, Christopher.[6] Elland, Rastrick, and St. Anne's were all chapels in the parish of Halifax. It would thus appear that there was a direct sequence between the groups represented by (*a*) Wigginton and Wilson; (*b*) Brereley, Webster, and Town; and (*c*) Thomas and Christopher Taylor, with the Seekers who were absorbed into Quakerism.

James Nayler comes into a similar sequence. Before Fox converted him to Quakerism,[7] Nayler was a member of the Congregational church at Woodkirk, *alias* West Ardsley, between Wakefield and Halifax, of which the minister was Christopher Marshall.[8] Marshall had been educated in New England, whence he took his first wife, a niece of Anne Hutchinson, whose Antinomianism is attributed by Winthrop to Grindletonian influence.[9] After Marshall's death his second wife married Gamaliel Marsden, another curate at St. Anne's, Halifax, and also a Congregationalist, whose brother, Jeremiah Marsden, again a Congregationalist, connects Halifax, Whalley, and

birthplace of the earlier Separatist leaders, Francis and George Johnson (cf. *D.N.B.*, *s.vv.*) and of another Thomas Taylor, perhaps of the same family, who entered into controversy with Robert Town, a clergyman accused of Grindletonianism (cf. *D.N.B.*, *s.v.* T. Taylor, and p. 158, n. 4, *sup.*; *C.R.*, *s.v.* R. Town).

[1] Cf. *B.Q.*, p. 80, n. 2, which assumes too much, perhaps, from the phrase in a letter by Taylor (Swarthmore MSS., I. 18) quoted above. The Vicar at Carleton from 1638 to 1674, Edward Price, was 'a constant preacher' and 'the best in these parts': C. Fairfax, in *Memorials of the Civil War*, ed. R. Bell, I. 310, 305.

[2] J. G. Miall, *Congregationalism in Yorkshire*, p. 13; he quotes Grindal's reference to Halifax as 'one poor parish in Yorkshire, which, by continued preaching, had been better instructed than the rest'.

[3] For R. Town, T. Robinson and R. Coore, cf. *C.R.*, *s.vv.*

[4] Cf. *Original Records of Nonconformity*, ed. G. L. Turner, I. 361, 496; III. 715. At Kildwick James Hartley, 'a notable Antinomian' (T. Jollie, *Autobiography* (Chetham Soc., N.S., XXXIII), p. 14) applied for a Congregational licence (*Orig. Records*, I. 225, 237).

[5] Cf. *First Publishers of Truth*, ed. N. Penney, p. 291, as Chappell in the Bryers.

[6] Cf. *D.N.B.*, *s.v.* T. Taylor.

[7] Following Fox's 'testimony' in W. Dewsbury, *Testimony*, *ad init.*; Braithwaite remarks that in his own account (*Works*, pp. 12 f.) Nayler makes no reference to Fox and was probably already 'travelling for himself the pathway of Quaker experience' (*B.Q.*, p. 62).

[8] Cf. *C.R.*, *s.v.*

[9] Cf. J. Winthrop, *History of New England, 1630–1649* (1853 edn.), I. 267.

Kendal as places where he ministered.[1] In 1589 a correspondent of Burghley's compared the people of Dentdale, near the foot of which Sedbergh lies, with those of Halifax:

> These people, situate amongst the wild mountains and savage fells, are generally affected to religion, quiet and industrious, equall with Hallyfax in this, excelling them in civility and temper of Lyfe, as well as abstaining from drink as from other excesses.[2]

Fox's journey from Wakefield 'where Ja Naylor had beene a member of an Independant Church ... Into Dent'[3] can thus again be seen to have had what may be called a spiritual axis as well as a geographical.

[1] Cf. *C.R.*, *s.vv.*
[2] Cf. T. Whitehead, *History of the Dales Congregational Churches*, p. 254.
[3] G. Fox, *Journal*, ed. N. Penney, I. 37, 41.

APPENDIX II

The extent within early Quakerism of the use of what may be termed Messianic language, and the sense in which such language is to be interpreted, form a difficult subject which, though mentioned in recent works, has not yet been adequately explored, and cannot be without a thorough acquaintance with the evidence provided in the Swarthmore and other early Quaker MSS. at Friends House. The judgements expressed in what follows must be regarded therefore as provisional.

That certain persons addressed James Nayler in language, and behaved towards him with actions, which suggested that they regarded him as the Messiah, is sufficiently notorious. Partly because the extravagant language was accompanied by adulatory action, Nayler's case attracted public attention. But, 'if we scrutinise the enthusiastic utterances of the rank and file addressed to Fox, we find them as exaggerated, though not as dramatic, as those addressed to Nayler'.[1] Some examples[2] follow:

> let not that beastly power which keepes us in bondage seperate thy bodyly prsence from us, who reignes as king above it, & would reioyce to see thy kingly power here triumph over it . . .[3]
> the wante of thy shewinge forth unto Israell[4] . . .
> My Deare everlasting 'ābh [father] . . .[5]
> Grant that I may live with thee for ever & be cload with thy righteousnesse . . .[6]

These are from letters to Fox. The next two passages refer to him.

> how will thou answer this to Him who hath given him a Name better than every name to which every knee must bow . . .[7]

---

[1] E. Fogelklou, *James Nayler: the Rebel Saint*, tr. L. Yapp, p. 231.

[2] Some of these are collected by E. Bates, *An Appeal to the Society of Friends*.

[3] M. Fell to G. Fox, 1652 (cf. p. 54, *sup.*); cf. G. Fox to O. Cromwell, 1654, in *Journal*, ed. N. Penney, I. 161: 'my kingdome is not of this world'.

[4] H. Norton to G. Fox, 1656, in *Journal*, ed. N. Penney, I. 246; T. E. Harvey, *ib.*, introd., I. xxvi, n. a, says this letter 'is an instance less strong than many' in the Swarthmore MSS. 'of the intense and almost idolizing affection of his friends for Fox'.

[5] J. Stubbs to G. Fox, *s.a.*, quoted in *B.Q.*, p. 499, with a biblical reference to *Isa.* ix. 6: for later tampering with this 'Messianic' opening, cf. I. Sharp, in *Friends' Quarterly Examiner*, XXXVI. 266.

[6] A. Curtis to G. Fox, 1660, quoted by E. Bates, *op. cit.*, p. 21.

[7] M. Fell to J. Nayler, 1656, quoted in *B.Q.*, pp. 249 f.; cf. G. Fox to O. Cromwell: 'who is of the world called George ffox who A new name hath which the world knowes not': *Journal*, ed. N. Penney, I. 162; quoted on p. 131, n. 8, *sup.*

he is a blessinge to ye nations and ye Joy off his people ye second appearance of him whoe Is blessed for ever.[1]

The question arises: Did the Quakers' belief in the personal indwelling of the Holy Spirit lead some of them to regard Fox, and others to regard Nayler, as the Messiah?

1. One must remember the widespread extravagance with which language was used at this period, especially in religious circles of a Ranter complexion. Writing of the Nayler episode, Alexander Gordon says, 'Quakerism had not yet emerged from its ranter stage', and on Nayler's words to Dorcas Erbury, 'Dorcas, arise,' comments, 'in ranter language this merely meant that he had revived her spirits'.[2] Most of the letters containing extravagant language appear to date from this early period, though this is not so in the case of the last passage quoted above, of which the date is 1675 and the writer is Thomas Lower, who was no fanatic. The fact is that, whether Ranters or not, men felt passionately and wrote vehemently; and, in seeking to recover and to express a religious experience of the biblical type, they naturally adopted a biblical phraseology, itself often extreme, which they knew in a version still consonant with contemporary usage. The 'Messianic' language has to be set over against the 'filthy' language applied to opponents:[3] 'when abuse so far overpassed the bounds of propriety, it was not unnatural that praise should err equally on the other side'.[4]

2. If such language is blasphemous, the blasphemy arises only from a failure to distinguish between the Spirit of God within and the earthly vessel. This was realized by some of the more enlightened at Nayler's trial. 'If you hang every man that says, Christ is in you the hope of glory,' said Henry Lawrence, the Lord President,[5] 'you will hang a good many. . . . I do not believe that James Nayler thinks himself to be the only Christ, but that Christ is in him in the highest measure.' 'That which sticks most with me', said Colonel William Sydenham, a Congregationalist, 'is the nearness of this

---

[1] T. Lower to G. and M. Fox, 1675, quoted in E. Bates, *op. cit.*, p. 22; for references to other 'offensive phrases' in unpublished letters, sometimes, but not always, later erased by Fox, cf. *B.Q.*, p. 105, n. 1.

[2] A. Gordon, in *D.N.B.*, *s.v.*; cf. *eund., ib., s.v.* G. Fox, on 'the ranter swell' in M. Fell's letter to Fox quoted above.

[3] Cf., e.g., this opening of a paper by Fox: 'Your Tables are full of vomits, that the shameful spewing and vomiting your filth before the children of light is seen': H. J. Cadbury, *Annual Catalogue of G. Fox's Papers*, p. 57, no. 78 B, *s.a.* 1656.

[4] M. R. Brailsford, *A Quaker from Cromwell's Army: James Nayler*, p. 109.

[5] Lawrence, who was a Baptist, thought Quakers were 'to be pittied . . . out of a tendernes towards such poore deluded persons': *Extracts from State Papers relating to Friends*, ed. N. Penney, pp. 33 f.

opinion to that which is a most glorious truth, that the Spirit is personally in us.'[1] Braithwaite thus wisely sums up the matter:

> We may admit that the first Friends held a very imperfect doctrine of human nature. . . . But their imperfect conception of human nature is no valid ground for denying the reality of the spiritual experience which possessed them.[2]

One need add only that the fact that Fox 'never appears to have undergone any travail over his own sins'[3] was perhaps not altogether beneficial in its effects, and that his doctrine of human nature might have been less imperfect, had he been, like (say) Erbury, more 'sensible of his present frailty',[4] with less 'enormous sacred Self-confidence'.[5]

3. The essence of the Quaker message, as we shall see, was that the Spirit of God was in every man. 'Now the Lord God opened to me by his invisible power,' says Fox, ' "that every man was enlightened by the divine light of Christ"; and I saw it shine through all';[6] 'the hope of Israel', said Nayler with equal clarity, 'stands in the Righteousnesse of the Father in whomsoever it is'.[7] There was evidently a real danger that some Quakers, in recognizing the presence of God's Spirit in their leaders, would exalt those leaders unduly, and that the leaders would be tempted to lack a due humility. The force of the language used towards Fox and Nayler is weakened, however, in proportion to the extent to which such language was used also towards others. Edward Burrough, for instance, could address Margaret Fell thus:

> O thou daughter of God . . . thou art comely in thy beauty . . . clothed with the sun and the moon under thy feet . . . thou art in thy life and glory to be above all things desired after.[8]

Possibly similar passages addressed to other leaders could be found among the Swarthmore MSS.

4. There was clearly some rivalry between Fox and Nayler.

---

[1] T. Burton, *Diary*, ed. J. T. Rutt, I. 62, 69.

[2] *B.Q.*, p. 277; cf. T. E. Harvey, in *op. cit.*, I. xxv.

[3] R. M. Jones, introd. to *B.Q.*, p. xxxii; quoted on p. 55, *sup.*

[4] J. Webster, in W. Erbury, *Testimony*, introd.; cf. E. Fogelklou, *op. cit.*, p. 255: 'Fox recognized clearly that the difficulties and the strife were caused by a spirit of arrogance. But he failed to see that he had harboured this spirit himself.'

[5] T. Carlyle, in *Letters and Speeches of O. Cromwell*, *ad fin.*

[6] G. Fox, *Journal* (1901 edn.), I. 34; quoted on p. 52, *sup.*

[7] *Narrative of the Examination, Tryall, and Sufferings of James Nayler* 657,(1) p. 23.

[8] E. Burrough to M. Fell, 1655, in Swarthmore MSS., III. 17; it is quoted without the marks of omission, in M. R. Brailsford, *op. cit.*, p. 109; from the letter as printed in *Letters of Early Friends*, ed. A. R. Barclay, p. 262, the passage is omitted entirely.

Baxter calls Nayler 'their chief Leader'[1] and does not mention Fox in his autobiography; elsewhere he refers to 'the contention between Naylor and his followers, and Fox and his followers'.[2] Bernardi, the Genoese ambassador, also says of Nayler *è capo dei Tremolanti*.[3] By some

> Fox was likened to a 'pope', the preachers to 'bishops'. Margaret Fell was said to 'adore Fox' and regard him as infallible. Fox was accused of putting himself 'in God's place' and ordering others about after his own pleasure.[4]

That there was some ground for these aspersions is suggested by Margaret Fell's letter to Nayler, quoted above, by Fox's harshness towards Nayler,[5] and by the exception taken later to Fox's 'tyrannical government' by William Mucklow.[6] In the event, Nayler was eclipsed and Fox correspondingly magnified. In her study of Nayler, Dr. Fogelklou is perhaps not entirely fair to Fox, but she shows effectively with what studied neglect Nayler is treated in the works of later leaders who had been under Fox's influence.[7] Only in the present century has justice been done to Nayler, as one who fell where (partly through his falling) Fox but slipped, and as 'a spirit of wonderful beauty',[8] in some respects Fox's superior.

[1] *R.B.*, i. 123.   [2] R. Baxter, *One Sheet against the Quakers*, p. 11.
[3] Cf. W. H. Dawson, *Cromwell's Understudy: John Lambert*, p. 217, n. 1.
[4] E. Fogelklou, *op. cit.*, p. 148.
[5] Nayler at his trial repudiated Fox as 'a lyer, and a fire-brand of hell': J. Deacon, *The Grand Impostor*, p. 19.
[6] Cf. p. 46, *sup.*   [7] *Op. cit.*, pp. 284 f.   [8] *Q.S.M.*, p. 135.

———

Addendum to p. 13, n. 2:
    'dear Saltmarsh, honest Erbury, . . . Divine Webster, . . . Joshua Sprigge' are, again, included in a long list of 'certain Friends to the Bridegroom, who longed to see this day of the Son in Man; but could not, he vanishing out of their sight' by a disaffected Quaker (cf. *D.N.B.*, *s.v.*), Robert Rich, *Love without Dissimulation* ⟨*post* 1666⟩, pp. 6 f.

APPENDIX III

p. 16, n. 13. prin y gallai dynnu geiriau ei galon o lyfr a gyhoeddwyd yn Saesneg y flwyddyn honno, ac nid yn 1641 fel y deallai Barclay.

p. 68, n. 7. disgwilied yn ddistaw, mae'r dydd yn gwawrio.

p. 81, n. 5. Maent yn scrifennu eu pregethau, ond oni bai gyflog dynion.

p. 86, n. 4. ffynnon . . . ynddynt yn ceisio tarddu.

p. 92, n. 6. y Cymro cyntaf i gymeryd lle amlwg a blaenllaw yng ngwaith gwleidyddol Prydain Fawr.

p. 104, n. 9. Pam yr wyti yn dyfod brydnhawn yn yr hwyr, ac nid yn y borau a'th newydd gennit? Am mai tua diwedd y bŷd y pregethir yr efengil dragwyddol.

p. 109, n. 1. Ond o ddechreuad y bŷd hyd y diluw yr oedd mil a chwechant ac vn mlynedd, ar bymtheg a deugain: felly mi a'th gynghoraf (O Eryr) i ddisgwil canys mae fo yn agos.

p. 111, n. 5. yn nechreu yr eilfed ganrif ar bymtheg nid oedd odid ardal yng Nghymru lle y ffynnai cymaint parch at lenyddiaeth ac addysg.

p. 112. disgwil fyth am Grist gartref, yn aelwyd dy galon dy hun.

p. 140. y llais anrhaethadwy yn yr ysbryd.

Pan fo'r gwir fugail yn llefaru, a dŷn yn i glywed, mae'r galon yn llosci oddifewn, a'r cnawd yn crynnu, a'r meddwl yn goleuo fel canwyll, a'r gydwybod yn ymweithio fel gwîn mewn llestr, a'r ewyllys yn plygu i'r gwirionedd: Ac mae'r llais main nefol nerthol hwnnw yn codi y marw i fyw, oi fedd ei hunan, i wisgo'r goron, ac yn newid yn rhyfedd yr holl fywyd i fyw fel oen Duw.

p. 144. Pa fodd yr adwaenost di lais yr ysbryd glân ymysg y cwbl? Oni wyddost ti y medr oen bâch adnabod llais ei fam ei hun ymmysg cant o ddefaid.

p. 148, n. 7. yr oedd ei gyfriniaeth yn rhan ohono ef ei hun. Delw Cymru, ac nid yr Almaen, sydd ar ei feddyliau.

p. 149. Colomen: Ond os myn nêb i wadu ei hun a dilyn yr oenyn yr ailenedigaeth, a pharhau hyd y diwedd, a bôd yn gadwedig, Na ddiffodded mor golau sydd yn ei gydwybod, ond chwythed ef i oleuo, a dilyned oleuni Duw, a'r seren forau ynddo, ac fe a gyfyd yr haul yn ddisclair arno.

Eryr: Pa beth yw'r seren forau honno?

Colomen: Sicrwydd gwybodaeth, Gwystl yr ysbryd, siŵr lygad ffydd, ernes perffeithrwydd, sêl Jehovah, a thŷst tri yn vn, angor yr enaid, a'r cwbl pan fo dŷn yn y goleuni yn adnabod cariad Duw atto, ynddo, a thrwyddo, mewn nerth a heddwch ryfedd.

nid eglwys ond yr ysbrydol, nid ysbryd ond yr ail Adda, nid teml i Dduw ond meddwl pûr dyn, nid teml barhaus i ddyn ond yr Hollalluog, a'r Oen, nid vndeb ond vndeb yr ysbryd tragywyddol, nid canu, nid cymmun, nid vno, nid gweddio, nid ymaelodi mewn vn Eglwys oni bydd ysbryd y pen yn rheoli mewn nerth.

Ni ddysgodd y Crynwyr ddim byd mwy plaen, ac nid aethant erioed ymhellach na hyn.

p. 152. A ydyw efe ymmysg y crynwyr? Pam y mae efe yn crynnu? goleuni newydd, dysceidiaeth ddwfn ddierth ddyrus.

mudion a byddariaid yn malu ewyn, yn llygadtynnu ac yn synnu'r gwirion.

p. 153. Gwir y maent hwy yn ei ddywedyd, ond nid yr holl wir.

Ond nid ydym ni yn darllain iddo gymmeryd erioed vn text o'r bibl, ond vnwaith allan o Esay.

Maent yn scrifennu eu pregethau, ond oni bai gyflog dynion.

Eryr: Pa brŷd y mae gweddi dŷn yn cyrhaeddyd monwes Duw?

Colomen: Pan fo ysbryd Duw yn ochneidio (yn ddigymmysg) mewn dyn . . .

Colomen: . . . Immanuel Duw gyda ni yn cnawd.

Eryr: Beth yw hynny? a ydyw efe yn ein cnawd ni?

Colomen: Ydiw os ydym ni yn ei ysbryd ef.

p. 154. Ac mae llyfr ymhôb dŷn. . . .

Ac mae rhai eraill (Druain) yn edrych am Dduw o hirbell, ac hefyd yn gweddi am dano oddiallan, heb weled fôd ffynnon a gwreiddyn ynddynt yn ceisio tarddu a thyfu drwyddynt. Canys mae fe gyda phôb dŷn er cynddrwg yw, yn goleuo pôb dŷn ar sydd yn dyfod i'r bŷd . . .

p. 155. lleidr o'r tu fewn yw synwyr dŷn, yn cloi drŵs pôb meddwl yn erbyn awel yr ysbryd glân.

SELECT BIBLIOGRAPHY

A. *Seventeenth-century Works*

(The *index* includes all seventeenth-century authors to whose works reference is made.)

Baillie, Robert: *Dissuasive from the Errours of the Time*, 1645.

Baxter, Richard: *The Quakers Catechism*, 1655.

Reliquiae Baxterianae, ed. M. Sylvester, 1696.

Practical Works, ed. W. Orme, 1830.

Brereley, Roger: *Of True Christian Liberty* (pub. 1677).

Bunyan, John: *Works*, ed. H. Stebbing, 1859.

Cook, John: *What the Independents would have*, 1647.

Cradock, Walter: *Divine Drops Distilled*, 1650.

Gospel-Holinesse, 1651.

Gospel-Libertie, 1648.

Cromwell, Oliver: *Letters and Speeches*, ed. T. Carlyle (1908 edn.).

Dewsbury, William: *Testimony* (pub. 1689).

Erbury, William: *Testimony* (pub. 1658).

Extracts from State Papers relating to Friends, 1654-1672, ed. N. Penney, 1913.

Fenstanton, Warboys and Hexham, Records of Churches of Christ gathered at, ed. E. B. Underhill (Hanserd Knollys Soc. Pubs., v), 1854.

First Publishers of Truth, ed. N. Penney, 1907.

Forbes, John: *How a Christian man may discerne the testimonie of Gods spirit, from the testimonie of his owne spirit*, 1616.

Fox, George: *Journal*, ed. T. Ellwood (1901 edn.).

Journal, ed. N. Penney, 1911.

The Great Mistery of the Great Whore, 1659.

Gospel-Truth Demonstrated, ed. G. Whitehead *et al.*, 1706.

Epistles, ed. G. Whitehead, 1698.

cf. also *Annual Catalogue of George Fox's Papers*, ed. H. J. Cadbury, 1939.

Goodwin, John: Πλήρωμα τὸ πνευματικόν, 1670 (in 1867 edn.).

Goodwin, Thomas: *Works*, ed. J. C. Miller, 1861.

Hollinworth, Richard: *The Holy Ghost on the Bench*, 1656.

Howe, John: *Works*, ed. H. Rogers, *s.a.* ⟨1863⟩.

Howgill, Francis: *Works (The Dawnings of the Gospel-Day)*, ed. E. Hookes, 1676.

Jones, John: Letters printed in *Transactions* of Lancashire and Cheshire Historic Society (New Series, I), 1861.

Letters of Early Friends, ed. A. R. Barclay, 1841.

Llwyd, Morgan: *Gweithiau*, ed. T. E. Ellis and J. H. Davies, 1899 and 1908.

Milton, John: *Works*, ed. J. A. St. John, 1848–53.

Muggleton, Lodowicke, and Reeve, John: *A Volume of Spiritual Epistles* (1820 edn.).

Owen, John: *Pro Sacris Scripturis Adversus hujus temporis Fanaticos Exercitationes*, 1658.
Of the *Divine Originall, Authority, self-evidencing Light, and Power of the Scriptures*, 1659.
Works, ed. W. H. Goold, 1850–5.
Πνευματολογία, 1674.
Petto, Samuel: *The Voyce of the Spirit*, 1654.
Roses from Sharon, 1654.
Quaker Queries (cf. p. 153, n. 3).
Robinson, John: *Works*, ed. R. Ashton, 1851.
Rogers, John: *Ohel or Bethshemesh*, 1653.
Works, printed in E. Rogers, *Life and Opinions of a Fifth-Monarchy-Man*, 1867.
Rous, Francis: *Works (Treatises and Meditations)*, 1657.
Saltmarsh, John: *Sparkles of Glory*, 1647 (in 1847 reprint).
Sibbes, Richard: *Works*, ed. A. B. Grosart, 1862.
Smyth, John: *Works*, ed. W. T. Whitley, 1915.
Sprigg, Joshua: *A Testimony to Approaching Glory*, 1649.
Sterry, Peter: *The Spirits Conviction of Sinne*, 1645.
Terrill, Edward: *Records of a Church of Christ meeting in Broadmead, Bristol*, ed. N. Haycroft (Bunyan Library, xiv), 1865.

B. *Later Works*

Barclay, Robert: *The Inner Life of the Religious Societies of the Commonwealth* (1879 edn.).
Braithwaite, W. C.: *The Beginnings of Quakerism* (1923 edn.).
The Second Period of Quakerism (1921 edn.).
Brayshaw, A. N.: *The Personality of George Fox* (1933 edn.).
The Quakers: their Story and Message (1938 edn.).
Brown, L. F. : *The Baptists and Fifth Monarchy Men*, 1912.
Calamy Revised, ed. A. G. Matthews, 1934.
Dexter, H. M.: *The Congregationalism of the Last Three Hundred Years as seen in its Literature*, 1879.
Dictionary of National Biography, ed. Sir L. Stephen and Sir S. Lee (1937–8 edn.).
Evans, E. L.: *Morgan Llwyd*, 1930.
Firth, C. H.: *Oliver Cromwell* (1935 edn.).
Gardiner, S. R.: *History of the Commonwealth and Protectorate* (1903 edn.).
Cromwell's Place in History (1899 edn.).
King, R. H.: *George Fox and the Light Within, 1650–1660*, 1940.
Miller, Perry: *The New England Mind: the seventeenth century*, 1939.
Richards, Thomas: *The Puritan Movement in Wales*, 1920.
Religious Developments in Wales, 1654–62, 1923.

Sippell, Theodor: *Zur Vorgeschichte des Quäkertums,* 1920 (cf. p. 13, n. 8).
   Werdendes Quäkertum, 1937.
Smith, Joseph: *Descriptive Catalogue of Friends' Books,* 1867.
   Bibliotheca Antiquakeriana, 1873.
Stoughton, John: *Religion in England* (1881 edn.).
Troeltsch, Ernst: *The Social Teaching of the Christian Churches,* tr. O. Wyon,
   1931.
Weingarten, Hermann: *Die Revolutionskirchen Englands,* 1868.
Whitley, W. T.: *A Baptist Bibliography,* 1916.
Woodhouse, A. S. P., introd. to *Puritanism and Liberty,* ed. A. S. P. Wood-
   house, 1938.

INDEX NOMINUM

Names of modern writers are included only if mentioned at least once in the text.

189